# *Light Within*

## *Conversations with God*

*M.L. Bennett*

**Light Within**
Conversations with God

© 2021 by M.L. Bennett

ISBN: 978-1-63110-473-2

Printed in the United States of America by
Graphic Connections Publishing
Chesterfield, Missouri 63005

Copyediting by Karen L. Tucker and Andrew Doty of
Editwright (editwright.com)

# Dedication

To all the holy sons and daughters of God

who by their loving deeds shine with a light within.

# Acknowledgments

Susan Lowe, for her dedicated labor of love of formatting, editing, and consulting.

Rev. Nancy Wagner and Kate Fox, for their faith that this manuscript can invite a deepened relationship with God.

Srs. Antoinette Temporiti, CPPS; Lucy Meissen, CPPS; Barb Schlatter, CPPS; and Sandy Bay, SSND, for their wisdom and critique as this book was birthed.

Karen Berry, OSF, Leslie Conway, Suellyn Fahey, Elsie Gorski, Jody Uding, Scott Uding, and Ann Pierce, for their encouragement and presence in prayer.

Andrew Doty, at Editwright, for his expertise, kindness, and attention.

Kim Koenig, at Graphic Connections Group, for her responsiveness and skill in guiding the publication process.

You each are a blessing!!

# Invitation

Dear Reader,

I wish you blessing as you peruse these passages.
>May you meet your God playing in a thousand places in your life.
>May you know our earth-home as God's joy to share with you.
>May you dare to open your soul's secret sanctuary to the One
>who knows your heart.
>May you labor toward the family gathering in justice and delight.
>May you find peace and contentment in your years' twists and
>turns by trusting your Maker.
>May you discover your light within.
>May we walk each other home.

M.L. Bennett

Journalist Malcolm Muggeridge describes his crew filming Mother Teresa and her sisters as they prayed. The cameraman was dismayed when he entered the chapel and saw it was dimly lit. One of his crew encouraged them to film anyway. To their astonishment, the footage turned out to be brightly lit; the inside of the building glowed with a mysterious warm light. Muggerridge wrote of the overflowing love that registered on the faces of the sisters picked up in the photographic film.

Malcolm Muggeridge

*Something Beautiful for God*

# January

1. Journey
2. Horizons
3. Suspicion
4. Waver
5. Backfires
6. Snow Gift
7. Wilderness
8. Wonder
9. Threshold
10. Attention
11. Rush
12. Suffering
13. Companioning
14. Worry
15. Returning and Emptying
16. Sunset's Rest
17. The Pouring Forth
18. Music
19. Hope
20. Gentle Things
21. Guiding Star
22. Treasure
23. Steady
24. Whitewash
25. Embedded
26. Ashes
27. Rinse
28. Exhaustion
29. Coma
30. Elephant
31. Pristine

## Journey

**God:**

Come, dear traveler,
I am walking you home.
Skip, trudge, keep on moving.
I know your pace isn't mine.
Together we will meet the day.

**My soul:**

I am on the way
because You are faithful.
I can't see the destination
but You are my path.
I share the flight of eagles and butterflies.
I invite Your wading of creeks with me
and the stones' music.
Urge me onward, Light within!
You are my soul's companion.

**Acts 9:1-8**

*¹Meanwhile Saul, still breathing threats and murder against the disciples of the Lord, went to the high priest ² and asked him for letters to the synagogues at Damascus, so that if he found any who belonged to the Way, men or women, he might bring them bound to Jerusalem. ³ Now as he was going along and approaching Damascus, suddenly a light from heaven flashed around him. ⁴ He fell to the ground and heard a voice saying to him, "Saul, Saul, why do you persecute me?" ⁵ He asked, "Who are you, Lord?" The reply came, "I am Jesus, whom you are persecuting. ⁶ But get up and enter the city, and you will be told what you are to do." ⁷ The men who were traveling with him stood speechless because they heard the voice but saw no one. ⁸ Saul got up from the ground, and though his eyes were open, he could see nothing; so they led him by the hand and brought him into Damascus.*

Are you skipping or trudging along the way?
What light breaks through to convert you along the way?

## Horizons

**God:**

Seeker Soul, can you come to the horizon?
I want to meet you there.
Let the mountain rocks invite your climb.
Let the sea span call your own tide of heart.
Let trees like redwoods bring
your eyes upward to their reach.
While the skyline keeps eluding,
know that I am where you are
in the muck and stone and endless waves.
I want to share your world.

**My soul:**

Infinite Stretch of Life,
are you trying to deceive me?
I can only imagine arriving at the horizon's edge.
It moves before me like a mirage, so how can I meet you there?
Impossible goals make me want to quit trying.
God who creates the cosmos, find me where I am, please.
I am weighed down. I am covered with spent effort.
I am longing with no end evident.
You say You want to be where I am.
Are You sure? Because I can't see You.

**John 20:11-14**

¹¹ *But Mary stood weeping outside the tomb. As she wept, she bent over to look into the tomb;* ¹² *and she saw two angels in white, sitting where the body of Jesus had been lying, one at the head and the other at the feet.* ¹³ *They said to her, "Woman, why are you weeping?" She said to them, "They have taken away my Lord, and I do not know where they have laid him."* ¹⁴ *When she had said this, she turned around and saw Jesus standing there, but she did not know that it was Jesus.*

What is your horizon where you meet God?
Describe where it is that God will find you.

## Suspicion

**My soul:**

My hunches sit in shadows, God of Pure Light.
I entertain suspicion.
Do not let me mistrust when I breathe and grow and savor.
May doubt unlock curiosity.
May puzzlement bring humility.
May intuition carry me to Your presence.
I need You.

**God:**

I've done well in your making, restless child.
Scratch the uncertainties.
Hold to your truth.
Grand Canyons and Victoria Falls
hang in breathless mist
like your own precariousness.
I know what I am doing.

### John 18:33-38

*³³ Then Pilate entered the headquarters again, summoned Jesus, and asked him, "Are you the King of the Jews?" ³⁴ Jesus answered, "Do you ask this on your own, or did others tell you about me?" ³⁵ Pilate replied, "I am not a Jew, am I? Your own nation and the chief priests have handed you over to me. What have you done?" ³⁶ Jesus answered, "My kingdom is not from this world. If my kingdom were from this world, my followers would be fighting to keep me from being handed over to the Jews. But as it is, my kingdom is not from here." ³⁷ Pilate asked him, "So you are a king?" Jesus answered, "You say that I am a king. For this I was born, and for this I came into the world, to testify to the truth. Everyone who belongs to the truth listens to my voice." ³⁸ Pilate asked him, "What is truth?" After he had said this, he went out to the Jews again and told them, "I find no case against him.*

Of what are you suspicious?
What great holes in your precariousness proclaim God's wonder?

# Waver

**My soul:**

I waver,
God of steady foot beats.
How do I take the sea flutter
of my heart to mirrored glass?
I falter and hesitate.
Only You can urge my vacillations
to a swift unbending surge.
Let me move in Your rhythms.

**God:**

Catch My light in your movements.
Quivering one, match your heart song to Mine.
Hold back nothing.
Weave your breath strands in love's attention.
I can take your breath away if only you see Me.

**Hebrews 10:23-25**

²³ *Let us hold fast to the confession of our hope without wavering, for he who has promised is faithful.* ²⁴ *And let us consider how to provoke one another to love and good deeds,* ²⁵ *not neglecting to meet together, as is the habit of some, but encouraging one another, and all the more as you see the Day approaching.*

When you see your friends, what happens to your judgment?
How do you walk with Jesus's steadiness?

## Backfires

**God:**

I hear the backfire, intent one.
There is backlash to your miscalculations.
You labor to control.
You attempt effects that boomerang.
Catch the Spirit's fire and trust.
What looks like all has backfired
explodes into sunrise glory.
I want this for you.

**My soul:**

Teach me to surrender,
God who knows my purpose.
My renegade self eats apples to be somebody,
and there is blowback!
I want to do Your will.

**Matthew 6:10-13**

*¹⁰ Your kingdom come. Your will be done, on earth as it is in heaven. ¹¹ Give us this day our daily bread. ¹² And forgive us our debts, as we also have forgiven our debtors. ¹³ And do not bring us to the time of trial, but rescue us from the evil one.*

When have your plans backfired?
When do your intentions to be somebody crumble?

## Snow Gift

**God:**

I send you snow today.
It is fragile.
It can disappear with a sweep of your hand.
It lives on the cusp.
When cold temperatures barrel
across rain-soaked heights, it descends
and makes the universe dance.

**My soul:**

We pause
delighted,
surprised by joy even when predicted.
In the quiet soul escape from duty,
I feel Your nearness.
Sometimes,
when I can hold the cold and dare to play,
I can even move to Your rhythm.
Out of my wondrous single falling,
I meet the welcome soft pillowing of the snow bank.

### Luke 23:39-43

[39] One of the criminals who were hanged there kept deriding him and saying, "Are you not the Messiah? Save yourself and us!" [40] But the other rebuked him, saying, "Do you not fear God, since you are under the same sentence of condemnation? [41] And we indeed have been condemned justly, for we are getting what we deserve for our deeds, but this man has done nothing wrong." [42] Then he said, "Jesus, remember me when you come into your kingdom." [43] He replied, "Truly I tell you, today you will be with me in Paradise."

Where do you live on the cusp?
Where are you holding the cold?

## Wilderness

**My soul:**

I am a misfit.
Everyone else with determined gait
is stomping out their whys.
Busyness is buried in my horizon's edge.
I enter darkness enveloped by pause.
I hold my breath; even my heart vibration whispers.
Here, where danger is barred
and crazy monkey thoughts dissipate like mist,
I cast my silence to the sky's purple demarcation and wait.

**God:**

I hear your lonely ache.
In My spaciousness
I call your name
in My language.
My embrace secures your purpose.
Together, we are present.

**Mark 1:12-14**

*12 And the Spirit immediately drove him out into the wilderness. 13 He was in the wilderness forty days, tempted by Satan; and he was with the wild beasts; and the angels waited on him. 14 Now after John was arrested, Jesus came to Galilee, proclaiming the good news of God.*

Why do you think you don't fit in?
How is danger barred?

# Wonder

**My soul:**

A baby is born.
I glimpse my stretch
into a new and separate life.
How is it passion,
in its rush of mighty wind,
fits the puzzle of trust and surrender
and life receives its pattern?

**God:**

And so cosmos is born.
Your thread, your knot,
bubbles forth My image
larger than your grasp.

**Acts 17:23-26**

*²³ For as I went through the city and looked carefully at the objects of your worship, I found among them an altar with the inscription, 'To an unknown god.' What therefore you worship as unknown, this I proclaim to you. ²⁴ The God who made the world and everything in it, he who is Lord of heaven and earth, does not live in shrines made by human hands, ²⁵ nor is he served by human hands, as though he needed anything, since he himself gives to all mortals life and breath and all things. ²⁶ From one ancestor he made all nations to inhabit the whole earth, and he allotted the times of their existence and the boundaries of the places where they would live.*

You have come from a long line of life.
Are you a surviving thread or a knot?
What new life have you wondered at, a baby freshly showing God?

# Threshold

**God:**

Come to My house today.
At My threshold
stomp your feet, rub clean your soles!
Let the husks of life fall away
so the grain can fall clear.
I beckon from My hearth.
Sit in My rocker.
Let's share tea.

**My soul:**

I come to Your threshold.
Let the fuzz of my mind sift away.
I long to sit and share a cup of tea.

### Ruth 3:1-5

¹ *Naomi her mother-in-law said to her, "My daughter, I need to seek some security for you, so that it may be well with you. ² Now here is our kinsman Boaz, with whose young women you have been working. See, he is winnowing barley tonight at the threshing floor. ³ Now wash and anoint yourself, and put on your best clothes and go down to the threshing floor; but do not make yourself known to the man until he has finished eating and drinking. ⁴ When he lies down, observe the place where he lies; then, go and uncover his feet and lie down; and he will tell you what to do." ⁵ She said to her, "All that you tell me I will do."*

What must you clean from your shoes? Clear from your mind?
How are you daring to come to God's threshing floor?

## Attention

**God:**

I sent you breath today.
I hope you will pay attention.
Now is the time to live where there is no clutter.
Scatter the dust from your mind.
Notice.
Open your heart.

**My soul:**

I sit in Your sun's beam like a clam in the sun.
I am waiting.
Underneath I feel You.
Your warmth reaches my soul,
and the energy of waiting is my receiving.
I choose to live.

**Judges 6:11-14**

*¹¹ Now the angel of the Lord came and sat under the oak at Ophrah, which belonged to Joash the Abiezrite, as his son Gideon was beating out wheat in the wine press, to hide it from the Midianites. ¹² The angel of the Lord appeared to him and said to him, "The Lord is with you, you mighty warrior." ¹³ Gideon answered him, "But sir, if the Lord is with us, why then has all this happened to us? And where are all his wonderful deeds that our ancestors recounted to us, saying, 'Did not the Lord bring us up from Egypt?' But now the Lord has cast us off, and given us into the hand of Midian." ¹⁴ Then the Lord turned to him and said, "Go in this might of yours and deliver Israel from the hand of Midian; I hereby commission you."*

When have you entertained an angel coming to call your attention?
Has God's presence stirred your soul from the waiting?

## Rush

**My soul:**

My leaves are caught in my gutter,
jagged-toothed and stuck
until a wind picked up
and sang its music in my chimes.
Soon dancing from my eaves
comes the freed bounty.
They bounce and flit and swoop
along the earth,
unstuck and laughing
with their own swish.
Do they feel it as danger and risk?
Do they know the energy they shift?

**God:**

There is no prison in My world,
only a resting place, a pause.
Trust the mighty wind's advance.
I enjoy the dance,
the laws of catch and hold and gravity.
I have you in My grasp.
With My baton, you enter the symphony, soul-caught and splendid.
Trust Me.

**Genesis 1:1-2**

¹ *In the beginning when God created the heavens and the earth,* ² *the earth was a formless void and darkness covered the face of the deep, while a wind from God swept over the face of the waters.*

Where are you stuck?
When have you responded to God's music in your soul?

# Suffering

**My soul:**

Out of the crack of my life,
my inside bruises well up.
"Why" surges in my tears
but "no" loudly yells.
I feel stripped of normal
and feel the creak of love bending.
How do I bear pain
and not let it seep over all my days?

**God:**

You know I hold you tenderly.
I feel your river jams of ordinary disrupted.
In your soul-stripping,
I see your beauty.
Keep your eyes on Me.
I will carry you through.

**Isaiah 40:27-31**

*²⁷ Why do you say, O Jacob, and speak, O Israel, "My way is hidden from the Lord, and my right is disregarded by my God"? ²⁸ Have you not known? Have you not heard? The Lord is the everlasting God, the Creator of the ends of the earth. He does not faint or grow weary; his understanding is unsearchable. ²⁹ He gives power to the faint, and strengthens the powerless. ³⁰ Even youths will faint and be weary, and the young will fall exhausted; ³¹ but those who wait for the Lord shall renew their strength, they shall mount up with wings like eagles, they shall run and not be weary, they shall walk and not faint.*

Where is your life cracking open?
What is jamming up your flow of ordinary happenings?

## Companioning

**God:**

I come to soul-walk with you on real roads.
I recognize the gift you give of shared heart.
I see your strong desire and your flagging strength.
I hear your fear to say your yes
and leave your comfort zone.
Do you see I match My pace to yours,
eating, drinking, and being merry with stories and with laughter?

**My soul:**

I know the bond You offer me to be part of your grand adventure.
When I follow step by step,
I learn and laugh and disregard the blisters.
But when I go alone,
when I wander wide afield in an independent streak,
I forget what I'm all about. So I want to walk with You.
I believe You walk with me. Put Your seal upon my soul.

**John 1:35-42**

*35 The next day John again was standing with two of his disciples, 36 and as he watched Jesus walk by, he exclaimed, "Look, here is the Lamb of God!" 37 The two disciples heard him say this, and they followed Jesus. 38 When Jesus turned and saw them following, he said to them, "What are you looking for?" They said to him, "Rabbi" (which translated means Teacher), "where are you staying?" 39 He said to them, "Come and see." They came and saw where he was staying, and they remained with him that day. It was about four o'clock in the afternoon. 40 One of the two who heard John speak and followed him was Andrew, Simon Peter's brother. 41 He first found his brother Simon and said to him, "We have found the Messiah" (which is translated Anointed). 42 He brought Simon to Jesus, who looked at him and said, "You are Simon son of John. You are to be called Cephas" (which is translated Peter).*

When do you act alone?
What do you imagine as God's great adventure with you?

## Worry

**My soul:**

I've got spikes in my head today, my God.
I've got fences around my world.
It is a maze where I cannot find my way.
Do You see I carry a bag of stones
that grind in my heart core
and feel like a mountain?
I worry.
My mask is fear, hiding love.
But I think it is love knowing the pitfalls,
guarding the chasms.
I am so right, stubborn, persistent,
a slave making slaves,
with eyes slit to all that may be.

**God:**

Ah, little one,
I hear your angst. I feel your burden.
You are such an architect of love.
You weave prisons to guard
in your fierce protectiveness.
Don't you know Me?
Have I failed you and not protected yours?
Yes, there are dark pathways. I am here.
"Where were you when I laid the foundation of the world?"
I carry your bag of rocks.
Let your soul breathe free.

**2 Corinthians 11:21, 12:10**

²¹ *To my shame, I must say, we were too weak for that! But whatever anyone dares to boast of—I am speaking as a fool—I also dare to boast of that.*
¹⁰ *Therefore I am content with weaknesses, insults, hardships, persecutions, and calamities for the sake of Christ; for whenever I am weak, then I am strong.*

What do you worry about?
Who do you imprison by your worry?

# Returning and Emptying

**God:**

I love circles.
My design of so much of life's movement
is the return to where it began.
Know your heart in its new skin was worn down to stand up anew.
Stretch out your old roots to your story's end reframed.
Flow to the sea humbled in the brine of your beginning.

**My soul:**

I can't see the end, my God,
as the line bends around my mountain.
But I am propelled on the switchbacks
around and up and again around.
A wild and roiling ocean
breaks and licks my shore and risks my falling.
To return to brine is fearful until I see my bending down is needful.
Circle me round, my God, as my life circles and winds.

**Philippians 2:1-7**

[1] *If then there is any encouragement in Christ, any consolation from love, any sharing in the Spirit, any compassion and sympathy,* [2] *make my joy complete: be of the same mind, having the same love, being in full accord and of one mind.* [3] *Do nothing from selfish ambition or conceit, but in humility regard others as better than yourselves.* [4] *Let each of you look not to your own interests, but to the interests of others.* [5] *Let the same mind be in you that was in Christ Jesus,* [6] *who, though he was in the form of God did not regard equality with God as something to be exploited,* [7] *but emptied himself taking the form of a slave being born in human likeness and being found in human form.*

What shape does returning take in your life?
What have switchbacks taught you?

# Sunset's Rest

### God:

Don't you like My sunset?
I've painted it in purples and reds and oranges so you would notice.
Come sit at the seaside with Me and breathe.
Walk home in the darkness after swallowing the light.
Dare your shadows to open wide your eye's pupil and see.

### My soul:

I put down the day's stones and allow the restless waters
of time to overflow their cups and empty.
It is for rest.
My days—all gifts from You—rise up and fall away
as I attend the ending of the day.
I dare the night shadows because I have seen Your sunset.

### 2 Samuel 12:1-7

*¹ and the Lord sent Nathan to David. He came to him, and said to him, "There were two men in a certain city, the one rich and the other poor. ² The rich man had very many flocks and herds; ³ but the poor man had nothing but one little ewe lamb, which he had bought. He brought it up, and it grew up with him and with his children; it used to eat of his meager fare, and drink from his cup, and lie in his bosom, and it was like a daughter to him. ⁴ Now there came a traveler to the rich man, and he was loath to take one of his own flock or herd to prepare for the wayfarer who had come to him, but he took the poor man's lamb, and prepared that for the guest who had come to him." ⁵ Then David's anger was greatly kindled against the man. He said to Nathan, "As the Lord lives, the man who has done this deserves to die; ⁶ he shall restore the lamb fourfold, because he did this thing, and because he had no pity." ⁷ Nathan said to David, "You are the man!"*

What stories of sunset have you tended?
What are today's stones that you have laid down?

# The Pouring Forth

**God:**

Beautiful one, you are my clay pot.
From your deep recesses, the elixir of life
laughs in your eyes,
beats from your drum,
pours seeds from your basket,
and the riverbed of your heart blooms.

**My soul:**

You take my breath away.
In my enclosed garden, feel welcome, my God.
I trust that from my rough bulbs,
You will sprout beauty.
From my cave-soul, the music of life will trickle.
From my barren taut skin, vibration will burst,
and I can serve.

**John 12:3-7**

³ *Mary took a pound of costly perfume made of pure nard, anointed Jesus' feet, and wiped them with her hair. The house was filled with the fragrance of the perfume.* ⁴ *But Judas Iscariot, one of his disciples (the one who was about to betray him), said,* ⁵ *"Why was this perfume not sold for three hundred denarii and the money given to the poor?"* ⁶ *(He said this not because he cared about the poor, but because he was a thief; he kept the common purse and used to steal what was put into it.)* ⁷ *Jesus said, "Leave her alone. She bought it so that she might keep it for the day of my burial."*

How does life's elixir pour forth from you?
What music finds vibration in your life?

# Music

### God:

Dissonant child, come catch My music.
Know in your blood flow and heartbeat
the rhythm of My longing. I give you harmony.
I set astir vibrations in the wind and sea to call you to Me.
Let your bones rise up to dance with My grace.
Let your soul swell to singing.
You belong to Me.

### My soul:

Conductor God,
freedom is Your music in my soul.
Let me catch Your wind,
to dance like leaves
the rhythm of Your heart.
I whistle joy with a deep desire for oneness.
Like at new birth, I raise a mighty chorus.
May I praise You always,
God who directs my life.

### Luke 2:13-15

[13] *And suddenly there was with the angel a multitude of the heavenly host, praising God and saying,* [14] *"Glory to God in the highest heaven, and on earth peace among those whom he favors!"* [15] *When the angels had left them and gone into heaven, the shepherds said to one another, "Let us go now to Bethlehem and see this thing that has taken place, which the Lord has made known to us."*

How does oneness with God make music in your life?
What new births give rise to a whistling of joy?

# Hope

**My soul:**

Today hope bubbles up
as I remember You, my Life Source.
It is the freshness of a newborn's skin.
It is the surprise in a splash of color.
It is a flower strong to breach black asphalt.
Come then, with Your feathers, to perch in my soul.

**God:**

I know it is over the rainbow,
this new day.
I know it is beyond you.
It is My sunrise where you see and move.
Forever it is linked with trust
that I am near, that I am here, that I am for you.

**Romans 8:24-25**

[24] *For in hope we were saved. Now hope that is seen is not hope. For who hopes for what is seen?* [25] *But if we hope for what we do not see, we wait for it with patience.*

How does hope come when we remember our God?
When have you known hope?

# Gentle Things

**My soul:**

Gentle—it carries more questions than answers:
feathers, violet petals,
escaped tears, dandelion fuzz!
Are they weakness or empathy or choice?
Are they born of a lover's heart,
so at one in breathing life?

**God:**

I come gently touching your cheek in wind kisses.
I come disguised in your own growing,
knowing of what hurts.
I come in love with you, beckoning your sight.
I come in the sea sparkles of a million God-glimpses.
Small one, believe!
In your faith, see!

**Mark 10:46-52**

⁴⁶ *They came to Jericho. As he and his disciples and a large crowd were leaving Jericho, Bartimaeus son of Timaeus, a blind beggar, was sitting by the roadside.* ⁴⁷ *When he heard that it was Jesus of Nazareth, he began to shout out and say, "Jesus, Son of David, have mercy on me!"* ⁴⁸ *Many sternly ordered him to be quiet, but he cried out even more loudly, "Son of David, have mercy on me!"* ⁴⁹ *Jesus stood still and said, "Call him here." And they called the blind man, saying to him, "Take heart; get up, he is calling you."* ⁵⁰ *So throwing off his cloak, he sprang up and came to Jesus.* ⁵¹ *Then Jesus said to him, "What do you want me to do for you?" The blind man said to him, "My teacher, let me see again."* ⁵² *Jesus said to him, "Go; your faith has made you well." Immediately he regained his sight and followed him on the way.*

When have you known "gentle" in yourself? In others?
How is "gentle" a disguise?

## Guiding Star

**My soul:**

Light of the world, I need a guiding star.
Here all is flat in sameness and in darkness.
I recognize nighttime's constellations shifting in their season.
Distance holds their form for me.
Can I walk the light-year's path by their gracious gift?

**God:**

Can you surrender to My distant light to trudge your mountain cliff paths?
I send these messages of fire hidden by the miles.
These balls of fire toss rock explosions in wild exhilaration,
but you see only tiny sparkles.
Each holds its own family of planets,
but to you from faraway, they give their message.

### Matthew 2:1-7, 9-10

¹ *In the time of King Herod, after Jesus was born in Bethlehem of Judea, wise men from the East came to Jerusalem,* ² *asking, "Where is the child who has been born king of the Jews? For we observed his star at its rising, and have come to pay him homage."* ³ *When King Herod heard this, he was frightened, and all Jerusalem with him;* ⁴ *and calling together all the chief priests and scribes of the people, he inquired of them where the Messiah was to be born.* ⁵ *They told him, "In Bethlehem of Judea; for so it has been written by the prophet:* ⁶ *'And you, Bethlehem, in the land of Judah are by no means least among the rulers of Judah; for from you shall come a ruler who is to shepherd my people Israel.'"* ⁷ *Then Herod secretly called for the wise men and learned from them the exact time when the star had appeared.* ⁹ *When they had heard the king, they set out; and there, ahead of them, went the star that they had seen at its rising, until it stopped over the place where the child was.* ¹⁰ *When they saw that the star had stopped, they were overwhelmed with joy.*

What is shrouded in sameness in your life, feeling flat and dark?
What stars from their distance speak direction to you?

# Treasure

**My soul:**

I want to stand erect, my Maker God, on sturdy bones.
I want to be like naked trees in winter,
waiting tall
with Your wind-music creaking, moaning,
even crashing dead wood.
Where do I find Your treasure?

**God:**

I feel your ache, dear one,
in your honeycombed bones,
with their spaces in between.
I fill them with my liquid gold.
I invite you to lean on Me.
Pain-swept breakings pour forth sweetness.

**Luke 12:34**

*³⁴ For where your treasure is, there your heart will be also.*

How can treasure be stored in fragile bones?
What is the ache in you that God sees?

## Steady

**God:**

I am your leaning post,
your steady and faithful Friend.
Lean on Me when you need balance.
We will walk the long way home.

**My soul:**

In the midst of the storm,
be my Rock.
Comfort and renew me,
for the way is long and I am so tired.

**Isaiah 40:1-5**

*¹ Comfort, O comfort my people, says your God. ² Speak tenderly to Jerusalem, and cry to her that she has served her term, that her penalty is paid, that she has received from the Lord's hand double for all her sins. ³ A voice cries out: "In the wilderness prepare the way of the Lord, make straight in the desert a highway for our God. ⁴ Every valley shall be lifted up, and every mountain and hill be made low; the uneven ground shall become level, and the rough places a plain. ⁵ Then the glory of the Lord shall be revealed, and all people shall see it together, for the mouth of the Lord has spoken."*

How do you claim the entitlement of rest?
When do you know God's companioning you home?

# Whitewash

**My soul:**

Truthful One,
I try to whitewash my life.
I know it is my own denial.
You who called me to be born know truth.
I can't stand my mars and imperfections.
I delude myself only.
Let Your loving gaze heal and catch my eyes.
I want to stand in truth.

**God:**

Little one,
I am an expert at whitewash.
I invented snow so you would know
you are not alone in covering up.
It doesn't take long, though, for slush and mud to show.
The truth is precious. You don't need to gloss over.
I love you as you are and as you are becoming. Look at Me.

**Mark 14:66-72**

⁶⁶ *While Peter was below in the courtyard, one of the servant-girls of the high priest came by.* ⁶⁷ *When she saw Peter warming himself, she stared at him and said, "You also were with Jesus, the man from Nazareth."* ⁶⁸ *But he denied it, saying, "I do not know or understand what you are talking about." And he went out into the forecourt. Then the cock crowed.* ⁶⁹ *And the servant-girl, on seeing him, began again to say to the bystanders, "This man is one of them."* ⁷⁰ *But again he denied it. Then after a little while the bystanders again said to Peter, "Certainly you are one of them; for you are a Galilean."* ⁷¹ *But he began to curse, and he swore an oath, "I do not know this man you are talking about."* ⁷² *At that moment the cock crowed for the second time. Then Peter remembered that Jesus had said to him, "Before the cock crows twice, you will deny me three times." And he broke down and wept.*

Where do you whitewash your life to yourself?
Can you look at God?

## Embedded

**God:**

My enclosed garden,
come be embedded in My life flow.
Offer no resistance.
Let My energy carry you to shine.
I need you.
What is so broken and beleaguered in
our world needs your touch.
You are not a foreign part of My inclusion.
They will see Me if you act.

**My soul:**

God of my delight,
I choose this day to be one with You.
Let all that moves in my life respond to You.
Use me to heal and companion all that feels astray.
We need Your binding of us with You.
Only then will we be whole.

**Acts 4:16-22**

*16 They said, "What will we do with them? For it is obvious to all who live in Jerusalem that a notable sign has been done through them; we cannot deny it. 17 But to keep it from spreading further among the people, let us warn them to speak no more to anyone in this name." 18 So they called them and ordered them not to speak or teach at all in the name of Jesus. 19 But Peter and John answered them, "Whether it is right in God's sight to listen to you rather than to God, you must judge; 20 for we cannot keep from speaking about what we have seen and heard." 21 After threatening them again, they let them go, finding no way to punish them because of the people, for all of them praised God for what had happened. 22 For the man on whom this sign of healing had been performed was more than forty years old.*

How do you experience resistance to God?
Where do you feel called to heal and companion?

# Ashes

**My soul:**

Am I reduced to ashes to be scattered to the winds?
My life shows dusty shadows settled over wanderings.
Who are You, my Origin and Goal?
Can You shape my days to meaning?
Can the fire's remnants still be gathered?
Mercy, Master!

**God:**

Bereft one,
your charred heart will be My drawing pen.
Where ashes catch the wind, there is a clearing for fresh breath.
All residue will feed a hope unearthed.
You are not wasted.
Your days are more than dust in the wind.
I call you to trust.

**Malachi 4:1-3**

*¹ See, the day is coming, burning like an oven, when all the arrogant and all evildoers will be stubble; the day that comes shall burn them up, says the Lord of hosts, so that it will leave them neither root nor branch. ² But for you who revere my name the sun of righteousness shall rise, with healing in its wings. You shall go out leaping like calves from the stall. ³ And you shall tread down the wicked, for they will be ashes under the soles of your feet, on the day when I act, says the Lord of hosts.*

What feels like ashes in your life?
What is God drawing with your charcoal heart?

# Rinse

### God:

Muddy child,
let Me soap you down and rinse away the filth.
I will wash clean
what dirt would cling.
My water gives refreshment.
What you carry as burden and as grime, I will clear!
What is caked-on crud, I will remove.
Come bathe in My freedom.

### My soul:

Launderer God,
Only You can love my mud-streaked face.
Tears and playing on garbage heaps
have left their marks.
Clean me and hold me and towel my hair.
Let me smell of Your fragrance.
Let me savor Your care.

### Mark 1:6-8

*⁶ Now John was clothed with camel's hair, with a leather belt around his waist, and he ate locusts and wild honey. ⁷ He proclaimed, "The one who is more powerful than I is coming after me; I am not worthy to stoop down and untie the thong of his sandals. ⁸ I have baptized you with water; but he will baptize you with the Holy Spirit."*

What are you carrying of burden and of grime?
What garbage heaps are you playing on?

# January 28

## Exhaustion

**My soul:**

Forever-young God,
exhaustion settles in my bones
like age draining color from my hair.
I am worn out from too many days of moving in fog.
Bring a bright blue day, Keeper of Color.
Put dance in my step, Spark of Energy.
Lift the weariness of my soul to again receive Your love.
You are my Ancient Newness.

**God:**

Enfeebled soul,
I raise you up once more on strong knees.
Like a capering goat, be free across the hills of your mind.
Where you are depleted of dreams,
let Me draw you to mountaintop vistas.
I will refresh you to know young love again.
The apple trees blossom again in your heart.

**Acts 2:17**

*¹⁷ 'In the last days it will be, God declares, that I will pour out my Spirit upon all flesh, and your sons and your daughters shall prophesy and your young men shall see visions, and your old men shall dream dreams.*

Where are you moving in a fog?
Where are you depleted of dreams?

## Coma

**God:**

Sleepwalker,
break out of your coma
of not enough,
of Pollyanna self-focus,
of making Me invisible.
You are here because I am here.
Come be conscious.
Awake to wonder.
For this, you are called to life.

**My soul:**

I hear You, my God and my All.
It is a new day!
Let me arise to Your sun
and today's possibilities.
You are not invisible.
May I be woke
like luminous comet dust obscuring solid mass;
race me to Your arms.
Let me know Your substance.

**Isaiah 43:19-21**

[19] *I am about to do a new thing; now it springs forth, do you not perceive it? I will make a way in the wilderness and rivers in the desert.* [20] *The wild animals will honor the jackals, the ostriches; and me for I give water in the wilderness, rivers in the desert, to give drink to my chosen people,* [21] *the people whom I formed for myself so that they might declare my praise.*

Where do you walk in a coma, unaware?
How do you see the God who is visible?

# Elephant

**My soul:**

God of big things,
elephants come lumbering to my mind.
How did You imagine them?
I long to have their big hearts
that grieve the loss of loved ones.
I yearn to learn their community circle
to secure safety and life.
I love their ears that fan in grace and humor.
And such trunks for playfulness and teasing.
God of imaginings, I want to know You, their Creator.

**God:**

Odd child,
you don't think elephants tell Me
their longings about humans?
In the circle of life, there is no up and down.
All are learners and yearners.
Come with Me and let's play in My world.
Look with My eyes. Hear with My ears.
Love with My heart and laugh.

**Isaiah 49:15, 20-22**

[15] *Can a woman forget her nursing child, or show no compassion for the child of her womb? Even these may forget, yet I will not forget you.* [20] *The children born in the time of your bereavement will yet say in your hearing: "The place is too crowded for me; make room for me to settle."* [21] *Then you will say in your heart, "Who has borne me these? I was bereaved and barren, exiled and put away—so who has reared these? I was left all alone—where then have these come from?"* [22] *Thus says the Lord God: I will soon lift up my hand to the nations, and raise my signal to the peoples; and they shall bring your sons in their bosom, and your daughters shall be carried on their shoulders.*

Where do you conceive life as up and down?
Who are the children brought of your longing?

## Pristine

**God:**

Look out at your vast universe.
It is pristine.
Colors sweep in swirls
of stars born of rocks and fire and nebulae.
And you, tiny one,
are on your small blue earth.
I choose you to live and make your mark.
You are fresh and beautiful.
I send you.

**My soul:**

Open my heart to Your sky,
Great Architect of Life.
As chaos clashes in the vastness,
I see Your order,
Your law,
Your hand.
Keep me looking at the stars
to know my calling.
I will not be afraid.
I am Yours.

### Zephaniah 3:12-13

¹² *For I will leave in the midst of you a people humble and lowly.*
*They shall seek refuge in the name of the Lord—*¹³ *the remnant of*
*Israel; they shall do no wrong and utter no lies, nor shall a deceitful*
*tongue be found in their mouths. Then they will pasture and lie*
*down, and no one shall make them afraid.*

How does feeling small invite your fearlessness?
How does looking at the stars tell you your mission in life?

# February

1. Mystery
2. Seal
3. Inconsolable
4. Curves
5. Penny
6. Lean
7. Follower
8. Loneliness
9. Snow
10. Hurry
11. Awkward
12. Tuft
13. Hazard
14. Stairway
15. Totem
16. Resistance
17. Picnic
18. Soil
19. Silence
20. Ancient Grove
21. Anguish
22. Icicles
23. Surprise
24. Swept Away
25. Feathers
26. Release
27. Wine Jug
28. Secret
29. Morning Dew

## February 1

# Mystery

**My soul:**

Mystery,
You are my secret Love.
You breathe into me life.
You know my private thoughts.
The enigma is that You who made
the universe would notice me!
In the power of Your gaze, may I walk tall and desired.
I want to respond lavishly as You have.
How do I do that, my Love?

**God:**

Shy and small one,
shout out your love for me.
Lose your reticence.
Let My touch stir your response.
What is invisible to a whole
unconscious world, you see!
Dare to feel the passion.
Risk My way of life.
Trust My love to move you.
I am here with you.

**Ephesians 1:17-19**

*17 I pray that the God of our Lord Jesus Christ, the Father of glory, may give you a spirit of wisdom and revelation as you come to know him, 18 so that, with the eyes of your heart enlightened, you may know what is the hope to which he has called you, what are the riches of his glorious inheritance among the saints, 19 and what is the immeasurable greatness of his power for us who believe, according to the working of his great power.*

Where and how do you want to respond lavishly?
What impels your life as you see God's love for you?

## February 2

## Seal

**My soul:**

My Chosen One,
set Your seal upon me.
Make tight my tie to You.
Confirm Your hold on my life.
I wear Your insignia on my heart
and beg to deepen this truth all the
days of my life.
By Your permission, I walk in Your light,
bearing Your name in my living.
Touch my days with Your ring of truth.

**God:**

My bride, My beloved,
don your white gown and know I wait.
On the long aisle you march,
have no eyes but for Me.
I claim you in liberty.
The seal is set on your heart.
We make home in love
a shelter for many of the earth.

**Song of Songs 7:10-12**

*¹⁰ I am my beloved's, and his desire is for me. ¹¹ Come, my beloved, let us go forth into the fields, and lodge in the villages; ¹² let us go out early to the vineyards, and see whether the vines have budded, whether the grape blossoms have opened and the pomegranates are in bloom. There I will give you my love.*

How are you walking in God's light?
How are you and your Beloved making home for many?

# Inconsolable

**God:**

Tender child,
you weep without stopping.
Inconsolable, you ache in your heart
for wholeness.
Let Me hold you.
I know you see a darkness
that blocks hope.
I hear your orphan wail.
I've got you, little one.

**My soul:**

Big and Mighty God,
I am so scared.
In the dark, I fumble around.
Are You here?
Will You hold me?
You are so big; I am so small.
Will You dry my tears?

**Luke 7:11-15**

[11] *Soon afterwards  he went to a town called Nain, and his disciples
and a large crowd went with him.* [12] *As he approached the gate of
the town, a man who had died was being carried out. He was his
mother's only son, and she was a widow; and with her was a large
crowd from the town.* [13] *When the Lord saw her, he had
compassion for her and said to her, "Do not weep."* [14] *Then he came
forward and touched the bier, and the bearers stood still. And he
said, "Young man, I say to you, rise!"* [15] *The dead man sat up and
began to speak, and Jesus gave him to his mother.*

What is the wail of your heart?
How does the Big God hold you?

## Curves

**My soul:**

God, my heart's desire,
all seems curves.
There are no straight lines to You.
In my unfolding days, life gets complicated.
The words I would speak, I don't.
The actions where I'd choose to be brave pass before me.
The freedom to serve clogs, and I stand passively.
May all my turnings draw me to You.
I can't do it alone.

**God:**

Bereft person,
aren't the curves beautiful?
You don't have to do it alone.
I send My Spirit. Listen and lean on Her.
With the wind, it will be effortless.
With Spirit fire, you will capture the urge.
You will be in harmony,
like geese on the move in autumn.
Open your life to My Spirit.

**Ezekiel 37:1-6**

¹ *The hand of the Lord came upon me, and he brought me out by
the spirit of the Lord and set me down in the middle of a valley; it
was full of bones.* ² *He led me all around them; there were very
many lying in the valley, and they were very dry.* ³ *He said to me,
"Mortal, can these bones live?" I answered, "O Lord God, you
know."* ⁴ *Then he said to me, "Prophesy to these bones, and say to
them: O dry bones, hear the word of the Lord.* ⁵ *Thus says the
Lord God to these bones: I will cause breath to enter you, and you
shall live.* ⁶ *I will lay sinews on you, and will cause flesh to come
upon you, and cover you with skin, and put breath in you, and
you shall live; and you shall know that I am the Lord."*

Where is your life complicated?
Where is your motivation stuck, freed?

# Penny

**God:**

Trader creature,
I sent you a penny today.
Did you see it dropped on your pathway?
Is it too small for you to notice?
What story holds its leaving?
Will you bend to pick up this treasure?
This coin of the realm waits for your attention,
like all My surprises along your way.

**My soul:**

Lord of my world,
I am a beggar in Your universe.
I am also a prince in Your realm.
Scattered on my way are
life exchanges of joy and wealth.
I see You in this fun.
Teach me to bend in Your game.

**Luke 15:8-10**

[8] *"Or what woman having ten silver coins, if she loses one of them, does not light a lamp, sweep the house, and search carefully until she finds it?* [9] *When she has found it, she calls together her friends and neighbors, saying, 'Rejoice with me, for I have found the coin that I had lost.'* [10] *Just so, I tell you, there is joy in the presence of the angels of God over one sinner who repents."*

How is God playing a game with you?
Where are you being called to be a beggar in order to discover your princely call?

## Lean

**My soul:**

Lavish Lord,
how do I learn to share?
These are lean times
when breath and food and energy are rare!
Catch to fullness my listing ship to Your wind.
Break open my cupboard of plenty to all who lack.
I lean on Your hold on me.

**God:**

Hoarder of earth's bounty,
do you see My skinny ones?
Let your heart be moved—these are your family.
What slants toward destruction can be righted.
Lean on Me.

**Lamentations 3:19-24**

*[19] The thought of my affliction and my homelessness is wormwood and gall! [20] My soul continually thinks of it and is bowed down within me. [21] But this I call to mind, and therefore I have hope: [22] The steadfast love of the Lord never ceases, his mercies never come to an end; [23] they are new every morning; great is your faithfulness. [24] "The Lord is my portion," says my soul, "therefore I will hope in him."*

How do you learn to share?
When do you know joy in the sharing?

# Follower

**God:**

Soul, gifted with life,
follow me to the edges of your world.
The adventure you are on
will have unbelievable sunrises and sunsets.
All that is in between
will entail meeting strangers
to jump-start their stops.
There will be bruises and blisters.
Your decisions will come from dreams and darkness.
But remember, you are never alone.
I am with you.

**My soul:**

Shining Son,
I come after You.
With all my spirit-longing, I yearn to travel alongside.
How do I conform to Your energy of making family?
How do I meet tigers and sharks
with signs of peace and not go nuclear?
How do I trace Your pathway? It was rejected!
Make me a brave follower. Send me Your Spirit.

**2 Kings 2:6, 9-10**

[6] *Then Elijah said to him, "Stay here; for the Lord has sent me to the Jordan." But he said, "As the Lord lives, and as you yourself live, I will not leave you." So the two of them went on.* [9] *When they had crossed, Elijah said to Elisha, "Tell me what I may do for you, before I am taken from you." Elisha said, "Please let me inherit a double share of your spirit."* [10] *He responded, "You have asked a hard thing; yet, if you see me as I am being taken from you, it will be granted you; if not, it will not."*

What strangers are you meeting who need jump-starts?
How are you called to conform to God's energy of making family?

## Loneliness

**My soul:**

Walker in my soul,
sadness creeps over me with a soul lonesomeness.
I am forlorn
as it soaks into my being.
Even in a crowd, I walk in solitary confinement
because I cannot unlock my heart.
Come, Maker of Joy,
play Your fiddle with gusto.
Call me to dance the jig.
Fill my body and my spirit with Your ties of community,
oozing out my loneliness.
I am Yours.

**God:**

Desolate one,
I know your heart.
I unlock it and put My feet up there.
I pull out my violin.
Do you hear the melody of love that I play for you?
Let the lilt lift you.
It will soon become the jig to build community.
For I send you forth with music in your soul.

**Acts 2:43-47**

*⁴³ Awe came upon everyone, because many wonders and signs were being done by the apostles. ⁴⁴ All who believed were together and had all things in common; ⁴⁵ they would sell their possessions and goods and distribute the proceeds to all, as any had need. ⁴⁶ Day by day, as they spent much time together in the temple, they broke bread at home and ate their food with glad and generous hearts, ⁴⁷ praising God and having the goodwill of all the people. And day-by-day the Lord added to their number those who were being saved.*

What keeps your heart locked?
What music are you being sent forth to play for others?

41

## Snow

**God:**

Frenetic one, it snows.
I lay My blanket on a very weary world.
Rest now.
Sleep.
The single path along once-traveled roads
invites your walk with Me.
Come, let's talk
of memories,
of mercies,
of the million gifts
scattered in your way.
It is Our time.
Let Us savor.

**My soul:**

God, content to be quiet,
our world covered in snow quiets my soul.
Be at home with me by the fire.
Speak to me of Your longing.
I hold it tenderly as I listen.
Awake me to You.
I want to walk in Your way.

**Mark 8:34-37**

[34] *He called the crowd with his disciples, and said to them, "If any want to become my followers, let them deny themselves and take up their cross and follow me. [35] For those who want to save their life will lose it, and those who lose their life for my sake, and for the sake of the gospel, will save it. [36] For what will it profit them to gain the whole world and forfeit their life? [37] Indeed, what can they give in return for their life?"*

How is snow time your time with God?
What does God speak to you in Her longing?

# Hurry

**My soul:**

All-seeing Master,
I hurry down the corridors of my days.
I rush headlong as the years gather.
Buckets fill precipitously with urgency of time's speed.
Do I believe heaven is now? I can slow to see You.
Do I move so fast, snapping pictures,
listing brimful schedules, posting notables,
and not breathe in Your beauty, Your omnipresence,
Your gaze on me that I pass by?
Is that what stalking death does?
Mercy, my Lord and God!

**God:**

Frantic person, slow down.
I yearn to catch your glance.
Your thoughts rush past like a windstorm.
You catch debris and follow its scattering
while I watch. I am here, waiting for you
to know you are loved.

**Mark 9:33-37**

*³³ Then they came to Capernaum; and when he was in the house he asked them, "What were you arguing about on the way?" ³⁴ But they were silent, for on the way they had argued with one another who was the greatest. ³⁵ He sat down, called the twelve, and said to them, "Whoever wants to be first must be last of all and servant of all." ³⁶ Then he took a little child and put it among them; and taking it in his arms, he said to them, ³⁷ "Whoever welcomes one such child in my name welcomes me, and whoever welcomes me welcomes not me but the one who sent me."*

Do you believe heaven is now?
When does God catch your glance?

# Awkward

**God:**

Awkward child,
I know you are clumsy.
You tumble and fumble at living.
I hear your stuttering prayers.
When I listen to your social conversation,
I see your hunger for connection is cumbersome.
You stumble over truth
like a needle in straw.
But I want you to know:
Nothing can separate you from My love.

**My soul:**

God of the big arms,
hold me when I wriggle and am ungainly.
I am awkward.
I lack grace.
Let Your love overflow within me
to all who, like me, are inept.
All of us are inelegant in expression.
I say it simply: I love You,
God who made me.

**Romans 8:37-39**

[37] *No, in all these things we are more than conquerors through him who loved us.* [38] *For I am convinced that neither death, nor life, nor angels, nor rulers, nor things present, nor things to come, nor powers,* [39] *nor height, nor depth, nor anything else in all creation, will be able to separate us from the love of God in Christ Jesus our Lord.*

Where are you stumbling over truth?
Where do you wriggle in God's hold?

## Tuft

**My soul:**

God of laughter,
are You smiling at the tuft
escaping from its ribbon?
My plumage is the million
monkey thoughts that take
me far afield from You.
It is a shock of hair
refusing to be tamed.
Like feathers on a peacock
shouting "Look at me,"
You have to laugh at my pretense.
I trust Your humor, Lord, at such buffoonery.

**God:**

Knotty one,
because I love you, I laugh
at your mind's cowlicks.
The ruff that pokes up
can hurt though.
So I comb your wild and wandering
thought clusters with My gentle hand.
Speak gently!
Pray with attention.
Have kind eyes.
You are My sign in a very jungled world.

### Colossians 3:1-4

*¹ So if you have been raised with Christ, seek the things that are above, where Christ is, seated at the right hand of God. ² Set your minds on things that are above, not on things that are on earth, ³ for you have died, and your life is hidden with Christ in God. ⁴ When Christ who is your life is revealed, then you also will be revealed with him in glory.*

What monkey thoughts do you hope God laughs at?
How are your thoughts showing up in behaviors?

# Hazard

### God:

I call you, my child, to see!
You hazard life
in your dangerous pursuit
of distraction.
The chance you take in disguise
is not innocence or inattention.
Beware of the dangers.
You risk My call to deepen.

### My soul:

I long to walk in the sunlight with You.
What mars and blinds,
I surrender to Your healing.
Dear Maker, I want to deepen,
but the precipice paralyzes
and I sit down.
Alas, in this, I refuse to grow.
Have mercy.
Please take my hand.

### Mark 8:22-26

*22 They came to Bethsaida. Some people brought a blind man to him and begged him to touch him. 23 He took the blind man by the hand and led him out of the village; and when he had put saliva on his eyes and laid his hands on him, he asked him, "Can you see anything?" 24 And the man looked up and said, "I can see people, but they look like trees, walking." 25 Then Jesus laid his hands on his eyes again; and he looked intently and his sight was restored, and he saw everything clearly. 26 Then he sent him away to his home, saying, "Do not even go into the village."*

What dangers do you meet by not seeing?
Where are you called to deepen?

# Stairway

**God:**

Dear one whose heart I know,
Jesus is your way.
Let Him be your stairway,
who calls you to climb.
The Spirit is your energy,
who sets your pace
and gives you breath.
I call to you
since I know you can't imagine
where this stairway leads.

**My soul:**

I know You,
Spark within me.
Keep me climbing.
I hold within the awesome vista,
even though enclosed,
because You urge me onward.

**John 16:4-7**

⁴ *"But I have said these things to you so that when their hour comes you may remember that I told you about them. I did not say these things to you from the beginning, because I was with you. ⁵ But now I am going to him who sent me; yet none of you asks me, 'Where are you going?' ⁶ But because I have said these things to you, sorrow has filled your hearts. ⁷ Nevertheless I tell you the truth: it is to your advantage that I go away, for if I do not go away, the Advocate will not come to you; but if I go, I will send him to you."*

What can you say of your pace of climbing?
What is your inner Spark revealing to you about your destination?

# Totem

**My soul:**

Holy One,
I'm given the totem of my community.
A cross is signed on my head
in ashes.
It is raised among us in wood carried from the forged crossroads
of our leader,
of our martyrs,
of my own suffering;
blood seals words and actions.

**God:**

Do you believe in me? Receive then, little follower,
the legacy you've been born into.
It is trial-tested.
It is the life-force bonding that you receive.
The cross enfolds My community.
It records the history of soul happenings
where trust is,
where you are raised up.
I've got you!

**1 Peter 1:20-21**

²⁰ *He was destined before the foundation of the world, but was revealed at the end of the ages for your sake. ²¹ Through him you have come to trust in God, who raised him from the dead and gave him glory, so that your faith and hope are set on God.*

How has the cross been a sign of our community?
How do you experience that God's got you?

# Resistance

**My soul:**

God of Amazing Grace,
I know resistance in me. It takes many forms.
It looks like a stubbornness that fiercely fights unfairness.
There is the vacuum of being hollowed out by loss that I rush to fill.
There is surrender to You, so much bigger than me,
that overwhelms and raises fear.
In Your grace, I intend no resistance.

**God:**

Free spirit, know I rejoice in your freedom.
I allow it leeway. I choose your loving.
Resistance is needed against passivity.
It is the shape of soul-gravity pushing against the lure.
I will hold you tightly when you rage and reach to harm,
but I will weep and wait a lifetime for you to welcome love.

**Matthew 23:37-39**

[37] *"Jerusalem, Jerusalem, the city that kills the prophets and stones those who are sent to it! How often have I desired to gather your children together as a hen gathers her brood under her wings, and you were not willing!* [38] *See, your house is left to you, desolate.* [39] *For I tell you, you will not see me again until you say, 'Blessed is the one who comes in the name of the Lord.'"*

Where do you resist?
How do you intend no resistance to the God who will hold you and the
God who will wait?

# Picnic

**My soul:**

Great and Generous Dreamer, as far as the eye can see
is a place of green grass.
Gather all of us who come to Your picnic.
We laugh and sing, build campfires, and set out the table.
These extend down valleys and up mountains,
on and on through time.
We tell the tales of Your love—it is the Kingdom.

**God:**

You are a dreamer with Me of such mighty sharing.
It is a feast of fun!
There is no one who doesn't belong,
and always there is enough!

**John 6:5-13**

⁵ *When he looked up and saw a large crowd coming toward him, Jesus said to Philip, "Where are we to buy bread for these people to eat?"* ⁶ *He said this to test him, for he himself knew what he was going to do.* ⁷ *Philip answered him, "Six months' wages would not buy enough bread for each of them to get a little."* ⁸ *One of his disciples, Andrew, Simon Peter's brother, said to him,* ⁹ *"There is a boy here who has five barley loaves and two fish. But what are they among so many people?"* ¹⁰ *Jesus said, "Make the people sit down." Now there was a great deal of grass in the place; so they sat down, about five thousand in all.* ¹¹ *Then Jesus took the loaves, and when he had given thanks, he distributed them to those who were seated; so also the fish, as much as they wanted.* ¹² *When they were satisfied, he told his disciples, "Gather up the fragments left over, so that nothing may be lost."* ¹³ *So they gathered them up, and from the fragments of the five barley loaves, left by those who had eaten, they filled twelve baskets.*

What is your dream of the Kingdom?
How is your sense of "enough" challenged?

## Soil

**God:**

Evolving creature,
I made you from the soil,
a receiver of nutrients,
a holder of moisture.
I want to see you bloom.
Do not be afraid of dirty smudges
or clay that clings.
This is humus where growing happens.
I've made your lavish banquet.

**My soul:**

Daring God,
I yearn to believe
in the soil of my becoming.
I need to trust to Your bounty my growing.
I love the feast You make for me
to blossom.
Come inhabit my land.

**Matthew 13:8**

*⁸ Other seeds fell on good soil and brought forth grain, some a hundredfold, some sixty, some thirty.*

Where are you afraid of dirty smudges and clinging clay?
How are you blossoming in your soil?

# Silence

**God:**

Hush, little one.
You are crowded inside and small
and cannot see Me.
Be still in your soul.
I am here!
Come through the white fog to my Presence.
Let silence reveal Me.

**My soul:**

I surrender moment by moment
the distractions and thoughts that clamor.
You are here, Holy One.
I let my bonds fall away
to hear beyond the noise
and to see You through the mist.
This pause of mind is pregnant.
Can I hold You?

**1 Kings 19:11-13**

*¹¹ He said, "Go out and stand on the mountain before the Lord, for the Lord is about to pass by." Now there was a great wind, so strong that it was splitting mountains and breaking rocks in pieces before the Lord, but the Lord was not in the wind; and after the wind an earthquake, but the Lord was not in the earthquake; ¹² and after the earthquake a fire, but the Lord was not in the fire; and after the fire a sound of sheer silence. ¹³ When Elijah heard it, he wrapped his face in his mantle and went out and stood at the entrance of the cave. Then there came a voice to him that said, "What are you doing here, Elijah?"*

How do you recognize God's presence?
How is the pause of your mind pregnant?

# Ancient Grove

**My soul:**

Here to this ancient grove I come.
I hear Your coming in the silence, Great One!
Here the tall and swaying trees
are witness to desperation.
They stir to a warrior song
touched by You, the music of life.
I hear in this gathering spot
all creation tending.
I bow and weep and seek!

**God:**

Rise up, child of my heart.
Here in this forest, I confirm your knighthood.
I send you forth,
walking and skipping and leaping, dancing to My song.
Lay down your fierce endeavor. Let me lead.

**Hosea 11:3-4**

³ *Yet it was I who taught Ephraim to walk, I took them up in my arms; but they did not know that I healed them.* ⁴ *I led them with cords of human kindness, with bands of love. I was to them like those who lift infants to their cheeks. I bent down to them and fed them.*

Which ancient grove draws you to meet the Holy One?
How does your knighthood call you to serve?

# Anguish

**God:**

I ache with you, bereft one.
I know the anguish of your soul.
I dwell in the cells of your being.
Life holds you.
Trust this!

**My soul:**

I cannot find you, Lord.
I know I live.
Is that how I know You?
My angst is buried in the truth of my limits.
I cannot see beyond my inner holes
to where You shine!
So all I can do is believe!

**Psalm 46:10**

¹⁰ *"Be still, and know that I am God! I am exalted among the nations, I am exalted in the earth."*

How do you feel your angst before God?
How does life hold you?

## Icicles

**God:**

Can you imagine icicles, my love?
Out of the freezing cold,
I created beauty in the melting.
From rocks and rooftops,
warmth drips crystal lines that catch light.
Beware because their falling can be dangerous.
Winter is on the move!

**My soul:**

Amazing God,
I love Your message in art.
In my own frozen time
buried in banks of snow,
please come and melt me.
Catch the movement of possibility and make it gleam.
The points of my changing can fall in danger to all who pass under.
In my frigid cold, I stand in Your sun and wait.

**Matthew 16:21-23**

²¹ *From that time on, Jesus began to show his disciples that he must go to Jerusalem and undergo great suffering at the hands of the elders and chief priests and scribes, and be killed, and on the third day be raised.* ²² *And Peter took him aside and began to rebuke him, saying, "God forbid it, Lord! This must never happen to you."* ²³ *But he turned and said to Peter, "Get behind me, Satan! You are a stumbling block to me; for you are setting your mind not on divine things but on human things."*

Where is winter keeping you frozen?
How can your changing endanger others like falling icicles?

## February 23

## Surprise

**God:**

Are you open to see? I send you a surprise!
Out of the ordinary appears the fresh, like magic:
a sunset, a troupe of deer, a present.
Do you realize My attention to you—
what you like, what you need.
Change comes ringing to let you know I love you.

**My soul:**

How can I who am so small see You, Invisible Master,
who are beyond my wildest grasp?
So You send surprises. You engage my tiny ways:
a parking spot, a healing hardly noticed, a connection once broken,
snow to the brown landscape.
I see Your gifts, and I want to scatter my days with gifts for You.

**Exodus 16:9-15**

⁹ *Then Moses said to Aaron, "Say to the whole congregation of the Israelites, 'Draw near to the Lord, for he has heard your complaining.'"* ¹⁰ *And as Aaron spoke to the whole congregation of the Israelites, they looked toward the wilderness, and the glory of the Lord appeared in the cloud.* ¹¹ *The Lord spoke to Moses and said,* ¹² *"I have heard the complaining of the Israelites; say to them, 'At twilight you shall eat meat, and in the morning you shall have your fill of bread; then you shall know that I am the Lord your God.'"* ¹³ *In the evening quails came up and covered the camp; and in the morning there was a layer of dew around the camp.* ¹⁴ *When the layer of dew lifted, there on the surface of the wilderness was a fine flaky substance, as fine as frost on the ground.* ¹⁵ *When the Israelites saw it, they said to one another, "What is it?" For they did not know what it was. Moses said to them, "It is the bread that the Lord has given you to eat."*

What surprises does God give you?
What gifts can you plant in your days for God?

## Swept Away

**My soul:**

God who designed gravity, the movement of the stars,
the seasons of our lives, and us humans,
please have mercy! We are being swept away!
The earth, our home, is overrun.
We've been rolled over by our choices and have no control.
I am being swept away, lifted high by passion.
Am I enjoying the exhilaration of "on the edge,"
having my heart caught up?
Dancing into safety, desires bubble up from my life force.

**God:**

Frightened child,
swept away in waves or wind or earthquake,
I am here in the sheer silence.
Wait in your cave for My passing.
On the long journey of fear, knowing death is tracking,
move in My energy.
There is no security yet you shall live.
I walk with you.
I am within you. Have courage.

**John 16:29-33**

*²⁹ His disciples said, "Yes, now you are speaking plainly, not in any figure of speech! ³⁰ Now we know that you know all things, and do not need to have anyone question you; by this we believe that you came from God." ³¹ Jesus answered them, "Do you now believe? ³² The hour is coming, indeed it has come, when you will be scattered, each one to his home, and you will leave me alone. Yet I am not alone because the Father is with me. ³³ I have said this to you, so that in me you may have peace. In the world you face persecution. But take courage; I have conquered the world!"*

How do you experience our earth being swept away beneath us?
Where is God walking with you in your fear?

## Feathers

**My soul:**

Gracious Giver,
I watched the ducks today,
marveled at their feathers' colors.
They can shake off and dry and lift and fly.
Oh to be so light, to so radiantly shine.

**God:**

These are your brother and sister creatures
who alert your heart to beauty.
Keep hope; you, too, are rain resistant.
See My way for you; you, too, can reach the sky.
Let My love abide in you; you, too, can shine!

### John 4:7-15

*⁷ A Samaritan woman came to draw water, and Jesus said to her, "Give me a drink." ⁸ (His disciples had gone to the city to buy food.) ⁹ The Samaritan woman said to him, "How is it that you, a Jew, ask a drink of me, a woman of Samaria?" (Jews do not share things in common with Samaritans.) ¹⁰ Jesus answered her, "If you knew the gift of God, and who it is that is saying to you, 'Give me a drink,' you would have asked him, and he would have given you living water." ¹¹ The woman said to him, "Sir, you have no bucket, and the well is deep. Where do you get that living water? ¹² Are you greater than our ancestor Jacob, who gave us the well, and with his sons and his flocks drank from it?" ¹³ Jesus said to her, "Everyone who drinks of this water will be thirsty again, ¹⁴ but those who drink of the water that I will give them will never be thirsty. The water that I will give will become in them a spring of water gushing up to eternal life." ¹⁵ The woman said to him, "Sir, give me this water, so that I may never be thirsty or have to keep coming here to draw water."*

How does God's way help you fly?
When in your life are you rain resistant?

## Release

### God:

My precious one,
I unlock the bars that confine you.
My earth is for your roaming.
Isn't it beautiful?
Let go of your inside shackles.
Untighten your fears.
You have what is needed.

### My soul:

My Falcon Lord,
fly me to freedom.
I surrender to Love.
In each new turn of my fate,
lift me up.
Open my heart.
Release me to laugh and to serve.

### Luke 22:39-46

[39] *He came out and went, as was his custom, to the Mount of Olives; and the disciples followed him.* [40] *When he reached the place, he said to them, "Pray that you may not come into the time of trial."* [41] *Then he withdrew from them about a stone's throw, knelt down, and prayed,* [42] *"Father, if you are willing, remove this cup from me; yet, not my will but yours be done."* [43] *Then an angel from heaven appeared to him and gave him strength.* [44] *In his anguish he prayed more earnestly, and his sweat became like great drops of blood falling down on the ground.* [45] *When he got up from prayer, he came to the disciples and found them sleeping because of grief,* [46] *and he said to them, "Why are you sleeping? Get up and pray that you may not come into the time of trial."*

What confines your heart?
Where would you roam in freedom?

**February 27**

# Wine Jug

**God:**

Little mind, are you scandalized that I
would choose to hide in wine? Let this be a sign to you!
That which carries the taint of looseness, debauchery, and numbing
also carries the shine of celebration, community, joy, and ME!

**My soul:**

Your ways are not my ways, my Lord.
I taste the richness of You carrying the mix of human life.
To drown my blues stands equal to toasting my bonds of victory.
There is the crushing and the juice.
There is the ferment of waiting
for the sugars to create my labors.
Come, Luscious Lord, come.

**John 2:1-10**

[1] *On the third day there was a wedding in Cana of Galilee, and the mother of Jesus was there.* [2] *Jesus and his disciples had also been invited to the wedding.* [3] *When the wine gave out, the mother of Jesus said to him, "They have no wine."* [4] *And Jesus said to her, "Woman, what concern is that to you and to me? My hour has not yet come."* [5] *His mother said to the servants, "Do whatever he tells you."* [6] *Now standing there were six stone water jars for the Jewish rites of purification, each holding twenty or thirty gallons.* [7] *Jesus said to them, "Fill the jars with water." And they filled them up to the brim.* [8] *He said to them, "Now draw some out, and take it to the chief steward." So they took it.* [9] *When the steward tasted the water that had become wine, and did not know where it came from (though the servants who had drawn the water knew), the steward called the bridegroom* [10] *and said to him, "Everyone serves the good wine first, and then the inferior wine after the guests have become drunk. But you have kept the good wine until now."*

When do you experience when the divine is hidden in the coarse?
How is there hope hidden in what is crushing you?

# Secret

**My soul:**

Playful Master,
I've had a glimpse of Your secret.
Planted, hidden, You are shining all around.
My attention keeps getting distracted by
grains of nothingness.
Do not let me miss You
enclosed in me.
How can You be so near
and I not know?
Secret of my soul, I adore.

**God:**

I ache to be known.
Can you hear My truth?
In mere whispers, I speak
so you won't be afraid.
It is My revealing of "pray always";
then you won't ever feel alone.

**1 Thessalonians 5:16-19**

*16 Rejoice always, 17 pray without ceasing, 18 give thanks in all circumstances; for this is the will of God in Christ Jesus for you. 19 Do not quench the Spirit.*

How do you know God's secret?
What is your secret?

## Morning Dew

**God:**

I know your callouses,
your hands and feet, worn and gnarled.
You see, I am the Ancient One.
You wear the work of days,
but I have made your way.
Where you wonder if you labor in vain,
I see your apple harvest.
Taste with Me the juice of your choices.
It is the astonishment of your glory.

**My soul:**

Light Within,
soften my thick and knobby soul with Your ever-fresh sunrise.
Come into the garden of my days to fertilize and prune.
Let Your morning dew refresh.
I want to go apple picking with You.

**Daniel 7:13-14**

*¹³ As I watched in the night visions, I saw one like a human being coming with the clouds of heaven. And he came to the Ancient One and was presented before him.¹⁴ To him was given dominion and glory and kingship, that all peoples, nations, and languages should serve him. His dominion is an everlasting dominion that shall not pass away, and his kingship is one that shall never be destroyed.*

When do you wonder if you labor in vain?
What sunrises soften your callouses?

# March

1. Labyrinth
2. Courtyard
3. Heroine
4. Wings
5. Roots
6. Make Room
7. Heart Listening
8. Hospitality
9. May I?
10. Exile
11. Bird Song
12. Enough
13. Weavings
14. Longing
15. Mirror
16. Beehive
17. Sapphire
18. Rocks
19. Sands
20. Well
21. Breathing
22. Ladder
23. Candle
24. Dust
25. Time
26. Forest
27. Fireflies
28. Birches
29. Scorched
30. Talisman
31. Tapestry

## March 1

# Labyrinth

**My soul:**

It is otherworldly, God to whom I cling.
I feel so near my Center,
and then my path veers backward
and I trudge sightless
and hungry for a goal.
Let me feel You near.
I hold with whitened knuckles to Your hand,
for I am caught in this endless circle
and I fear.

**God:**

I walk with you, nearsighted girl.
The way meanders, calling you to watch
the path of turns and stones.
Let your heart be free to trust.
You are not lost on this holy walk,
though you do not see the end,
for I hold your hand.

**Exodus 16:1-4**

*¹ The whole congregation of the Israelites set out from Elim; and Israel came to the wilderness of Sin, which is between Elim and Sinai, on the fifteenth day of the second month after they had departed from the land of Egypt. ² The whole congregation of the Israelites complained against Moses and Aaron in the wilderness. ³ The Israelites said to them, "If only we had died by the hand of the Lord in the land of Egypt, when we sat by the fleshpots and ate our fill of bread; for you have brought us out into this wilderness to kill this whole assembly with hunger." ⁴ Then the Lord said to Moses, "I am going to rain bread from heaven for you, and each day the people shall go out and gather enough for that day. In that way I will test them, whether they will follow my instruction or not."*

How are you circling forward and retreating in your life?
What goal leads you onward, and how do you feel God's hand?

# Courtyard

### God:

Let's walk, beloved, you and I!
In this courtyard of flowers and fountain,
proclaim to all who gather
that you are one with Me.
In this public square, be attached.
Raise up hope beyond seeing that love endures.

### My soul:

Seer who knows my ways,
You would be seen with me, taking my side?
In this enclosed garden,
my eyes see only You.
I who am scarred and soiled belong to You.
I take your hand, my God,
and all has changed.

### Luke 22:66-71

⁶⁶ *When day came, the assembly of the elders of the people, both chief priests and scribes, gathered together, and they brought him to their council.* ⁶⁷ *They said, "If you are the Messiah, tell us." He replied, "If I tell you, you will not believe;* ⁶⁸ *and if I question you, you will not answer.* ⁶⁹ *But from now on the Son of Man will be seated at the right hand of the power of God."* ⁷⁰ *All of them asked, "Are you, then, the Son of God?" He said to them, "You say that I am."* ⁷¹ *Then they said, "What further testimony do we need? We have heard it ourselves from his own lips!"*

How do you experience that being in love with God gives hope?
When does the truth of your scars and grime shame you to fear and
resist God's invitation?

# Heroine

### God:

Come, dear one of my heart, receive your commission.
I sent you forth to risk callouses, foot washings, blood, and sweat.
The vision that claims your life is to know the poor ones
and act with them against their greed and addiction,
your greed and addiction.
It is the crossroads where a heroine is born.

### My soul:

Warrior God, I follow You.
If I look into Your eyes, I can act. I can stand tall
and live the truth to which You call.
Mighty deeds have no great trumpet,
but only the heart that sings its love.
What moves me, then, to courage
is not fear but fierce and faithful love.

### Joshua 2:1-7

¹ *Then Joshua son of Nun sent two men secretly from Shittim as spies, saying, "Go, view the land, especially Jericho." So they went, and entered the house of a prostitute whose name was Rahab, and spent the night there.* ² *The king of Jericho was told, "Some Israelites have come here tonight to search out the land."* ³ *Then the king of Jericho sent orders to Rahab, "Bring out the men who have come to you, who entered your house, for they have come only to search out the whole land."* ⁴ *But the woman took the two men and hid them. Then she said, "True, the men came to me, but I did not know where they came from.* ⁵ *And when it was time to close the gate at dark, the men went out. Where the men went I do not know. Pursue them quickly, for you can overtake them."* ⁶ *She had, however, brought them up to the roof and hidden them with the stalks of flax that she had laid out on the roof.* ⁷ *So the men pursued them on the way to the Jordan as far as the fords. As soon as the pursuers had gone out, the gate was shut.*

Where is the crossroads of your own commission?
How is love moving you to act more than fear?

# Wings

**God:**

I know you want to fly.
Your desire is for the long view.
Can you brace against My wind?
Can your bony frame stretch to embrace it all?
From My sky kingdom with a world at your feet,
can your feathers speak to earth?

**My soul:**

My Maker God, Awesome One,
yes, I want to fly!
I see the eagle and the monarch.
How do we join the great migrations?
In the long haul, speak to my soul of freedom, endurance, and play.
With my brother birds and sister insects,
let me catch Your currents and trust.

**Matthew 6:26**

[26] *Look at the birds of the air; they neither sow nor reap nor gather into barns, and yet your heavenly Father feeds them. Are you not of more value than they?*

What is your long view?
When have you known migration?

## Roots

**God:**

Do you feel your roots today,
stretched deep into a black hole,
gnarled, twisted around the rocks of ordinary?
Will you draw moisture from your soil,
be unafraid to get entwined with mud and stones,
deepen into your steadiness?
Embrace your earth in its seasons
so you can stand in the dark
and become an ancient grove.

**My soul:**

My God, Holy One,
I have a jumble of roots and am, from my darkness,
playfully wondering if I am a cedar or oak,
red bud or birch.
How do I bear the mud
that would nourish my earth-bound seeking?
How do I trust as I stretch my tendrils
to the edge of my longing?
It is a way of endless blackness,
but the pulse within knows the juice of yearning.
Come, Maker, shake loose my lethargy.

**Ephesians 3:16-19**

*[16] I pray that, according to the riches of his glory, he may grant that you may be strengthened in your inner being with power through his Spirit, [17] and that Christ may dwell in your hearts through faith, as you are being rooted and grounded in love. [18] I pray that you may have the power to comprehend, with all the saints, what is the breadth and length and height and depth, [19] and to know the love of Christ that surpasses knowledge, so that you may be filled with all the fullness of God.*

What longing allows you to bear the darkness?
How do you know your life is rooted in love?

# Make Room

**God:**

Come under the shadow of My wing.
I make room.
Beyond your comfort zone, I call the world to you.
Speak your welcome
as you see with your heart and attend with your soul.
There is a secret garden here.

**My soul:**

Do you know it's crowded here,
dear Keeper of the earth?
Pushing and jostling to serve tea and chat and sleep—
where is Your quiet?
Making welcome upsets my apple cart.
As we nestle into Your enlarged tent,
I must shift and give way. Welcomes cost.
The foreigner, the vagabond, the runaway, the broken
are all wanting in.
It is Your great sweep of shelter
where all of us are beggars.
Help me make room.

**John 17:20-24**

²⁰ *"I ask not only on behalf of these, but also on behalf of those who will believe in me through their word,* ²¹ *that they may all be one. As you, Father, are in me and I am in you, may they also be in us, so that the world may believe that you have sent me.* ²² *The glory that you have given me I have given them, so that they may be one, as we are one,* ²³ *I in them and you in me, that they may become completely one, so that the world may know that you have sent me and have loved them even as you have loved me.* ²⁴ *Father, I desire that those also, whom you have given me, may be with me where I am, to see my glory, which you have given me because you loved me before the foundation of the world.*

Where are you being moved to make welcome? Who wants in?
How does your seeing and attending make room?

## Heart Listening

**God:**

I listen to your heart, the beat of its music.
I know the texture of your fears
and spread My wings of safety.
I hear your restless pacing
and give My staff to share My purpose.
I touch your broken pain
and feel your searing ache.
I know you; will you know Me?

**My soul:**

Deep within, my Lover God,
You placed a heart of flesh.
Out of my loneliness, I know You hear.
You share Your great heart with me.
Yes, oh yes,
I want to know You.
I want to heart-listen to the magic of the big bang—
our beginning.
I want to know Your longing for the lost in me and others.
I hear Your walk among us on dusty roads—
with laughter and resistance.
I taste with You your hunger for our abundant life.
Give me, please, a heart that listens.

**Ezekiel 36:26-28**

²⁶ *A new heart I will give you, and a new spirit I will put within you; and I will remove from your body the heart of stone and give you a heart of flesh.* ²⁷ *I will put my spirit within you, and make you follow my statutes and be careful to observe my ordinances.* ²⁸ *Then you shall live in the land that I gave to your ancestors; and you shall be my people, and I will be your God.*

How do you let God know you?
Where do you hear God's heart in your world?

## Hospitality

**My soul:**

My God, whose image scatters
like stars in a desert night,
come to my table. We break bread.
My heart-reach lays before You my truth.
In the feast of soul, I see You. I receive You.
I hear Your urge: "Child within, hold on to life."

**God:**

I love your invitation.
Comfort wears your attention.
In safety, a new world emerges
with My look, with My heart.
After the weariness,
I put My feet up in your house,
at your hearth.

### Luke 10:38-41

*³⁸ Now as they went on their way, he entered a certain village, where a woman named Martha welcomed him into her home. ³⁹ She had a sister named Mary, who sat at the Lord's feet and listened to what he was saying. ⁴⁰ But Martha was distracted by her many tasks; so she came to him and asked, "Lord, do you not care that my sister has left me to do all the work by myself? Tell her then to help me." ⁴¹ But the Lord answered her, "Martha, Martha, you are worried and distracted by many things.*

When have you known the hospitality that is a feast of soul?
Where are you inviting God to put His feet up?

# May I?

**My soul:**

God, who imagined us, may I be, sing,
come into alignment with all You want.
You call me to choose, design, love!
In my lowly unknowing, I feel my separateness.
Join me with You in the pulsing blood
of my brother beast and my sister flower.
With respect, I kneel before You.
In our aloneness, may I?

**God:**

Small one,
I see you in your darkness,
in the caverns of your longing to stand in My sun.
I hear your "May I?"
From the sounding of your solitary ache, break open in your song.
I will echo.

### 1 Kings 19:1-6

¹ *Ahab told Jezebel all that Elijah had done, and how he had killed all the prophets with the sword.* ² *Then Jezebel sent a messenger to Elijah, saying, "So may the gods do to me, and more also, if I do not make your life like the life of one of them by this time tomorrow."* ³ *Then he was afraid; he got up and fled for his life, and came to Beer-sheba, which belongs to Judah; he left his servant there.* ⁴ *But he himself went a day's journey into the wilderness, and came and sat down under a solitary broom tree. He asked that he might die: "It is enough; now, O Lord, take away my life, for I am no better than my ancestors."* ⁵ *Then he lay down under the broom tree and fell asleep. Suddenly an angel touched him and said to him, "Get up and eat."* ⁶ *He looked, and there at his head was a cake baked on hot stones, and a jar of water. He ate and drank, and lay down again.*

When has your God humbled Herself to echo your song?
Where do you feel the caverns of your longing?

# Exile

**My soul:**

I'm torn from my home,
out of my skin, exiled.
You, who flow in my being, are gone.
Who am I in this alien place,
sent forth with nothing?
My tasseled joy, bundled on my shoulder,
has been ripped from my grasp.
My child is taken.
His wail echoes day upon day in my heart.
Bereft, all is lost,
invisible where my inquiries bounce unseen,
unheard on concrete walls
through cyclone fences,
and dissipates like fog.

**God:**

I've got you!
I've got your son.
Your exile shall not last forever.
You will come into a place of welcome, of feasting,
and of belonging,
where the son of your tears and longing waits for you.

**Isaiah 24:3-4, 25:9-10**

³ *The earth shall be utterly laid waste and utterly despoiled; for the Lord has spoken this word.* ⁴ *The earth dries up and withers, the world languishes and withers, the heavens languish together with the earth.*
⁹ *It will be said on that day, Lo, this is our God; we have waited for him, so that he might save us. This is the Lord for whom we have waited; let us be glad and rejoice in his salvation.* ¹⁰ *For the hand of the Lord will rest on this mountain. The Moabites shall be trodden down in their place as straw is trodden down in a dung-pit.*

How are you out of your skin?
What promise of God breaks through your exile?

# Bird Song

**God:**

I send you secrets in my bird song.
Can you attend to the music of juice and life?
It is My language of falling in love.
It is the hope vibration of My winged Self.

**My soul:**

I know this melody opens my heart.
Its variations repeated call me to hear.
Let me know You in the springtime, urge of life
that can't be silenced.
May my own life force echo to Yours.

**Matthew 13:32**

*³² It is the smallest of all the seeds, but when it has grown it is the greatest of shrubs and becomes a tree, so that the birds of the air come and make nests in its branches.*

What bird song of life returns your attention to God?
How can attending to bird's music open your heart?

# Enough

**God:**

Is it not enough that I should come to you?
Is it not enough that I should walk in your skin?
Is it not enough that I should speak your language?
My love, I come close.
See Me. Hold Me. Listen.

**My soul:**

Your enough, my God, exceeds my grasp.
I am afraid. I run and flee.
Open wide my silence.
Let my emptiness enfold You.
Is it too much for me?
Enough can't hold it, so I grasp
distraction, hoarding, overflowing.
My gutter drips a stream of winter
water shining in Your sun.
Enough—come enter the cavern
of my loneliness, my hunger, my nakedness.
Even for my thimble, You are enough, Beloved.

**Song of Songs 3:1-3**

*¹ Upon my bed at night I sought him whom my soul loves;
I sought him, but found him not; I called him, but he gave no
answer ² "I will rise now and go about the city, in the streets and
in the squares; I will seek him whom my soul loves." I sought him,
but found him not. ³ The sentinels found me, as they went about in
the city. "Have you seen him whom my soul loves?"*

Where is enough the echo of emptiness in your life?
Do you live with enough? Where is contentment?

# Weavings

**God:**

Isn't the weaving of your being amazing—
the blood streams, the nerve patterns, your skeleton
and all else layered with sinew for life.
I pulled you from stardust
and wove your history from ancient ones.
Your fingerprint is like no other,
your life force destined to make your mark.

**My soul:**

Creator God,
thank You that I am fearfully, wonderfully made,
that You chose me for life.
How in this maze of shadows do I focus Your shine?
How can the stardust I hold give hope and direction
on our stumbling earth?
When I remember all the mothers and fathers who came before,
let me trust what You are doing.
I will laugh at Your wonder in me.

**Psalm 139:13-18**

*¹³ For it was you who formed my inward parts; you knit me together in my mother's womb. ¹⁴ I praise you, for I am fearfully and wonderfully made. Wonderful are your works; that I know very well. ¹⁵ My frame was not hidden from you, when I was being made in secret, intricately woven in the depths of the earth. ¹⁶ Your eyes beheld my unformed substance. In your book were written all the days that were formed for me, when none of them as yet existed. ¹⁷ How weighty to me are your thoughts, O God! How vast is the sum of them! ¹⁸ I try to count them—they are more than the sand. I come to the end—I am still with you.*

Look at your fingerprints; what is the destiny only you can accomplish?
How do you experience your ancestors counting on you for this time?

# Longing

**My soul:**

I am entangled with unseen skeins
that hold my longing paralyzed.
I ache in the pain
mired and bound by inaction.
I feel helpless in my desire,
my leaning into what is not yet.

**God:**

My little bird, let your wings stretch. You will fly.
Hope blankets the earth beneath you.
Your nest is a brief home
for you to see and test and grow.
Trust the longing of your heart.

**Psalm 13:5, 16:1-11**

⁵ *But I trusted in your steadfast love; my heart shall rejoice in your salvation.*
¹ *Protect me, O God, for in you I take refuge.* ² *I say to the Lord, "You are my Lord; I have no good apart from you."* ³ *As for the holy ones in the land, they are the noble, in whom is all my delight.* ⁴ *Those who choose another god multiply their sorrows; their drink offerings of blood I will not pour out or take their names upon my lips.* ⁵ *The Lord is my chosen portion and my cup you hold my lot.* ⁶ *The boundary lines have fallen for me in pleasant places; I have a goodly heritage.* ⁷ *I bless the Lord who gives me counsel; in the night also my heart instructs me.* ⁸ *I keep the Lord always before me because he is at my right hand, I shall not be moved.* ⁹ *Therefore my heart is glad, and my soul rejoices; my body also rests secure.* ¹⁰ *For you do not give me up to Sheol or let your faithful one see the Pit.* ¹¹ *You show me the path of life. In your presence there is fullness of joy; in your right hand are pleasures forevermore.*

When has hope blanketed your life?
How is your longing entangled?

## Mirror

**My soul:**

Holy One, come be welcome within,
where my hollowed-out self makes space.
Here in the quiet, my water can reflect Jesus
if my eyes stay intent on Him.
When ripples distort, my mirror speaks my truth:
shaky, restless, troubled.
Calm my inner storms in Your great mercy.

**God:**

I send you as a mirror
for those who want to see Me.
Be true to your calling.
Mirrors can distract and catch your self-absorption.
But if you keep your eyes on Me,
I will quiet your soul.

### Matthew 19:13-14

*¹³ Then little children were being brought to him in order that he might lay his hands on them and pray. The disciples spoke sternly to those who brought them; ¹⁴ but Jesus said, "Let the little children come to me, and do not stop them; for it is to such as these that the kingdom of heaven belongs."*

Where do you see Jesus?
Do you mirror the Infinite or are you self-absorbed?

## March 16

## Beehive

**God:**

My love, may I gather your sweetness.
I hear your hum,
busy across the land,
visiting clover and lavender,
milling honey in your comb.
One alone can be your lead.
In danger, the queen will call the swarm
to stings of war and fight.
Harm will come
to these wandering refugees of soul.
It is the way of nature.

**My soul:**

Creator God, You would have me savor
the land of milk and honey.
You order the gathering of fragrance in cooperation.
The Kingdom of God is near.
May I do my work that all may be one!

**John 17:10-11**

¹⁰ *All mine are yours, and yours are mine; and I have been glorified in them. ¹¹ And now I am no longer in the world, but they are in the world, and I am coming to you. Holy Father, protect them in your name that you have given me, so that they may be one, as we are one.*

Where are your fields of lavender and clover?
How are you called to work that all may be one?

# Sapphire

**God:**

I gift you with a sapphire,
child who delights My heart.
It is of the earth.
Let it whisper courage,
the true blue of faithfulness.
It is cut to shine,
polished to mirror light.
Trust My process.

**My soul:**

Thank you, my Maker, for gifts and signs.
I want to be true blue.
Help me be brave to let Your facets shine.
That You would gift me this precious stone—ahh!
I wear my heart's desire.

**1 Kings 10:9-10**

*⁹ Blessed be the Lord your God, who has delighted in you and set you on the throne of Israel! Because the Lord loved Israel forever, he has made you king to execute justice and righteousness." ¹⁰ Then she gave the king one hundred twenty talents of gold, a great quantity of spices, and precious stones; never again did spices come in such quantity as that which the queen of Sheba gave to King Solomon.*

What signs or gifts call you to courage?
How are you being cut, and what does it take to trust the process?

# Rocks

**My soul:**

My God of Mercy,
I am full of jagged rocks
tumbling in my heart,
scattered by the ice floe
by mountains and cliffs
of danger and blockage.
Please make Your way through.
Help me see clear through granite piles and broken geodes,
where You shine in surprises.

**God:**

Be patient, bruised soul, to stop and see the beauty.
Rocks at seaside are water-colored,
smoothed and shaped by My touch.
My love heals.

**Isaiah 32:2-3**

*² Each will be like a hiding place from the wind, a covert from the tempest, like streams of water in a dry place, like the shade of a great rock in a weary land. ³ Then the eyes of those who have sight will not be closed, and the ears of those who have hearing will listen.*

Where are you too bruised to see the beauty?
What rocks tumble in your heart with their jagged edges?

# Sands

**God:**

Build your life on Me, your Rock.
Then you who are so small will be strong.
Unlike the sands that shift and move,
you, dear precious one, will be secure.
The mountains may fall.
The seas may engulf.
Enemies may hold you to account,
but I know you.
My love will keep you safe.

**My soul:**

My God,
I place my trust in You.
Help me believe that You care.
I am a mere grain of sand
in the vast expanse of the seashore.
Do You see me?
Hidden and nondescript, can You care, really?
I need to see Your face, my Love.
My heart longs to know You.
Can my small being bring You a pearl?

**Matthew 7:24-27**

[24] *"Everyone then who hears these words of mine and acts on them will be like a wise man who built his house on rock.* [25] *The rain fell, the floods came, and the winds blew and beat on that house, but it did not fall, because it had been founded on rock.* [26] *And everyone who hears these words of mine and does not act on them will be like a foolish man who built his house on sand.* [27] *The rain fell, and the floods came, and the winds blew and beat against that house, and it fell—and great was its fall!"*

Where do you feel small, shifting, and insecure?
How do you see God's face today?

## Well

**My soul:**

I come to the well, my daily chore! I need water.
It is the gathering place for news and laughter.
Can I meet You here, Lord of my longing, at this trysting place?
Can You draw from my deep?
You are refreshment; You accept me just as I am, really seeing me.
Can I wish like Rebekah and Rachel to know You, my life's love?
Can I like the Samaritan woman confront my soul's belonging?
Would You like some water, my Lord?

**God:**

I have sought you, My beautiful dove, through the ages.
My eyes scanned many wells to find you.
I know your heart.
I see into your depths to know My image mirrored there.
Come, dance at this well with Me.
I have found you.
Your heart will announce who I am.
Together we will drink of the water of life that I prepared for you.

**Genesis 24:42-46**

*⁴² I came today to the spring, and said, 'O Lord, the God of my master Abraham, if now you will only make successful the way I am going! ⁴³ I am standing here by the spring of water; let the young woman who comes out to draw, to whom I shall say, "Please give me a little water from your jar to drink," ⁴⁴ and who will say to me, "Drink, and I will draw for your camels also"—let her be the woman whom the Lord has appointed for my master's son. ⁴⁵ Before I had finished speaking in my heart, there was Rebekah coming out with her water jar on her shoulder; and she went down to the spring, and drew. I said to her, 'Please let me drink.' ⁴⁶ She quickly let down her jar from her shoulder, and said, 'Drink, and I will also water your camels.' So I drank, and she also watered the camels.*

When have you known God seeks for you?
How is God's image mirrored in your deep well?

## Breathing

**God:**

I choose to breathe life within you.
I come close and share My energy of the big bang,
of the juice of life,
of vibration for you to ring your own amazing life song.
Don't forget in your movement in and out
that invisibly I touch you.

**My soul:**

Wow, I receive!
I receive what is unconscious and taken for granted.
I accept in awe!
It is wholly a holy gift.
Beyond thought, I am alive!
In breathing, I honor my kinship with all living things.
In Your God-choice, I live and breathe!
Let me trust this exchange as foundation
to resuscitate our ailing earth.

**Matthew 27:50-54**

*⁵⁰ Then Jesus cried again with a loud voice and breathed his last. ⁵¹ At that moment the curtain of the temple was torn in two, from top to bottom. The earth shook, and the rocks were split. ⁵² The tombs also were opened, and many bodies of the saints who had fallen asleep were raised. ⁵³ After his resurrection they came out of the tombs and entered the holy city and appeared to many. ⁵⁴ Now when the centurion and those with him, who were keeping watch over Jesus, saw the earthquake and what took place, they were terrified and said, "Truly this man was God's Son!"*

How does breathing speak God's touch in you?
How can your breathing resuscitate our ailing earth?

# Ladder

**God:**

Put the stone beneath your head and sleep.
I give you dreams,
ladders with angels going up and down.
What climbing up satisfies your soul but Me?
What coming down satisfies My heart but you?
I am no dream. Hold Me in your heart, little one.

**My soul:**

Is it really not a dream?
Did You really walk in skin,
sail in boats,
tell tales that speak Your wisdom?
Can I dare to see You touch and heal?
What have I done that You are broken and bruised?
How could You die on a cross?
My God and my All!

**Genesis 28:10-15**

*¹⁰ Jacob left Beer-Sheba and went toward Haran. ¹¹ He came to a certain place and stayed there for the night, because the sun had set. Taking one of the stones of the place, he put it under his head and lay down in that place. ¹² And he dreamed that there was a ladder set up on the earth, the top of it reaching to heaven; and the angels of God were ascending and descending on it. ¹³ And the Lord stood beside him and said, "I am the Lord, the God of Abraham your father and the God of Isaac; the land on which you lie I will give to you and to your offspring; ¹⁴ and your offspring shall be like the dust of the earth, and you shall spread abroad to the west and to the east and to the north and to the south; and all the families of the earth shall be blessed in you and in your offspring. ¹⁵ Know that I am with you and will keep you wherever you go, and will bring you back to this land; for I will not leave you until I have done what I have promised you."*

What angels come to you in dreams?
When has God's love gotten through to you?

# Candle

**My soul:**

Light of my world, come be the heart wick for my candle glow.
In Your light, darkness will be dispelled.
May I spend the wax and fragrance of my life
in praise of You.
May You find my life force at the service of Your way.

**God:**

Raise high your candle.
We are one.
I will shine for your world in you.
As you disappear, fear not, dear servant.
Your heart light burns My eternal flame.

**Matthew 5:14-16**

[14] *"You are the light of the world. A city built on a hill cannot be hid.* [15] *No one after lighting a lamp puts it under the bushel basket, but on the lampstand, and it gives light to all in the house.* [16] *In the same way, let your light shine before others, so that they may see your good works and give glory to your Father in heaven."*

When have you let your wax and fragrance
be praise for God, who is Light?
How are you called to raise high the light of your candle?

## Dust

**My soul:**

Fashioner of Life, I remember that we are dust,
particles blown by the wind,
held together by nothing.
You took a handful of dust and fashioned us.
It is from where we humans began.
Dust it is to where I am going.
How then could You join us, Jesus?
What conscious choice could bear such audacity?
I bow down in awe!

**God:**

Dust gatherer, I hope you remember as truthfully
that you are stardust.
I came in your frame, precious human,
so you know it
in the roots of your being.
That your destiny is full of light and energy,
a beacon in the darkness.
I believe in you.

**Genesis 2:7**

*⁷ Then the Lord God formed man from the dust of the ground, and breathed into his nostrils the breath of life; and the man became a living being.*

When do you feel held together by nothing?
How do you experience being full of light?

# Time

### God:

I give you the time of your life, My child.
Receive its passage to grow and savor.
Observe and engage the turn of its seasons
within your earth, within your days.
Now is your time to love!
Let it flourish in your birthdays, play days, and brave days.

### My soul:

My God of Forever Time,
There is no measure to Your giving or Your living.
Jesus, You break into our time to heal, comfort, create.
Yet it feels sometimes that time has marched over my life,
scattering memory seeds, making grooves and wrinkles, dusting my
head.
And then again, I breathe into my heart
and dance and ski and cartwheel with an ease and pleasure.
In my beginning and my end, I praise and thank You, Lord of Life.

### Ecclesiastes 3:1-8

*¹ For everything there is a season, and a time for every matter under heaven: ² a time to be born, and a time to die; a time to plant, and a time to pluck up what is planted; ³ a time to kill, and a time to heal; a time to break down, and a time to build up; ⁴ a time to weep, and a time to laugh; a time to mourn, and a time to dance; ⁵ a time to throw away stones, and a time to gather stones together; a time to embrace, and a time to refrain from embracing ⁶ a time to seek, and a time to lose; a time to keep, and a time to throw away; ⁷ a time to tear, and a time to sew; a time to keep silence, and a time to speak; ⁸ a time to love, and a time to hate; a time for war, and a time for peace.*

How do you observe and engage your life seasons?
When has God broken into your time?

# Forest

**God:**

Come, roam in the woods with Me, dear playmate.
See what is lovely, dark and deep,
and full of promise.
There is mystery in the quiet.
Pathways stir the chatting of My kingdom of creatures,
and sunbeams shine through.

**My soul:**

In the forest wilderness full of brambles and tangles,
I long for You.
The dense green covers the hills with straight trunks,
and I feel lost.
Send Your light rays to shine the path.
Lift my fear and aloneness.
Alas, we create our own forests of skyscrapers.

**Revelations 22:1-2**

*¹ Then the angel showed me the river of the water of life, bright as crystal, flowing from the throne of God and of the Lamb ² through the middle of the street of the city. On either side of the river is the tree of life with its twelve kinds of fruit, producing its fruit each month; and the leaves of the tree are for the healing of the nations.*

In the wilderness of forest or city, where have you felt lost?
How do you hear God's promise?

## Fireflies

**My soul:**

Awesome One,
what a wondrous gift of glow You send
in the gathering gloom!
As dusk settles,
You break the night with their pulsing light,
sparking promise and hope.

**God:**

Wondering child,
fireflies are beautiful, aren't they?
See the community sending its lightning signals of love
to a darkening world.
Hold them tenderly,
gently,
and give them freedom.
I bestow this hope from them to you.

**Isaiah 60:1-2**

¹ *Arise, shine; for your light has come, and the glory of the Lord has risen upon you.* ² *For darkness shall cover the earth, and thick darkness the peoples; but the Lord will arise upon you, and his glory will appear over you.*

What is the promise and hope you see today?
How does your community of light send love?

# Birches

**God:**

Wandering one,
do you like My "lady" trees?
Birches stretch their charm into bright blue skies.
They thrive in the cold with curled bark like hair.
They tell tales in their forest clans.
Even their lying down weeps beauty.
Wander, and know kinship.

**My soul:**

Wondrous Creative God, I love birches.
I love the northern pathways through their gatherings.
Their scarred skins and knotted trunks
speak to me of courage.
Do I dare such surrender to the cold?
Can I lay down my life with such grace?

**Isaiah 52:13-14**

*[13] See, my servant shall prosper; he shall be exalted and lifted up, and shall be very high. [14] Just as there were many who were astonished at him—so marred was his appearance, beyond human semblance, and his form beyond that of mortals.*

What community listens to your heart?
How are you feeling your scarred skin and call to surrender in the cold?

# Scorched

**My soul:**

I come before you humbled, Great Ruler of my heart.
I am marked, scorched, lightning-scarred.
Your fire came from the heavens;
it kindled pain.
We are split, one from the other—
defeated in our division.
Have mercy and heal us,
You who made us.

**God:**

I know your heart's burning,
kindled by My Spirit.
I see the marring that such fierce fire leaves.
Trust the kinship that is forming.

**Luke 12:49-53**

⁴⁹ *"I came to bring fire to the earth, and how I wish it were already kindled!* ⁵⁰ *I have a baptism with which to be baptized, and what stress I am under until it is completed!* ⁵¹ *Do you think that I have come to bring peace to the earth? No, I tell you, but rather division!* ⁵² *From now on five in one household will be divided, three against two and two against three;* ⁵³ *they will be divided: father against son and son against father, mother against daughter and daughter against mother, mother-in-law against her daughter-in-law and daughter-in-law against mother-in-law."*

Where do you feel division that needs healing?
How is your pain and marring calling you to love?

# Talisman

**God:**

Can you read the message of this stone,
seeker of truth?
It is a talisman, a gift.
It is full of power for your walk with Me
because it takes your faith to see Me.
Know we are connected, child.
I give you My spirit.

**My soul:**

I hold it sacred, God of mystery.
I bear Your message: trust, trust.
When I feel most alone,
I carry this stone
as Presence and power
to walk believing.

**Ezekiel 11:19-20**

*¹⁹ I will give them one heart, and put a new spirit within them; I will remove the heart of stone from their flesh and give them a heart of flesh, ²⁰ so that they may follow my statutes and keep my ordinances and obey them. Then they shall be my people, and I will be their God.*

How is your heart of stone turned to a heart of flesh?
What word within are you called to trust?

## Tapestry

**My soul:**

Your hand, Mighty Weaver, is on my life.
You take its strands
of scarlet sin and loss,
of green springtime hope,
of yellow sunny gladness,
and make my days a tapestry.
All that I am is in Your hands
as I wonder, ache, and trust.

**God:**

I am about art with you
as you swirl color around your loom.
I am the Master Artist,
so know when knots of pain
and holes of loneliness
assault your life, it is as it
should be, princess child.
I have chosen you to be,
so trust My reverence of your tiny life.

### Isaiah 55:10-11

*¹⁰ For as the rain and the snow come down from heaven, and do not return there until they have watered the earth, making it bring forth and sprout, giving seed to the sower and bread to the eater, ¹¹ so shall my word be that goes out from my mouth; it shall not return to me empty, but it shall accomplish that which I purpose, and succeed in the thing for which I sent it.*

Where are you being challenged to trust the art of your life?
How do you trust the knots and holes of your life are purposefully in the hands of the Master Artist?

# April

1. Warrior
2. Hurt
3. Prison
4. Breakfast Dishes
5. Brick Wall
6. Fragrant
7. Absence
8. Mirage
9. Trapdoor
10. Radiance
11. Bereft
12. Home
13. Chimney
14. Obscurity
15. Tiger
16. Epiphany
17. Deafness
18. Indolence
19. Waiting
20. Conforming
21. Robin
22. Privilege
23. Goats and Sheep
24. Incandescence
25. Passover
26. Reverence
27. Desire
28. Gardens
29. Velocity
30. Current

# Warrior

**God:**

I see you.
I name you warrior.
You have been in training
in this age's discipline of soul.
You are My elite,
knowing My heart
and willing to risk your comfort,
your way of life, your very self.

**My soul:**

Can I be Your warrior, Unseen God?
Am I strong enough,
wise enough,
selfless enough
to lay down my life for Your own?
I see You—glimpses that take my breath away.
Because of You
I don my pack and march in defense
of those who cannot see
or walk or embrace.
I hear Your marching song.
I follow Your lead.

**Mark 10:28-31**

²⁸ *Peter began to say to him, "Look, we have left everything and followed you." ²⁹ Jesus said, "Truly I tell you, there is no one who has left house or brothers or sisters or mother or father or children or fields, for my sake and for the sake of the good news, ³⁰ who will not receive a hundredfold now in this age—houses, brothers and sisters, mothers and children, and fields, with persecutions—and in the age to come eternal life. ³¹ But many who are first will be last, and the last will be first."*

How is your warrior heart called to know God's heart?
What are you called to see that inclines you to pick up and march in
God's elite?

# Hurt

**God:**

I see you are hurt.
Come, let Me hold you
and wipe away your tears.
Let your scars shine
with courage and with love.
I know you weep
because you have come close enough to life to be hurt.

**My soul:**

Comforter God,
I am full of pain.
Each part of me screams
for what I've known of peace and life.
Can I believe that You, the great and mighty One,
do hold me close?
In Your arms, I weep.
Have mercy, Lord.

**Luke 8:43-48**

⁴³ *Now there was a woman who had been suffering from hemorrhages for twelve years; and though she had spent all she had on physicians, no one could cure her.* ⁴⁴ *She came up behind him and touched the fringe of his clothes, and immediately her hemorrhage stopped.* ⁴⁵ *Then Jesus asked, "Who touched me?" When all denied it, Peter said, "Master, the crowds surround you and press in on you."* ⁴⁶ *But Jesus said, "Someone touched me; for I noticed that power had gone out from me."* ⁴⁷ *When the woman saw that she could not remain hidden, she came trembling; and falling down before him, she declared in the presence of all the people why she had touched him, and how she had been immediately healed.* ⁴⁸ *He said to her, "Daughter, your faith has made you well; go in peace."*

How are you close enough to life to be hurt?
What does trusting your vulnerability to God look like?

## Prison

**My soul:**

I hear the clanging of bars,
the slamming shut!
You hear it, too, Just Companion.
My life is arrested,
enclosed in this barren cell.
The others have the power.
They say I am a danger
and therefore have no right
to walk the sunlit paths.
I curl up, so scared and judged.
Receive my tiny life now, my God.

**God:**

Prisoner in My heart,
I know you are shut down and wait.
I hear you speak, "There is no waiting; this is it! Only death can free me."
That is why I am with you.
Climb on My eagle wings and we shall fly.
I love you.

**Mark 15:16-20**

*[16] Then the soldiers led him into the courtyard of the palace (that is, the governor's headquarters); and they called together the whole cohort. [17] And they clothed him in a purple cloak; and after twisting some thorns into a crown, they put it on him. [18] And they began saluting him, "Hail, King of the Jews!" [19] They struck his head with a reed, spat upon him, and knelt down in homage to him. [20] After mocking him, they stripped him of the purple cloak and put his own clothes on him. Then they led him out to crucify him.*

Where are you imprisoned and judged?
How does God invite you to freedom on His eagle wings?

# Breakfast Dishes

### God:

I want to have breakfast with you.
Break open the day with gratitude and newness.
With this day untouched yet, I believe in you.
Receive my sunlight, bird song, and nourishment.
At the start of this new day, I want to be familiar to your pattern of life.

### My soul:

Please be welcome, Host of Life!
Let me drink in the gift of moment-by-moment life
and give worship and thanks.
Let Your energy flow through my bones to move me for good today.
I love You with my whole being and consciousness.

### John 21:9-14

*⁹ When they had gone ashore, they saw a charcoal fire there, with fish on it, and bread. ¹⁰ Jesus said to them, "Bring some of the fish that you have just caught." ¹¹ So Simon Peter went aboard and hauled the net ashore, full of large fish, a hundred fifty-three of them; and though there were so many, the net was not torn. ¹² Jesus said to them "Come and have breakfast." Now none of the disciples dared to ask him, "Who are you?" because they knew it was the Lord. ¹³ Jesus came and took the bread and gave it to them, and did the same with the fish. ¹⁴ This was now the third time that Jesus appeared to the disciples after he was raised from the dead.*

To what does God's belief in you call you?
How does breakfast and bounty bond you to tend His sheep?

# Brick Wall

**My soul:**

I see a brick wall in my heart,
hardened and resistant.
It divides me from grace
and movement to open in spaciousness.
I must rise from my paralysis.
Break down what divides and shrivels and arrests,
God of Jericho.

**God:**

Do not be afraid, little girl.
*Talitha cumi!*
I've marched around your life all its days,
waiting and trumpeting.
Trust that I know how to win you over.

## Luke 8:40-42, 49-56

*⁴⁰ Now when Jesus returned, the crowd welcomed him, for they were all waiting for him. ⁴¹ Just then there came a man named Jairus, a leader of the synagogue. He fell at Jesus' feet and begged him to come to his house, ⁴² for he had an only daughter, about twelve years old, who was dying. As he went, the crowds pressed in on him. ⁴⁹ While he was still speaking, someone came from the leader's house to say, "Your daughter is dead; do not trouble the teacher any longer." ⁵⁰ When Jesus heard this, he replied, "Do not fear. Only believe, and she will be saved." ⁵¹ When he came to the house, he did not allow anyone to enter with him, except Peter, John, and James, and the child's father and mother. ⁵² They were all weeping and wailing for her; but he said, "Do not weep; for she is not dead but sleeping." ⁵³ And they laughed at him, knowing that she was dead. ⁵⁴ But he took her by the hand and called out, "Child, get up!" ⁵⁵ Her spirit returned, and she got up at once. Then he directed them to give her something to eat. ⁵⁶ Her parents were astounded; but he ordered them to tell no one what had happened.*

What is your brick wall of resistance?
How will you know that God wins your heart?

# Fragrant

**God:**

Lost child,
come be near My fragrance.
Know I am near,
in evergreen freshness,
in lilac's lushness,
in the autumn leaves.
I send My perfume
to comfort and encourage.
What you cannot see and what you even doubt
is My dimension of love and courage.
What wafts is what holds you.

**My soul:**

Like the smell of rain over broken soil,
come, my Lord, be near.
Let me know again my young love of yes.
Break open my dullness and lassitude.
You surprise my heart.
I bow in Your fragrance.
Please stay.

**2 Corinthians 2:14-17**

[14] *But thanks be to God, who in Christ always leads us in triumphal procession, and through us spreads in every place the fragrance that comes from knowing him.* [15] *For we are the aroma of Christ to God among those who are being saved and among those who are perishing;* [16] *to the one a fragrance from death to death, to the other a fragrance from life to life. Who is sufficient for these things?* [17] *For we are not peddlers of God's word like so many; but in Christ we speak as persons of sincerity, as persons sent from God and standing in his presence.*

What perfume of God comforts and encourages you?
What young love surprises your heart?

## Absence

**My soul:**

O Absent One, my soul aches for You today.
I sit and brood, burying my attentions
in myriad nonessentials.
There are black holes inside me unknown,
where my dark spirit is lonely.
I long for You, my Lord.

**God:**

Break open your heart in song, dear one.
I am not absent, just unseen.
Stir up your faith
by the miracles all around.
You can see Me.
I am here even as you are here.
Breathe in my life.

**Jeremiah 3:19-24**

¹⁹ *I thought how I would set you among my children, and give you a pleasant land, the most beautiful heritage of all the nations. And I thought you would call me, My Father, and would not turn from following me.* ²⁰ *Instead, as a faithless wife leaves her husband, so you have been faithless to me, O house of Israel, says the Lord.* ²¹ *A voice on the bare heights is heard, the plaintive weeping of Israel's children because they have perverted their way, they have forgotten the Lord their God:* ²² *Return, O faithless children. I will heal your faithlessness. "Here we come to you; for you are the Lord our God.* ²³ *Truly the hills are a delusion, the orgies on the mountains. Truly in the Lord our God is the salvation of Israel.* ²⁴ *"But from our youth the shameful thing has devoured all for which our ancestors had labored, their flocks and their herds, their sons and their daughters."*

How are your soul's black holes burying your sense of God?
In what ways do you experience God's mercies renewed each morning?

# April 8

## Mirage

**My soul:**

I am not separate
except for Your choice.
It is illusion that my breath,
my stories, my labels,
exist to shape my meaning.
Mighty cosmic Lord,
apart from me, myself, and I
is the life that is You, that is All.
In the lifting of mirage
is the shedding of desire and my
mind's tricks of pretense,
and I consent.

**God:**

My creature, I know you,
your shadows and your secrets,
your patterns and your mind's foils.
Fear not, I hold you in My arms.
The light within Me
shines through you.

**Genesis 25:29-34**

*²⁹ Once when Jacob was cooking a stew, Esau came in from the field, and he was famished. ³⁰ Esau said to Jacob, "Let me eat some of that red stuff, for I am famished!" (Therefore he was called Edom) ³¹ Jacob said, "First sell me your birthright." ³² Esau said, "I am about to die; of what use is a birthright to me?" ³³ Jacob said, "Swear to me first." So he swore to him, and sold his birthright to Jacob. ³⁴ Then Jacob gave Esau bread and lentil stew, and he ate and drank, and rose and went his way. Thus Esau despised his birthright.*

Where do you experience the illusion of yourself as separate?
How do you know God holds you in Her arms?

## Trapdoor

**My soul:**

I am hiding behind this trapdoor.
Am I secured from tornadoes in security's illusion?
Protector God, you know I am
weak and at risk.
Open wide the hatch to Your
embracing love.
Lift from me the fear to live.

**God:**

I am here, hiding child.
Come out of the prison of your smallness.
Claim your patrimony!
You are My child.
There will be high winds and war.
You will know devastation.
If you know I am with you,
you will carry your scars
like the daughter of the King.

### John 3:1-5

¹ *Now there was a Pharisee named Nicodemus, a leader of the Jews.* ² *He came to Jesus by night and said to him, "Rabbi, we know that you are a teacher who has come from God; for no one can do these signs that you do apart from the presence of God."* ³ *Jesus answered him, "Very truly, I tell you, no one can see the kingdom of God without being born from above."* ⁴ *Nicodemus said to him, "How can anyone be born after having grown old? Can one enter a second time into the mother's womb and be born?"* ⁵ *Jesus answered, "Very truly, I tell you, no one can enter the kingdom of God without being born of water and Spirit."*

What scars do you bear with dignity?
How are you knowing and living the illusion of security?

# Radiance

**God:**

I am Who I am,
present and giving you radiance.
Let your way be guided by My light
because My heart suffers
with those who do not belong.
Fill up your longing with the glow of My love and shine!

**My soul:**

Your brightness bows me in fear and in awe.
How do I come so close?
Who can hold Your intensity?
Let me laugh at the absurdity that I am chosen.
Clear my being for Your great heart.

**Wisdom 3:1-9**

*¹ But the souls of the righteous are in the hand of God, and no torment will ever touch them. ² In the eyes of the foolish they seemed to have died, and their departure was thought to be a disaster, ³ and their going from us to be their destruction; but they are at peace. ⁴ For though in the sight of others they were punished, their hope is full of immortality. ⁵ Having been disciplined a little, they will receive great good, because God tested them and found them worthy of himself; ⁶ like gold in the furnace he tried them, and like a sacrificial burnt offering he accepted them. ⁷ In the time of their visitation they will shine forth, and will run like sparks through the stubble. ⁸ They will govern nations and rule over peoples, and the Lord will reign over them forever. ⁹ Those who trust in him will understand truth, and the faithful will abide with him in love, because grace and mercy are upon his holy ones, and he watches over his elect.*

When are you terrified that God is present and calling you?
How does being chosen make you laugh?

# Bereft

**My soul:**

Where are You, Invisible One?
I am orphaned, abandoned, bereft,
left on my own to make sense of it all!
I am in the midst of the puzzle of who I am now.
No one has my back.
I search for a kind eye, a hearth for rest, food to be shared,
a place to belong.

**God:**

I birthed you, child of my own.
Believe that with every breath you take that I am with you.
You are not alone.
I bring you to feast on juicy tomatoes and luxuriant wheat.
I fight your fights in near misses, fearless sleep, and
stranger's smiles.
You are mine.
I am here.

**Genesis 37:23-28**

²³ *So when Joseph came to his brothers, they stripped him of his robe, the long robe with sleeves that he wore;* ²⁴ *and they took him and threw him into a pit. The pit was empty; there was no water in it.* ²⁵ *Then they sat down to eat; and looking up they saw a caravan of Ishmaelites coming from Gilead, with their camels carrying gum, balm, and resin, on their way to carry it down to Egypt.* ²⁶ *Then Judah said to his brothers, "What profit is it if we kill our brother and conceal his blood?* ²⁷ *Come, let us sell him to the Ishmaelites, and not lay our hands on him, for he is our brother, our own flesh." And his brothers agreed.* ²⁸ *When some Midianite traders passed by, they drew Joseph up, lifting him out of the pit, and sold him to the Ishmaelites for twenty pieces of silver. And they took Joseph to Egypt.*

How are you abandoned?
How is God securing your life?

# Home

### God:

Chosen creature, come be at home in My heart.
You belong. Let down your hair.
Meet your needs here because
you, My beloved, are accepted, received, listened to.
Stretch the shape of your life
into art and emotion and womb because you are safe.

### My soul:

Heart of my Lord and Master, I release all fear and breathe easy.
I am at home in my Father's house. Here I relax and can sleep.
Let me awaken to Your laughter and surprises.
Let me savor the wafting of Your home cooking—all that satisfies.
Here, let me know Your heart.

### Luke 1:26-33

*26 In the sixth month the angel Gabriel was sent by God to a town in Galilee called Nazareth, 27 to a virgin engaged to a man whose name was Joseph, of the house of David. The virgin's name was Mary. 28 And he came to her and said, "Greetings, favored one! The Lord is with you." 29 But she was much perplexed by his words and pondered what sort of greeting this might be. 30 The angel said to her, "Do not be afraid, Mary, for you have found favor with God. 31 And now, you will conceive in your womb and bear a son, and you will name him Jesus. 32 He will be great, and will be called the Son of the Most High, and the Lord God will give to him the throne of his ancestor David. 33 He will reign over the house of Jacob forever, and of his kingdom there will be no end."*

How is being at home stretching life?
What laughter of God do you hear in your Father's house?

# Chimney

**My soul:**

Who built the first chimney, God of life?
Chimneys carry remnants and create art of wispy clouds.
Soot clings in sticky resin.
Ashes rest from burned out fires,
but spirits lift and are thinned out
in wide open spaces.

**God:**

So you like My art tools, student observer of life?
Burned out fires that give warmth and light
leave only dust and ash.
I invite you to keep the fire burning.
Watch it glow.
Feed its coals.
Let what snaps and sizzles send to the sky its beautiful spew.
Trust your searing soul!

**Deuteronomy 4:5-8**

*⁵ See, just as the Lord my God has charged me, I now teach you statutes and ordinances for you to observe in the land that you are about to enter and occupy. ⁶ You must observe them diligently, for this will show your wisdom and discernment to the peoples, who, when they hear all these statutes, will say, "Surely this great nation is a wise and discerning people!" ⁷ For what other great nation has a god so near to it as the Lord our God is whenever we call to him? ⁸ And what other great nation has statutes and ordinances as just as this entire law that I am setting before you today?*

What soot sticks to your soul like resin?
How are you freed of poisons so you can give warmth and light?

# Obscurity

**My soul:**

Invisible One,
I hide in the mighty sweep of eons unnoticed, obscure.
In this concealment, I claim the illusion of security
away from prying cameras and satellites.
And on the other extreme, I dare being noticed,
flaunt a secret anonymity, aching to be somebody.

**God:**

Precious child,
I hear your shout to the skies
that is truly a mere squeak
against such obscurity.
Know you are forever known and loved.
The design of your longing
depends on My key.
I have made you. I notice.
I invite your noticing Me.

**Matthew 15:21-28**

²¹ *Jesus left that place and went away to the district of Tyre and Sidon.* ²² *Just then a Canaanite woman from that region came out and started shouting, "Have mercy on me, Lord, Son of David; my daughter is tormented by a demon."* ²³ *But he did not answer her at all. And his disciples came and urged him, saying, "Send her away, for she keeps shouting after us."* ²⁴ *He answered, "I was sent only to the lost sheep of the house of Israel."* ²⁵ *But she came and knelt before him, saying, "Lord, help me."* ²⁶ *He answered, "It is not fair to take the children's food and throw it to the dogs."* ²⁷ *She said, "Yes, Lord, yet even the dogs eat the crumbs that fall from their masters' table."* ²⁸ *Then Jesus answered her, "Woman, great is your faith! Let it be done for you as you wish." And her daughter was healed instantly.*

What cravings urge you beyond obscurity?
How do you recognize God's key to your heart?

# Tiger

**God:**

Caretaker child,
I did a fine job with our tiger, didn't I?
Guard this fierce, courageous cat
as her life is at risk in your world.
She roars her message of anger and protection.
Her stealthy shape-shifting
comes to you with prophecy.

**My soul:**

God of Humor and Art,
I love our tiger!
I fear her prophecy.
Our world crowds and games and disregards
what is sacred and rare.
I send my tigress sister
to leap and to transform,
to survive!
Thank you, my Lord and Master,
for tigers.

**Psalm 84:1-4**

*¹ How lovely is your dwelling place, O Lord of hosts! ² My soul longs, indeed it faints for the courts of the Lord; my heart and my flesh sing for joy to the living God. ³ Even the sparrow finds a home, and the swallow a nest for herself, where she may lay her young, at your altars, O Lord of hosts, my King and my God. ⁴ Happy are those who live in your house, ever singing your praise.*

How do you protect your own fierce courage?
How is your leaping and transforming helping you survive?

# Epiphany

**God:**

Come, unseeing one, open your eyes!
I reveal to you My heart.
Know in My epiphany
you will understand good and evil,
pain and loss, and incredible light,
loneliness and union.
It is your finding of the whole fabric
of which you are a part.

**My soul:**

Light and Life of creation's weaving, yes!
I hunger for this watershed moment of Your unveiling.
I know the glimpses of You
in synchronicities, in harmonies,
in breathtaking beauties, in unconditional love.
Otherwise, I walk in faith.
"Help thou my unbelief."

**Mark 15:33-39**

*³³ When it was noon, darkness came over the whole land until three in the afternoon. ³⁴ At three o'clock Jesus cried out with a loud voice, "Eloi, Eloi, lema sabachthani?" which means, "My God, my God, why have you forsaken me?" ³⁵ When some of the bystanders heard it, they said, "Listen, he is calling for Elijah." ³⁶ And someone ran, filled a sponge with sour wine, put it on a stick, and gave it to him to drink, saying, "Wait, let us see whether Elijah will come to take him down." ³⁷ Then Jesus gave a loud cry and breathed his last. ³⁸ And the curtain of the temple was torn in two, from top to bottom. ³⁹ Now when the centurion, who stood facing him, saw that in this way he breathed his last, he said, "Truly this man was God's Son!"*

What watershed moment marks your faith? How do you feel its power?
In knowing God's heart, why do you know pain, loneliness, and evil?

## Deafness

**God:**

I see you are blocked, lost one!
In your deafness to My voice,
I see your caution and uncertainty.
The pathways to My world
are closed and impenetrable.
Take My hand.
With the earth's mud, I will open our connection
because I want you to know Me.

**My soul:**

My God who comes close,
I long for the melody of Your voice.
Without hearing, I am isolated from all Your ways of speaking—
from the brook's rush over stones,
from the wren's mating in spring,
from sirens and gunshots and weeping,
all of it that binds me to You.
All of it is life.
You walk among us full of Life.
Come touch me, my Lord of Life.

### Mark 7:31-35

³¹ *Then he returned from the region of Tyre, and went by way of Sidon towards the Sea of Galilee, in the region of the Decapolis.* ³² *They brought to him a deaf man who had an impediment in his speech; and they begged him to lay his hand on him.* ³³ *He took him aside in private, away from the crowd, and put his fingers into his ears, and he spat and touched his tongue.* ³⁴ *Then looking up to heaven, he sighed and said to him, "Ephphatha," that is, "Be opened."* ³⁵ *And immediately his ears were opened, his tongue was released, and he spoke plainly.*

How is your hearing blocked?
When has God's touch opened your heart to all of life?

# Indolence

**My soul:**

God of explosive expansion,
I'm stuck.
"What for?" slides across my consciousness
with oil-slick ease.
I put off the push for life.
The lack of motivation cocoons me in apathy.
Stir within me the juices for spring.
Let the boredom of indolence lift.
I am Your child.
Smoldering somewhere within is Your energy.
Why can't I feel it?

**God:**

You who are My slacker,
is this your time of hibernation?
Let the mother bear within you awaken.
Fierce and inexorable is your arising.
Sloth will not imprison the running of sap.
Trust Me. I will stir within you.

**2 Samuel 16:11-14**

¹¹ *David said to Abishai and to all his servants, "My own son seeks my life; how much more now may this Benjaminite! Let him alone, and let him curse; for the Lord has bidden him.* ¹² *It may be that the Lord will look on my distress, and the Lord will repay me with good for this cursing of me today."* ¹³ *So David and his men went on the road, while Shimei went along on the hillside opposite him and cursed as he went, throwing stones and flinging dust at him.* ¹⁴ *The king and all the people who were with him arrived weary at the Jordan; and there he refreshed himself.*

How do you know the "what for?" in your days?
What does the rising of mother bear within you look like in your daily life?

# Waiting

**God:**

Will you wait for Me, impatient one?
Through the seasons of your life,
I invite you:
in your childhood's earnest longing for Christmas, birthdays, summer;
the ache and search for what reason you are here;
the pregnant mom's longing to see her child;
the discovery of your own gifts for use;
the weary work of days too long for ready energy;
your pause near life's end for My next revealing.
It is all waiting.
Gird yourself with faith for the long evolution.

**My soul:**

God within my search, how do I stay alert?
Waiting feels like darkness before the dawn.
It is the soul work of doing nothing but trusting.
Time slows to absorbing concentration.
When are You coming, my Lord?

**Luke 12:35-37**

[35] *"Be dressed for action and have your lamps lit;* [36] *be like those who are waiting for their master to return from the wedding banquet, so that they may open the door for him as soon as he comes and knocks.* [37] *Blessed are those slaves whom the master finds alert when he comes; truly I tell you, he will fasten his belt and have them sit down to eat, and he will come and serve them."*

When is waiting most difficult for you?
What is your soul work of doing nothing?

# Conforming

**My soul:**

You are my pattern, Jesus, my God.
Let there be no resistance within me to follow Your flow.
Give my heart Your shape.
I conform to my deepest calling
at Your hand, to be the child of Your creation.
Make me malleable in Your hands.

**God:**

Conforming to My ways means choosing symmetry, chosen one.
Trust My will!
I will bring your life to harmony.
The music shaping your days will be love.
Then will you know Me!

**Romans 12:1-2**

*¹ I appeal to you therefore, brothers and sisters, by the mercies of God, to present your bodies as a living sacrifice, holy and acceptable to God, which is your spiritual worship. ² Do not be conformed to this world, but be transformed by the renewing of your minds, so that you may discern what is the will of God—what is good and acceptable and perfect.*

Where do you feel resistance in your life to God's way?
Where are you malleable?

## Robin

**God:**

My child who notices,
I send you robins today.
In the dark of winter's last chill,
they know the rising of hope.
Worms wriggle unseen to all but My robin.
Food and spring bring fresh energy.
Aren't they signs of joy?

**My soul:**

God who speaks,
I hear Your bird message.
What fun!
Yes, I am worn down with
coats and gloves and mufflers
and need the daring risk
of faith for food and warmth.
Their chubby rust breasts
announce the winter famine's over.
Thank You, Lord of coming springtime.

### Ruth 1:1, 3-6

¹ *In the days when the judges ruled, there was a famine in the land, and a certain man of Bethlehem in Judah went to live in the country of Moab, he and his wife and two sons.* ³ *But Elimelech, the husband of Naomi, died, and she was left with her two sons.* ⁴ *These took Moabite wives; the name of the one was Orpah and the name of the other Ruth. When they had lived there about ten years,* ⁵ *both Mahlon and Chilion also died, so that the woman was left without her two sons and her husband.* ⁶ *Then she started to return with her daughters-in-law from the country of Moab, for she had heard in the country of Moab that the Lord had considered his people and given them food.*

What signs of joy announce a new springtime in your life?
What gives you hope at the end of your long winters?

# Privilege

**God:**

Dear child, My mere grain of dust,
know privilege in being My child.
More than deserved, you have immunity,
protection, and rare opportunity!
Walk tall in My special consideration.
Laugh with the right of adoption.

**My soul:**

God, my Father, what rights do I boast?
How do I dare to speak?
You have shaped my life in Your truth, put Your spark of light within me.
Let me not be callous, uncomprehending, and unappreciative.
You, the God of the universe, are my Parent.
I honor and am in awe. I am swept away in Your choice!

**Ephesians 1:3-10**

³ *Blessed be the God and Father of our Lord Jesus Christ, who has blessed us in Christ with every spiritual blessing in the heavenly places, ⁴ just as he chose us in Christ before the foundation of the world to be holy and blameless before him in love. ⁵ He destined us for adoption, as his children through Jesus Christ, according to the good pleasure of his will, ⁶ to the praise of his glorious grace that he freely bestowed on us in the Beloved. ⁷ In him we have redemption through his blood, the forgiveness of our trespasses, according to the riches of his grace ⁸ that he lavished on us. With all wisdom and insight ⁹ he has made known to us the mystery of his will, according to his good pleasure that he set forth in Christ, ¹⁰ as a plan for the fullness of time, to gather up all things in him, things in heaven and things on earth.*

How are you aware of your privilege as a child of God?
In what ways are you sucked into incomprehension and callousness?

## Goats and Sheep

**My soul:**

It is the trumpet time.
Before You, Judge (and Shepherd), I come,
part of the human assembly. I am accountable.
Have I nourished my truth?
In this end-time, what shape is my soul before You?
Have I gathered Your little ones with food and shelter and welcome
and bridged the great separation?
Am I Your sheep or a wildly unruly goat?

**God:**

I see you. I have always seen you.
There are strains of both goat and sheep in you.
Out of your blind raucous rollicking,
you've denied your entitlements, your indulgent brashness.
But I see your meager heart
weeping and touching your child's sleepless night,
the child separated from her parent at your border.
My mercy covers all you are,
my dear unruly goat and my dear lost sheep.

**Matthew 25:31-36**

³¹ *When the Son of Man comes in his glory, and all the angels with him, then he will sit on the throne of his glory. ³² All the nations will be gathered before him, and he will separate people one from another as a shepherd separates the sheep from the goats, ³³ and he will put the sheep at his right hand and the goats at the left. ³⁴ Then the king will say to those at his right hand, 'Come, you that are blessed by my Father, inherit the kingdom prepared for you from the foundation of the world; ³⁵ for I was hungry and you gave me food, I was thirsty and you gave me something to drink, I was a stranger and you welcomed me, ³⁶ I was naked and you gave me clothing, I was sick and you took care of me, I was in prison and you visited me.'*

How do you experience your soul?
How are you knowing God's mercy?

# Incandescence

**God:**

You, whom I created, glow!
On the spectrum of responsiveness you shine!
May I be your filament!
May you be the light of My world!

**My soul:**

Sunlight that breaks through clouds makes me happy.
God who casts out darkness,
I want to be your light-giver.
Stir up Your shine within.
Let Your incandescence
radiate hope, for our world is dark.

**John 12:34-36**

[34] *The crowd answered him, "We have heard from the law that the Messiah remains forever. How can you say that the Son of Man must be lifted up? Who is this Son of Man?"* [35] *Jesus said to them, "The light is with you for a little longer. Walk while you have the light, so that the darkness may not overtake you. If you walk in the darkness, you do not know where you are going.* [36] *While you have the light, believe in the light, so that you may become children of light." After Jesus had said this, he departed and hid from them.*

How do you experience God as the filament of light within you?
Where do you shine in the darkness of our world?

# Passover

**God:**

Do you remember Passover, enslaved one?
Instructions were to share the lamb,
to eat standing with staff in hand.
It was the feast
of moving from slavery to freedom.
Keep what is passed from
generation to generation
in sacred memory.
I am your Lamb of sacrifice.

**My soul:**

This is the moment of demarcation.
Savior God, You lead me out
by cloud and by fire.
In the strength of Your feast
I follow.
I remember the tale told by my ancestors.
We were slaves.
You heard our cry of anguish.
You laid down Your life.
You, Lamb of God, bought my freedom.

**John 13:1**

*¹ Now before the festival of the Passover, Jesus knew that his hour had come to depart from this world and go to the Father. Having loved his own who were in the world, he loved them to the end.*

How are you standing, staff in hand, ready for the march to freedom?
How is Jesus buying your freedom?

# Reverence

**My soul:**

God who comes near,
I reverence You.
You have let me know Your heart.
I bow before You, Creator and Master!
As You are gentle and tender with me,
I want to show Your face in my life.
Make me transparent with Your love.

**God:**

Do you know, child of My longing,
that your heart will be broken wide?
If you would show My love, it would be in callouses and blood.
But I am with you.
Fear not.

**Matthew 20:20-28**

*²⁰ Then the mother of the sons of Zebedee came to him with her sons, and kneeling before him, she asked a favor of him. ²¹ And he said to her, "What do you want?" She said to him, "Declare that these two sons of mine will sit, one at your right hand and one at your left, in your kingdom." ²² But Jesus answered, "You do not know what you are asking. Are you able to drink the cup that I am about to drink?" They said to him, "We are able." ²³ He said to them, "You will indeed drink my cup, but to sit at my right hand and at my left, this is not mine to grant, but it is for those for whom it has been prepared by my Father." ²⁴ When the ten heard it, they were angry with the two brothers. ²⁵ But Jesus called them to him and said, "You know that the rulers of the Gentiles lord it over them, and their great ones are tyrants over them. ²⁶ It will not be so among you; but whoever wishes to be great among you must be your servant, ²⁷ and whoever wishes to be first among you must be your slave; ²⁸ just as the Son of Man came not to be served but to serve, and to give his life a ransom for many."*

Where does knowing God's heart bring you in your life?
How is your broken heart leading you to reverence?

## Desire

**My soul:**

Delight of my heart,
I come and place my desire at Your feet.
My want is to love fiercely like You do.
Set fire to my energy to follow Your way,
to empty myself for You.

**God:**

Trust My desire for you, My child.
I know the journey you walk,
its detours, its shadows, its switchbacks.
I come with you.
I am at work in your life shaping your transparency
as well as your resistance.
Learn to see Me and know my nearness.
I yearn to share My heart.

**Psalm 36:7-9**

*7 How precious is your steadfast love, O God! All people may take refuge in the shadow of your wings. 8 They feast on the abundance of your house, and you give them drink from the river of your delights. 9 For with you is the fountain of life; in your light we see light.*

What ways are you being called to love fiercely as God loves?
How is God's work in you leading to greater transparency?

# Gardens

**God:**

I love walking in the garden of your life.
It satisfies Me to see your season's faithfulness.
Your tulips stand tall and vibrant red
in defiance of leftover cold.
Your flowering crab apple cascades its petals in the wind.
Your yellow mums laugh in the unexpected frost.
And sedum endures beneath the ice and snow.
Oh, and peaches, juicy and weighty.
Do you see Me walking among your plantings?

**My soul:**

Oh yes, my God, I see You.
You shine in all that blooms.

### Song of Songs 2:13-17

*¹³ The fig tree puts forth its figs, and the vines are in blossom; they give forth fragrance. Arise, my love, my fair one, and come away. ¹⁴ O my dove, in the clefts of the rock, in the covert of the cliff, let me see your face, let me hear your voice; for your voice is sweet, and your face is lovely. ¹⁵ Catch us the foxes, the little foxes, that ruin the vineyards—for our vineyards are in blossom." ¹⁶ My beloved is mine and I am his; he pastures his flock among the lilies. ¹⁷ Until the day breathes and the shadows flee, turn, my beloved, be like a gazelle or a young stag on the cleft mountains.*

How are you growing tulips in your early spring?
How do you feel God's walk in the garden of your life?

## Velocity

**My soul:**

God whom I approach,
my life is gaining velocity.
You are my frame of reference
that calls my days to attention.
Break open what impedes.
Displace the obstacles.
Let the direction of my longing
rush my days into Your arms.

**God:**

Come, gray-haired girl of My longing.
Feel the impulse of gathering speed
as your limbs saunter and your spirit races forward.
I wait for you in each discovery,
in every twilight,
as each fresh day dawns.
I am your Light and your contentment.

**John 8:12**

¹² *Again Jesus spoke to them, saying, "I am the light of the world.
Whoever follows me will never walk in darkness but will have the
light of life."*

How is God calling your attention?
How is God your life's contentment?

## Current

**God:**

Feel my current, tiny reservoir.
I am your inexhaustible Source.
Energy rushes your life, impelling love.
You let Me touch the pain, confusion, despair to heal.
In your great heart, I am here.

**My soul:**

Mover of Life, Shaker of Dreams,
come let me be Your passage for flow.
Our earth groans with its pressure.
You are power to renew.

**Acts 7:30-34**

[30] *"Now when forty years had passed, an angel appeared to him in the wilderness of Mount Sinai, in the flame of a burning bush.* [31] *When Moses saw it, he was amazed at the sight; and as he approached to look, there came the voice of the Lord:* [32] *'I am the God of your ancestors, the God of Abraham, Isaac, and Jacob.' Moses began to tremble and did not dare to look.* [33] *Then the Lord said to him, 'Take off the sandals from your feet, for the place where you are standing is holy ground.* [34] *I have surely seen the mistreatment of my people who are in Egypt and have heard their groaning, and I have come down to rescue them. Come now, I will send you to Egypt.'"*

How is God touching pain through you?
Where do you experience God's power renewing the earth?

# May

1. Blame
2. Participation
3. Course
4. Hew
5. Impossible
6. Disparate
7. Knight
8. Horses
9. Enjoyment
10. Intimate
11. Loon
12. Integrity
13. Indignant
14. Determined
15. Fog
16. Tangle
17. Praise
18. Loss
19. Summons
20. Stumble
21. Stranger
22. Sting
23. Refuse
24. Sea
25. Payment
26. Meet
27. Mindful
28. Meditate
29. Keep
30. Justice
31. Run

## May 1

# Blame

**God:**

Shriveled child, you cannot grow on blame.
You pretend to push away your guilt
in a thrust on someone else,
in judgment and in criticism.
Blame permeates the air with negativity.
No one can move in such mire.
You must forgive.

**My soul:**

God of mercy,
I am afraid.
I strike in blame
because I am responsible.
Teach me Your way of seeing the world.
The burden I carry
I shove onto others.
Yoke me to You, mighty One.

**Matthew 11:25-27**

*25 At that time Jesus said, "I thank you, Father, Lord of heaven and earth, because you have hidden these things from the wise and the intelligent and have revealed them to infants; 26 yes, Father, for such was your gracious will. 27 All things have been handed over to me by my Father; and no one knows the Son except the Father, and no one knows the Father except the Son and anyone to whom the Son chooses to reveal him."*

Where do you blame? How do you own up to your own responsibility?
When do you experience God's yoking to you?

# Participation

**God:**

I invite you, my little echo, to share my life energy.
You have a flickering flame within that partakes of My shine.
Let your heart involvement
hear the burden of loving.
Join it, tiny light quiver, like sound caresses its echo.

**My soul:**

I want to act, Mighty Source of Action,
with my own puzzle piece of life.
You call me to participate.
Let me carry Your steel of purpose,
Your tender fierceness of love.
I know it gratefully as Your gift.

**Daniel 6:19-23**

[19] *Then, at break of day, the king got up and hurried to the den of lions.* [20] *When he came near the den where Daniel was, he cried out anxiously to Daniel, "O Daniel, servant of the living God, has your God whom you faithfully serve been able to deliver you from the lions?"* [21] *Daniel then said to the king, "O king, live forever!* [22] *My God sent his angel and shut the lions' mouths so that they would not hurt me, because I was found blameless before him; and also before you, O king, I have done no wrong."* [23] *Then the king was exceedingly glad and commanded that Daniel be taken up out of the den. So Daniel was taken up out of the den, and no kind of harm was found on him, because he had trusted in his God.*

Where is your heart hearing the burden of involvement?
How are you participating in God's purpose?

## Course

**My soul:**

Playful Lord of Creation,
of course, naturally, obviously,
You have scattered Your laughter
in signs all over our universe.
In this field of play,
let Your rich and royal blood of life
course within me.
Be my way, my God of wit and irony!

**God:**

I am so humored
that you get Me, dear child of perception.
I've spread out My course for your learning.
Come know My way of truth!
Enjoy!

**Genesis 18:11-15**

*[11] Now Abraham and Sarah were old, advanced in age; it had ceased to be with Sarah after the manner of women. [12] So Sarah laughed to herself, saying, "After I have grown old, and my husband is old, shall I have pleasure?" [13] The Lord said to Abraham, "Why did Sarah laugh, and say, 'Shall I indeed bear a child, now that I am old?' [14] Is anything too wonderful for the Lord? At the set time I will return to you, in due season, and Sarah shall have a son." [15] But Sarah denied, saying, "I did not laugh"; for she was afraid. He said, "Oh yes, you did laugh."*

How do you experience God's blood of life coursing in you?
What course of learning is God setting before you?

# Hew

**God:**

Daring warrior child,
the fight in you will hew the cluttered wood.
It is debris of soul scattered and fired to ash.
Fear not, I fight the war in you.

**My soul:**

Mighty Maker God,
I bow my ax before You.
Sift my shavings as You choose me
so I can faithfully follow.
I give You my allegiance.

**2 Samuel 22:1-7**

¹ *David spoke to the Lord the words of this song on the day when the Lord delivered him from the hand of all his enemies, and from the hand of Saul.* ² *He said: The Lord is my rock, my fortress, and my deliverer,* ³ *my God, my rock, in whom I take refuge, my shield and the horn of my salvation, my stronghold and my refuge, my savior; you save me from violence.* ⁴ *I call upon the Lord, who is worthy to be praised, and I am saved from my enemies.* ⁵ *For the waves of death encompassed me, the torrents of perdition assailed me;* ⁶ *the cords of Sheol entangled me, the snares of death confronted me.* ⁷ *In my distress I called upon the Lord, to my God I called. From his temple he heard my voice, and my cry came to his ears.*

What debris in your soul does God turn to ash?
How does God's choice of you call forth your allegiance?

# Impossible

**God:**

Have you noticed, child of wonder,
I do the impossible?
When you think all is lost, I come!
When doors are shut and all is hopeless,
I throw open windows for the breeze of My Spirit.
When you are weary and cannot take another step,
I restore you to run once again.
Where there is no life, birth stirs and death bows down.
Believe in My springtime.

**My soul:**

My amazing Friend,
You come when all within me is blocked.
You hold me to Your heart.
The impossible melts into reality.
I can begin anew singing Your song of trust.

**Luke 1:35-38**

*³⁵ The angel said to her, "The Holy Spirit will come upon you, and the power of the Most High will overshadow you; therefore the child to be born will be holy; he will be called Son of God. ³⁶ And now, your relative Elizabeth in her old age has also conceived a son; and this is the sixth month for her who was said to be barren. ³⁷ For nothing will be impossible with God." ³⁸ Then Mary said, "Here am I, the servant of the Lord; let it be with me according to your word." Then the angel departed from her.*

How do you know the impossible happens?
How has God's holding you to His heart brought a song in your life?

# Disparate

**My soul:**

God, Companion of my Solitude,
You know the division of my heart.
Gather all that is dispersed in me,
my separate inclinations.
Let all be focused in You
that I may love as You do.

**God:**

I see what is disparate in you,
dear home of My longing.
Let the music of your disharmony find resolution
in trusting My work.
All that is distinct and jarring
can come to concord
if you only trust.

**Luke 9:51-56**

*⁵¹ When the days drew near for him to be taken up, he set his face to go to Jerusalem. ⁵² And he sent messengers ahead of him. On their way they entered a village of the Samaritans to make ready for him; ⁵³ but they did not receive him, because his face was set toward Jerusalem. ⁵⁴ When his disciples James and John saw it, they said, "Lord, do you want us to command fire to come down from heaven and consume them?" ⁵⁵ But he turned and rebuked them. ⁵⁶ Then they went on to another village.*

How are you God's home of longing?
Where are you called to trust God's forming of you?

# Knight

**My soul:**

Knight of my soul,
keep guard in the vigil
over the covenant You call me to live.
Too often, You are encrusted in armor
where I do not see You,
Warrior God, fight for my freedom to serve You,
faithful to my pledge.

**God:**

You know Me!
I have lifted the visor of My presence
for your glimpse of My eyes on you.
Let this fire of My love
enflame your quest.
Hold fast the faith that I entrust to you.
You are mine.

**Song of Songs 8:6-7**

*⁶ Set me as a seal upon your heart, as a seal upon your arm; for love is strong as death, passion fierce as the grave. Its flashes are flashes of fire, a raging flame. ⁷ Many waters cannot quench love, neither can floods drown it. If one offered for love all the wealth of one's house, it would be utterly scorned.*

What pledge do you make to your God to serve?
How do you endure because you've seen God lift the visor of His armor?

# Horses

**God:**

Do you know horses?
I created these wild and strong
creatures of grace
to speak to your heart
of freedom and play,
of loyalty and endurance.
They partner with you
as you learn discipline and love.

**My soul:**

They are beautiful, Delight of my heart.
I am astride the world
as they make their way o'er rocks and streams.
Steady and protective,
we listen to each other's fears and longings
to weld a poetry of movement and peace!

**Zechariah 1:8-11**

*8 In the night I saw a man riding on a red horse! He was standing among the myrtle trees in the glen; and behind him were red, sorrel, and white horses. 9 Then I said, "What are these, my lord?" The angel who talked with me said to me, "I will show you what they are." 10 So the man who was standing among the myrtle trees answered, "They are those whom the Lord has sent to patrol the earth." 11 Then they spoke to the angel of the Lord who was standing among the myrtle trees, "We have patrolled the earth, and lo, the whole earth remains at peace."*

Who partners with you in discipline and love?
How does listening to fears and longings bring peace in your life?

## May 9

## Enjoyment

**God:**

I give you joy, my child who wonders.
It envelops, surrounds, and bubbles up from within.
Be awake to open your eyes, your lap, your heart.
Receive!

**My soul:**

My God who sweeps me away,
it is in Your gift
that I wonder and am lifted and carried away.
I am so little and empty.
Your joy in me expands my heart in gratitude.
Thank You.

**Romans 5:1-5**

*¹ Therefore, since we are justified by faith, we have peace with God through our Lord Jesus Christ, ² through whom we have obtained access to this grace in which we stand; and we boast in our hope of sharing the glory of God. ³ And not only that, but we also boast in our sufferings, knowing that suffering produces endurance, ⁴ and endurance produces character, and character produces hope, ⁵ and hope does not disappoint us, because God's love has been poured into our hearts through the Holy Spirit that has been given to us.*

Where do you find joy?
How is God's love poured out in your heart stretching you?

# Intimate

**My soul:**

I want so much, my God,
to be close to You.
I want to know Your heart.
Let me sit with You.
Yet to quiet my soul is
like climbing a mountain.

**God:**

How can you know Me?
I am ancient. I made you.
How dare you be so casual
to climb on My lap
and curl My hair with your fingers.
Is it to rub off My shine,
or does love impel you?
Can you share My agony,
My disappointments, My betrayal, My labor?

**John 15:12-16**

[12] *"This is my commandment, that you love one another as I have loved you.* [13] *No one has greater love than this, to lay down one's life for one's friends.* [14] *You are my friends if you do what I command you.* [15] *I do not call you servants any longer, because the servant does not know what the master is doing; but I have called you friends, because I have made known to you everything that I have heard from my Father.* [16] *You did not choose me but I chose you. And I appointed you to go and bear fruit, fruit that will last, so that the Father will give you whatever you ask him in my name."*

When do you know the heart of God?
Do you know God wants to be intimate with you? How?

# Loon

**My soul:**

I hear the cry of the loon at dusk.
It stirs the ache for more.
Companion of my solitude, You are here.
In my blindness, let me be here too.

**God:**

At this edge of night,
come sit and know My dreams for you.
Unfurl your wildest dancing by the campfire.
I have stirred your longings
with the night sounds.
Only I will satisfy.

**Matthew 14:22-33**

*²² Immediately he made the disciples get into the boat and go on ahead to the other side, while he dismissed the crowds. ²³ And after he had dismissed the crowds, he went up the mountain by himself to pray. When evening came, he was there alone, ²⁴ but by this time the boat, battered by the waves, was far from the land, for the wind was against them. ²⁵ And early in the morning he came walking toward them on the sea. ²⁶ But when the disciples saw him walking on the sea, they were terrified, saying, "It is a ghost!" And they cried out in fear. ²⁷ But immediately Jesus spoke to them and said, "Take heart, it is I; do not be afraid." ²⁸ Peter answered him, "Lord, if it is you, command me to come to you on the water." ²⁹ He said, "Come." So Peter got out of the boat, started walking on the water, and came toward Jesus. ³⁰ But when he noticed the strong wind, he became frightened, and beginning to sink, he cried out, "Lord, save me!" ³¹ Jesus immediately reached out his hand and caught him, saying to him, "You of little faith, why did you doubt?" ³² When they got into the boat, the wind ceased. ³³ And those in the boat worshiped him, saying, "Truly you are the Son of God."*

How do you experience a hunger for more?
What do you know of God's dreams for you?

# Integrity

**My soul:**

God of Light, You call me to
the truth of my smallness,
my weakness, my sin.
How do I hear this?
You, who are the pure and mighty One,
would still desire me near?
Your ways are not my ways.
I will not walk away.
By Your overwhelming mercy, I stay.

**God:**

Integrity calls you to truth,
brokenhearted child.
Come see the cracks of your life
filled with my Light,
dripping My water to quench the earth's thirst.
You are whom I send.

**Jeremiah 1:4-10**

⁴ *Now the word of the Lord came to me saying,* ⁵ *"Before I formed you in the womb I knew you, and before you were born I consecrated you; I appointed you a prophet to the nations."* ⁶ *Then I said, "Ah, Lord God! Truly I do not know how to speak, for I am only a boy."* ⁷ *But the Lord said to me, "Do not say, 'I am only a boy'; for you shall go to all to whom I send you, and you shall speak whatever I command you.* ⁸ *Do not be afraid of them, for I am with you to deliver you, says the Lord."* ⁹ *Then the Lord put out his hand and touched my mouth; and the Lord said to me, "Now I have put my words in your mouth.* ¹⁰ *See, today I appoint you over nations and over kingdoms, to pluck up and to pull down, to destroy and to overthrow, to build and to plant."*

How does the truth of your soul want you to walk away?
How do you know your brokenness gives drink to the thirsty?

# Indignant

### God:

Tiny echo of My love,
let the spark within you set a mighty conflagration.
Roar your indignation!
Like Me, you hear the cry of My people.
See their misery and know their suffering!
They are made slaves. They are starving.
Their taskmasters revel in their oppression.
I send you to give them freedom.

### My soul:

Weeping God, I know Your wild and aching protest.
It rises up in me like a searing lightning. Where is truth?
How to free those who are used for money and for pleasure?
How to not be paralyzed by those who wreak terror in addiction and
despair? How to heal our ravaged earth?
Let Your great heart touch mine to hope and to move.

### Matthew 17:14-20

¹⁴ *When they came to the crowd, a man came to him, knelt before him,* ¹⁵ *and said, "Lord, have mercy on my son, for he is an epileptic and he suffers terribly; he often falls into the fire and often into the water.* ¹⁶ *And I brought him to your disciples, but they could not cure him."* ¹⁷ *Jesus answered, "You faithless and perverse generation, how much longer must I be with you? How much longer must I put up with you? Bring him here to me."* ¹⁸ *And Jesus rebuked the demon, and it came out of him, and the boy was cured instantly.* ¹⁹ *Then the disciples came to Jesus privately and said, "Why could we not cast it out?"* ²⁰ *He said to them, "Because of your little faith. For truly I tell you, if you have faith the size of a mustard seed, you will say to this mountain, 'Move from here to there,' and it will move; and nothing will be impossible for you."*

Where do you feel God's indignation?
How does God's great heart move you to hope and to move?

# Determined

**God:**

Shattered one, I have determined your glory.
It was declared to all your people
that you are chosen.
I await your open hands.

**My soul:**

Mystery of my election, I wait to see You.
I listen in silence for Your Word.
I ache in longing amidst my paralysis.
Make strong my soul to receive You.
Shape my being to dance to Your music,
to dance with You who call my name.
Let my stride walk among Your hurt ones
to heal and comfort.

**John 21:3-9, 12**

*³ Simon Peter said to them, "I am going fishing." They said to him, "We will go with you." They went out and got into the boat, but that night they caught nothing. ⁴ Just after daybreak, Jesus stood on the beach; but the disciples did not know that it was Jesus. ⁵ Jesus said to them, "Children, you have no fish, have you?" They answered him, "No." ⁶ He said to them, "Cast the net to the right side of the boat, and you will find some." So they cast it, and now they were not able to haul it in because there were so many fish. ⁷ That disciple whom Jesus loved said to Peter, "It is the Lord!" When Simon Peter heard that it was the Lord, he put on some clothes, for he was naked, and jumped into the sea. ⁸ But the other disciples came in the boat, dragging the net full of fish, for they were not far from the land, only about a hundred yards off. ⁹ When they had gone ashore, they saw a charcoal fire there, with fish on it, and bread. ¹² Jesus said to them, "Come and have breakfast." Now none of the disciples dared to ask him, "Who are you?" because they knew it was the Lord.*

Like Peter, how do you respond to the resurrected Lord?
When are you dancing with your God?

# Fog

**My soul:**

I am lost in fog, my Unseen God.
Where are You in this time
when my soul flounders?
There is no goal in sight.
The next step is shrouded and in danger.
So I am stopped, paralyzed to movement.

**God:**

I am your Mover.
I am your Goal.
All along the way where you
feel terror, I've got you.
You belong to Me, so fear not.

**2 Peter 1:19-21**

[19] *So we have the prophetic message more fully confirmed. You will do well to be attentive to this as to a lamp shining in a dark place, until the day dawns and the morning star rises in your hearts.* [20] *First of all you must understand this, that no prophecy of scripture is a matter of one's own interpretation,* [21] *because no prophecy ever came by human will, but men and women moved by the Holy Spirit spoke from God.*

Where do you find yourself unable to move?
How do you experience that God has you?

# Tangle

**My soul:**

My soul is a tangle of twisted scatterings.
God of order and peace, unbind me.
Let my love flow free.
I know it is time-consuming
to comb my matted life.
Have mercy, for I am caught.

**God:**

Do you know that I see your beauty?
We have a lifetime to untwist
all that jungle of soul to freedom.
It is My privilege, little one.

### John 15:1-5

¹ *"I am the true vine, and my Father is the vine grower.* ² *He removes every branch in me that bears no fruit. Every branch that bears fruit he prunes to make it bear more fruit.* ³ *You have already been cleansed by the word that I have spoken to you.* ⁴ *Abide in me as I abide in you. Just as the branch cannot bear fruit by itself unless it abides in the vine, neither can you unless you abide in me.* ⁵ *I am the vine, you are the branches. Those who abide in me and I in them bear much fruit, because apart from me you can do nothing."*

What tangle holds you fast?
How do you know impatience that does not align with God's time?

# Praise

**My soul:**

I praise You, Creator Parent,
with each day's rising.
I honor You
with the sea's ebb and flow,
with the wren's songs,
and the call of the heart.
I give tribute
with gifts You have given me,
inspired, surrendered, serving, laying down my life.

**God:**

In My great weaving of life,
I've planted a mighty alleluia: astonishments, courage,
fierce faithful love.
Jesus gathers you all in praise.

## 1 Corinthians 1:26-31

*²⁶ Consider your own call, brothers and sisters: not many of you were wise by human standards, not many were powerful, not many were of noble birth. ²⁷ But God chose what is foolish in the world to shame the wise; God chose what is weak in the world to shame the strong; ²⁸ God chose what is low and despised in the world, things that are not, to reduce to nothing things that are, ²⁹ so that no one might boast in the presence of God. ³⁰ He is the source of your life in Christ Jesus, who became for us wisdom from God, and righteousness and sanctification and redemption, ³¹ in order that, as it is written, "Let the one who boasts, boast in the Lord."*

How do you praise God?
Where does God astonish your foolishness?

# Loss

**My soul:**

My path to You, Companion of my soul, is loss.
I scatter all I've gathered of treasure along the way.
Unencumbered, I rush to meet You,
whom my soul knows.
In the surrender, my weakness and decline show.
Gather me in, my Lord.

**God:**

Your going forth feels
as injury and wound
as you grieve your loss.
Trust.
All you have surrendered and forfeited,
you will find again in Me.

**Philippians 3:7-11**

*⁷ Yet whatever gains I had, these I have come to regard as loss because of Christ. ⁸ More than that, I regard everything as loss because of the surpassing value of knowing Christ Jesus my Lord. For his sake I have suffered the loss of all things, and I regard them as rubbish, in order that I may gain Christ ⁹ and be found in him, not having a righteousness of my own that comes from the law, but one that comes through faith in Christ, the righteousness from God based on faith. ¹⁰ I want to know Christ and the power of his resurrection and the sharing of his sufferings by becoming like him in his death, ¹¹ if somehow I may attain the resurrection from the dead.*

What treasures are you leaving behind?
Where is the challenge to forfeit?

## Summons

**My soul:**

I have heard Your summons,
Voice that impels!
The order that repeats in my heart
is one I cannot resist.
I choose to appear in readiness
that my life may shine You.

**God:**

Blossoming child, I have placed
within your being a lure.
It is the pulley that will draw you back to me.
As you come and are present
in the court of My truth,
all that is dross, all that is chaff, will fly away.
Do not be afraid but surrendered.

### Luke 22:54-62

⁵⁴ *Then they seized him and led him away, bringing him into the high priest's house. But Peter was following at a distance.* ⁵⁵ *When they had kindled a fire in the middle of the courtyard and sat down together, Peter sat among them.* ⁵⁶ *Then a servant-girl, seeing him in the firelight, stared at him and said, "This man also was with him."* ⁵⁷ *But he denied it, saying, "Woman, I do not know him."* ⁵⁸ *A little later someone else, on seeing him, said, "You also are one of them." But Peter said, "Man, I am not!"* ⁵⁹ *Then about an hour later still another kept insisting, "Surely this man also was with him; for he is a Galilean."* ⁶⁰ *But Peter said, "Man, I do not know what you are talking about!" At that moment, while he was still speaking, the cock crowed.* ⁶¹ *The Lord turned and looked at Peter. Then Peter remembered the word of the Lord, how he had said to him, "Before the cock crows today, you will deny me three times."* ⁶² *And he went out and wept bitterly.*

When do you feel God's summons in your life?
How are you being cleansed in the court of God's truth?

# Stumble

**God:**

I see you stumble.
In your unsteady gait toward Me,
I watch and steady you.
Like a foal who trips and staggers,
your pathway is uneven.
Grow into your grace.
I will catch you before you fall.

**My soul:**

It is embarrassing, Beautiful Lord,
to be so clumsy.
I wander on cliff edges and near sinkholes.
Keep my eyes on You.

**Luke 23:34**

[34] *Then Jesus said, "Father, forgive them; for they do not know what they are doing." And they cast lots to divide his clothing.*

What is the grace into which God is calling you to grow?
Near what cliff edges and sinkholes are you wandering?

## Stranger

**My soul:**

Are we strangers, my God? You made me!
I ache to know You
and fear the utter blackness
at the door—
"I do not know You."
How do I hear the ache of Your heart
and not be arrested at Your art,
not be stopped in my hungers?
I listen for Your footsteps in the silence.

**God:**

I made you, creature of My dream.
I will not let the quicksand of My earth
grab you from Me.
Listen to Me in the wind and the wren.
Feel Me in the morning sun and the lashing rain.
Long for Me in the homeless and despairing
where you are kin.
I am with you now.

**Matthew 8:18-20**

¹⁸ *Now when Jesus saw great crowds around him, he gave orders to go over to the other side.* ¹⁹ *A scribe then approached and said, "Teacher, I will follow you wherever you go." * ²⁰ *And Jesus said to him, "Foxes have holes, and birds of the air have nests; but the Son of Man has nowhere to lay his head."*

Where do you block God's coming by saying, "I do not know You?"
What quicksand draws all your desperation?

# Sting

**God:**

I know you feel a sting.
You wonder if you've been conned, taken advantage of,
felt the bite of too much trust.
You walk in a world where bees object to your presence,
where you smart from gossip,
where the hurt, greed, and deceit would use you.
Keep your eyes on Me. I am trustworthy.
I hold you precious in My sight.

**My soul:**

Ground my being, to whom else should I go?
Faith is walking without certainty,
but I remember Your mercy, Your miracles,
and Your healing presence.
I come so small on Your wide ocean and give You my trust.

**Mark 15:6-15**

*⁶ Now at the festival he used to release a prisoner for them, anyone for whom they asked. ⁷ Now a man called Barabbas was in prison with the rebels who had committed murder during the insurrection. ⁸ So the crowd came and began to ask Pilate to do for them according to his custom. ⁹ Then he answered them, "Do you want me to release for you the King of the Jews?" ¹⁰ For he realized that it was out of jealousy that the chief priests had handed him over. ¹¹ But the chief priests stirred up the crowd to have him release Barabbas for them instead. ¹² Pilate spoke to them again, "Then what do you wish me to do with the man you call the King of the Jews?" ¹³ They shouted back, "Crucify him!" ¹⁴ Pilate asked them, "Why, what evil has he done?" But they shouted all the more, "Crucify him!" ¹⁵ So Pilate, wishing to satisfy the crowd, released Barabbas for them; and after flogging Jesus, he handed him over to be crucified.*

What storms rage around you where you are called to trust?
How are you called to believe in a world that does not seem trustworthy?

# Refuse

**My soul:**

Healing Love,
I am at the end of the line silenced.
I do not want to refuse You.
I do not want to say no.
But with head bent, I lick my wounds
and fear that I will be refuse,
garbage, leftovers.
Let Your accepting presence give me courage
to show You my wounds.

**God:**

Out of your earth, your humus, crawling with life,
I call you to My sunlight.
Let my fresh warmth heal the ooze of your self-doubt and sullenness.
Sing your song of soul
to trust I know your beauty.

**1 Corinthians 4:9-13**

*⁹ For I think that God has exhibited us apostles as last of all, as though sentenced to death, because we have become a spectacle to the world, to angels and to mortals. ¹⁰ We are fools for the sake of Christ, but you are wise in Christ. We are weak, but you are strong. You are held in honor, but we in disrepute. ¹¹ To the present hour we are hungry and thirsty, we are poorly clothed and beaten and homeless, ¹² and we grow weary from the work of our own hands. When reviled, we bless; when persecuted, we endure; ¹³ when slandered, we speak kindly. We have become like the rubbish of the world, the dregs of all things, to this very day.*

How are you silent despite your being a child of God?
How do you confront your culture that reviles and slanders?

# Sea

**God:**

Come to My sea to know yourself, rider of the waves.
Ebbs and flows mirror your own reality.
Storms and placid days stir up your truth.
There is in you the urge to kiss the sky and caress your shores.
Your own womb origins are made of sea brine.

**My soul:**

God of wide horizons,
I can see no end of sea on our curving earth.
Gravity holds the wide and mighty oceans captive
even as the moon plays with the sea,
and I am so small. I bow in humility.

**2 Corinthians 11:21-29**

²¹ *To my shame, I must say, we were too weak for that! But whatever anyone dares to boast of—I am speaking as a fool—I also dare to boast of that. ²² Are they Hebrews? So am I. Are they Israelites? So am I. Are they descendants of Abraham? So am I. ²³ Are they ministers of Christ? I am talking like a madman—I am a better one: with far greater labors, far more imprisonments, with countless floggings, and often near death. ²⁴ Five times I have received from the Jews the forty lashes minus one. ²⁵ Three times I was beaten with rods. Once I received a stoning. Three times I was shipwrecked; for a night and a day I was adrift at sea; ²⁶ on frequent journeys, in danger from rivers, danger from bandits, danger from my own people, danger from Gentiles, danger in the city, danger in the wilderness, danger at sea, danger from false brothers and sisters; ²⁷ in toil and hardship, through many a sleepless night, hungry and thirsty, often without food, cold and naked. ²⁸ And, besides other things, I am under daily pressure because of my anxiety for all the churches. ²⁹ Who is weak, and I am not weak? Who is made to stumble, and I am not indignant?*

What truth do you know of yourself from storms and from placid seas?
How does Paul's boasting of his weakness invite you to be humble?

# Payment

**My soul:**

I am Your own with life given freely.
What payment do I owe to You,
Source and Sustainer?
What exchange could lift the debt
to One who owns the sky?
Can I comprehend that You have defrayed the cost
by loving me?

**God:**

I invite you into My love,
to keep your wings wide open
for the broken and scarred,
the fearsome and soulless, the loveless and ugly.
You are My belief in action
that each of My children
can know home.

**Hebrews 11:8-12**

*8 By faith Abraham obeyed when he was called to set out for a place that he was to receive as an inheritance; and he set out, not knowing where he was going. 9 By faith he stayed for a time in the land he had been promised, as in a foreign land, living in tents, as did Isaac and Jacob, who were heirs with him of the same promise. 10 For he looked forward to the city that has foundations, whose architect and builder is God. 11 By faith he received power of procreation, even though he was too old—and Sarah herself was barren—because he considered him faithful who had promised. 12 Therefore from one person, and this one as good as dead, descendants were born, "as many as the stars of heaven and as the innumerable grains of sand by the seashore."*

How do you keep wings wide open in your life?
Does God's faith in you move you to bring heaven into your world?

## Meet

**My soul:**

God nearer to me than myself,
I meet You each day, yet long with all my soul to meet You.
You are elusive, Beloved.
Hidden, You call my name and draw me to listen in the silence
to your unknown language.
Hunger rises in me like the ache for Life
that You alone can fill.

**God:**

I come in surprises.
I stand at your back
delighting at blooming rhododendrons,
weeping at the chaos of lives driven and addicted,
believing in your great heart to pour out My love.
Know that I meet you in each turn.

### Genesis 24:15-21

[15] *Before he had finished speaking, there was Rebekah, who was born to Bethuel son of Milcah, the wife of Nahor, Abraham's brother, coming out with her water jar on her shoulder.* [16] *The girl was very fair to look upon, a virgin, whom no man had known. She went down to the spring, filled her jar, and came up.* [17] *Then the servant ran to meet her and said, "Please let me sip a little water from your jar."* [18] *"Drink, my lord," she said, and quickly lowered her jar upon her hand and gave him a drink.* [19] *When she had finished giving him a drink, she said, "I will draw for your camels also, until they have finished drinking."* [20] *So she quickly emptied her jar into the trough and ran again to the well to draw, and she drew for all his camels.* [21] *The man gazed at her in silence to learn whether or not the Lord had made his journey successful.*

How is God hiding from you when you most ache to meet God?
Where is God showing up and surprising you?

# Mindful

**My soul:**

In the channel of mindfulness,
I choose my pathway
of heart-rest to listen to You,
God present in life!
I cast aside the streams of litter—
the plans of what to cook,
the prayers for friends,
the analysis of conversations—
and lean in to let You hold my soul
like a shared foot rub.
Is it all the soothing preparation for where we are going?

**God:**

You harbor distraction like your coastline mooring.
Heaven is here and now, My child. Don't miss it.
Let your showing up with Me open your eyes to the
exquisite fullness of this moment.
Let the accouterments fall away.
I will hold you.

**Isaiah 33:17-21**

*[17] Your eyes will see the king in his beauty; they will behold a land that stretches far away. [18] Your mind will muse on the terror: "Where is the one who counted? Where is the one who weighed the tribute? Where is the one who counted the towers?" [19] No longer will you see the insolent people, the people of an obscure speech that you cannot comprehend, stammering in a language that you cannot understand. [20] Look on Zion, the city of our appointed festivals! Your eyes will see Jerusalem, a quiet habitation, an immovable tent, whose stakes will never be pulled up, and none of whose ropes will be broken. [21] But there the Lord in majesty will be for us a place of broad rivers and streams, where no galley with oars can go, nor stately ship can pass.*

How do you let God hold your soul?
How do you experience heaven on the way?

153

# Meditate

**My soul:**

I go, my Love, to that pool of love within me to find You.
It is today's carving of a sanctuary to be present.
I open wide my space of gratitude.
I try to rein my mustang wildness
to walk the cliff path safely.
I welcome You to comfort as my honored Guest.

**God:**

Believe in Me and walk My way,
My own spark.
I have made you and you are Mine.
In grace, I immerse you.
In mercy, I lead you.
In heaven, I reveal you.
In this parallel blue earth castle of your roaming,
I am here!

**Isaiah 55:6-9**

*⁶ Seek the Lord while he may be found, call upon him while he is near; ⁷ let the wicked forsake their way, and the unrighteous their thoughts; let them return to the Lord, that he may have mercy on them, and to our God, for he will abundantly pardon. ⁸ For my thoughts are not your thoughts, nor are your ways my ways, says the Lord. ⁹ For as the heavens are higher than the earth, so are my ways higher than your ways and my thoughts than your thoughts.*

How do you find God within you?
When does God light up your world with Her presence?

# Keep

**My soul:**

God, my Keeper,
You've written in my soul.
You've secured me in the tower of Your love.
Danger moves around me.
Keep my eyes on You,
where fear cannot own me.
My choice is You, my Lord.

**God:**

I've sheltered you in the center of My heart.
Explore its terrain.
Here are wonders beyond your dreaming.
Be of strong heart.
I keep you.

**Numbers 6:24-26**

*²⁴ The Lord bless you and keep you; ²⁵ the Lord make his face to shine upon you, and be gracious to you; ²⁶ the Lord lift up his countenance upon you, and give you peace.*

When do you experience being kept by God?
What do imagine of the terrain as you are kept in God's heart?

## Justice

**My soul:**

There is stirring in me a rage for justice.
I hear it in the world
in protest crowds, raised hands, and feet stomping.
Is it Your echo, God of right?
We live where there is not fairness,
but the chant calls for it in my soul.
Did we catch a glimpse of it,
so we know it's possible?

**God:**

I touch your helplessness
at roaring floods,
encroaching woes,
friends' betrayals,
and bodies' illnesses.
Even through these, I bring wholeness.
Justice is carried in My truth.
Let your doors wide open.

**Luke 18:2-7**

² *He said, "In a certain city there was a judge who neither feared God nor had respect for people. ³ In that city there was a widow who kept coming to him and saying, 'Grant me justice against my opponent.' ⁴ For a while he refused; but later he said to himself, 'Though I have no fear of God and no respect for anyone, ⁵ yet because this widow keeps bothering me, I will grant her justice, so that she may not wear me out by continually coming.'" ⁶ And the Lord said, "Listen to what the unjust judge says. ⁷ And will not God grant justice to his chosen ones who cry to him day and night? Will he delay long in helping them?*

Where do you ache for justice?
Where do you leave your doors wide open, even in a just world?

# Run

**God:**

Come run with Me.
I will pace your strength.
From jog to streak, I know your endurance.
Like a rivulet that can't be stopped,
I pour breath in you for life.

**My soul:**

Let the discipline of daily runs
breathe me to Your zone.
Great Mover and Shaker,
catch my breath,
feel my earth,
let me know Your life's embrace.
I am held in Your current
along Your way.

**Hebrews 12:1-2**

[1] *Therefore, since we are surrounded by so great a cloud of witnesses, let us also lay aside every weight and the sin that clings so closely, and let us run with perseverance the race that is set before us,* [2] *looking to Jesus the pioneer and perfecter of our faith, who for the sake of the joy that was set before him endured the cross, disregarding its shame, and has taken his seat at the right hand of the throne of God.*

What running is stretching your pace?
When do you feel in God's zone in your daily run?

# June

1. Cloak
2. Ruin
3. Summer
4. Sycamore
5. Swallow
6. Tale
7. Temple
8. Thirst
9. Revel
10. Plowshares
11. Obedience
12. Needle
13. Lodge
14. Likeness
15. Gain
16. Fox
17. Hobble
18. Dragonflies
19. Malaise
20. Petulant
21. Leach
22. Forfeit
23. Cataclysms
24. Charged
25. Crevices
26. Crescendo
27. Scrawny
28. Sea Glass
29. Squawk
30. Retrieve

**June 1**

# Cloak

**My soul:**

Cover me, Mercy Fullness, with Your cloak.
Let all that conceals my wounds fall away under Your mantle.
The mask of pretense that I am whole
is out in public view.
But You see truth.
Still, You receive me!

**God:**

I do know you, and My heart holds you.
It is a cape that keeps you warm.
Look around, dear one of disguise.
The whole of all who oppose you
are also under My cloak.
Can you accept that?

**Luke 8:16-18**

[16] *"No one after lighting a lamp hides it under a jar, or puts it under a bed, but puts it on a lampstand, so that those who enter may see the light. [17] For nothing is hidden that will not be disclosed, nor is anything secret that will not become known and come to light. [18] Then pay attention to how you listen; for to those who have, more will be given; and from those who do not have, even what they seem to have will be taken away."*

Where do you need God's cloak?
How do you know the "kinship of disguise"?

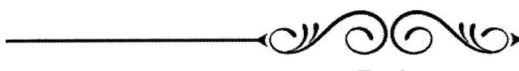

# Ruin

**God:**

I have made you fresh like the young girl
who pirouettes in life's garden.
And I have seen you age,
ruin, and scar and lay waste
in choices that only spoil.
Wake up again within My love
to let the wasteland of your soul
bloom like the desert.
Trust Me, princess child.

**My soul:**

Yes, God of my heart's springtime.
I open wide my arms
to embrace Your sunshine.
That You would still receive me—
ah, can I take it in?
Yes, I choose to awaken
to an ancient season that breaks
upon my desert soul.
Come, God of my knowing.
Be at home.

**Isaiah 35:1-4**

*¹ The wilderness and the dry land shall be glad, the desert shall rejoice and blossom; like the crocus ² it shall blossom abundantly, and rejoice with joy and singing. The glory of Lebanon shall be given to it, the majesty of Carmel and Sharon. They shall see the glory of the Lord, the majesty of our God. ³ Strengthen the weak hands, and make firm the feeble knees. ⁴ Say to those who are of a fearful heart, "Be strong, do not fear! Here is your God. He will come with vengeance, with terrible recompense. He will come and save you."*

Where do you see your wasteland bloom again?
What does choosing to awaken mean in your life?

# Summer

**God:**

It is your greening time, daughter mine.
Summer sets its pace in you:
warm,
playful,
growing.
Let the calcifications of your days free.
Let the riotous weeds of freedom know discipline.
Let summer ooze in all its juice toward harvest.

**My soul:**

Amazing Energy, Force of Love,
I stretch into my summertime
but so easily am self-focused.
Let my ground of daily living
open wide to rain and sun and wind.
May I do the labor of weed-pulling,
but even more, of letting You accomplish harvest.

**Matthew 13: 24-29**

²⁴ *He put before them another parable: "The kingdom of heaven may be compared to someone who sowed good seed in his field;* ²⁵ *but while everybody was asleep, an enemy came and sowed weeds among the wheat, and then went away.* ²⁶ *So when the plants came up and bore grain, then the weeds appeared as well.* ²⁷ *And the slaves of the householder came and said to him, 'Master, did you not sow good seed in your field? Where, then, did these weeds come from?'* ²⁸ *He answered, 'An enemy has done this.' The slaves said to him, 'Then do you want us to go and gather them?'* ²⁹ *But he replied, 'No; for in gathering the weeds you would uproot the wheat along with them.'"*

Where you see weeds grow among wheat, what does it stir in you?
What does God call you to in your summertime of greening?

## Sycamore

**God:**

Child of freedom,
do you like the sycamore trees like I do?
Their spotted trunks like brindled cows reach sturdy and tall.
They are climbing trees.
Bring your playful self to reach among the limbs.
And see Me and My world.

**My soul:**

God who laughs, let me climb.
Let me trust the call to heights where the wide world beckons.
It takes some do and dare. I feel the hunger push me higher
to hide from those who do not look up to catch a glimpse of You.

**Luke 19:1-10**

¹ *He entered Jericho and was passing through it.* ² *A man was there named Zacchaeus; he was a chief tax collector and was rich.* ³ *He was trying to see who Jesus was, but on account of the crowd he could not, because he was short in stature.* ⁴ *So he ran ahead and climbed a sycamore tree to see him, because he was going to pass that way.* ⁵ *When Jesus came to the place, he looked up and said to him, "Zacchaeus, hurry and come down; for I must stay at your house today."* ⁶ *So he hurried down and was happy to welcome him.* ⁷ *All who saw it began to grumble and said, "He has gone to be the guest of one who is a sinner."* ⁸ *Zacchaeus stood there and said to the Lord, "Look, half of my possessions, Lord, I will give to the poor; and if I have defrauded anyone of anything, I will pay back four times as much."* ⁹ *Then Jesus said to him, "Today salvation has come to this house, because he too is a son of Abraham.* ¹⁰ *For the Son of Man came to seek out and to save the lost."*

Where are you a climber, and for what?
Where do you choose to hide, and from what?

# Swallow

**My soul:**

I've swallowed hard
at the task You've set before me,
Great Other.
You think I can do this?
How do I take in Your great heart to love so fiercely?
It is all grace, and I thank You.
One step at a time!

**God:**

I've nourished you for this special moment.
All has trained your soul,
child of courage.
Follow Me and you'll have no fear.
Take My hand over the chasm.
Like a swallow, I'll teach you to fly.

**Isaiah 38:14-17**

*¹⁴ Like a swallow or a crane I clamor, I moan like a dove. My eyes are weary with looking upward. O Lord, I am oppressed; be my security! ¹⁵ But what can I say? For he has spoken to me, and he himself has done it. All my sleep has fled because of the bitterness of my soul. ¹⁶ O Lord, by these things people live, and in all these is the life of my spirit. Oh, restore me to health and make me live. ¹⁷ Surely it was for my welfare that I had great bitterness; but you have held back my life from the pit of destruction for you have cast all my sins behind your back.*

What task seems too much for you?
How have you been prepared for this moment in your life?

## Tale

**My soul:**

Comforter God,
night is near and I am weary.
I rest my head and listen to Your tale.
You weave of our lives and of our people a fabric of steel.
It lifts the burden and carves possibility.
Imagined endings, happy endings, where a wedding waits,
where a feast is served, where peace settles on the land.

**God:**

You got it!
It is the spell cast by campfire when the day is done.
Dreamer child, what you imagine is the first step for creating.
I am with you. Shape your dreams, your tales, by day.
I get excited with you.

**Matthew 1:18-25**

*18 Now the birth of Jesus the Messiah took place in this way. When his mother Mary had been engaged to Joseph, but before they lived together, she was found to be with child from the Holy Spirit. 19 Her husband Joseph, being a righteous man and unwilling to expose her to public disgrace, planned to dismiss her quietly. 20 But just when he had resolved to do this, an angel of the Lord appeared to him in a dream and said, "Joseph, son of David, do not be afraid to take Mary as your wife, for the child conceived in her is from the Holy Spirit. 21 She will bear a son, and you are to name him Jesus, for he will save his people from their sins." 22 All this took place to fulfill what had been spoken by the Lord through the prophet: 23 "Look, the virgin shall conceive and bear a son, and they shall name him Emmanuel," which means, "God is with us." 24 When Joseph awoke from sleep, he did as the angel of the Lord commanded him; he took her as his wife, 25 but had no marital relations with her until she had borne a son; and he named him Jesus.*

What tale do you find continually arising?
Did Joseph dream of fathering the Christ?

# Temple

**My soul:**

Mighty Energy, You fill our sacred space
with Your presence.
How do I hold the consciousness
that You want to come near?
In the temple of my heart,
of Your earth, of our community's
place of worship,
I come and kneel.
Let praise be my humble song.

**God:**

I see you, creature child.
I relish your song.
Here, I will speak the ancient wisdoms
and My love's secrets.
Let the silence of your soul
receive My embrace.
Do not be afraid.

**1 Samuel 3:1-3, 10-11**

¹ *Now the boy Samuel was ministering to the Lord under Eli. The word of the Lord was rare in those days; visions were not widespread.* ² *At that time Eli, whose eyesight had begun to grow dim so that he could not see, was lying down in his room;* ³ *the lamp of God had not yet gone out, and Samuel was lying down in the temple of the Lord, where the ark of God was.* ¹⁰ *Now the Lord came and stood there, calling as before, "Samuel! Samuel!" And Samuel said, "Speak, for your servant is listening."* ¹¹ *Then the Lord said to Samuel, "See, I am about to do something in Israel that will make both ears of anyone who hears of it tingle."*

What helps you hold awareness of God's presence in the temple?
What ancient wisdoms and love secrets have you heard in church?

# Thirst

**My soul:**

With a parched and driving thirst,
I come to You, Overflowing Fullness.
It draws me like desperation!
This need to drink impels a faith that wells up to be filled.
You are my thirst fulfilled and satisfied.

**God:**

I put that want within you so that you'll be drawn to Me.
Let that ache be felt and not distracted,
child of My longing.
Trust the craving for more
is borne of the stars within you.
I will satisfy your soul.

**Exodus 17:1-7**

¹ *From the wilderness of Sin the whole congregation of the Israelites journeyed by stages, as the Lord commanded. They camped at Rephidim, but there was no water for the people to drink.* ² *The people quarreled with Moses, and said, "Give us water to drink." Moses said to them, "Why do you quarrel with me? Why do you test the Lord?"* ³ *But the people thirsted there for water; and the people complained against Moses and said, "Why did you bring us out of Egypt, to kill us and our children and livestock with thirst?"* ⁴ *So Moses cried out to the Lord, "What shall I do with this people? They are almost ready to stone me."* ⁵ *The Lord said to Moses, "Go on ahead of the people, and take some of the elders of Israel with you; take in your hand the staff with which you struck the Nile, and go.* ⁶ *I will be standing there in front of you on the rock at Horeb. Strike the rock, and water will come out of it, so that the people may drink." Moses did so, in the sight of the elders of Israel.* ⁷ *He called the place Massah and Meribah, because the Israelites quarreled and tested the Lord, saying, "Is the Lord among us or not?"*

When is your thirst for the Lord a desperation?
How do you experience God satisfying your thirst?

## Revel

**God:**

Dancing child,
break open what restrains your joy.
I have called you to know merriment.
Soak in the caressing winds.
Let songbirds lift your spirit.
All this I wish for you.

**My soul:**

How do I savor Your Presence?
Your face is glimpsed in truth, in beauty, in goodness.
Let me not become arrested
in rowdy raucous revelry.
The hints of You intoxicate with my pouring out.
In the emptiness of learning Your language,
I want to know You.

**Exodus 32:1-6**

*¹ When the people saw that Moses delayed to come down from the mountain, the people gathered around Aaron, and said to him, "Come, make gods for us, who shall go before us; as for this Moses, the man who brought us up out of the land of Egypt, we do not know what has become of him." ² Aaron said to them, "Take off the gold rings that are on the ears of your wives, your sons, and your daughters, and bring them to me." ³ So all the people took off the gold rings from their ears, and brought them to Aaron. ⁴ He took the gold from them, formed it in a mold, and cast an image of a calf; and they said, "These are your gods, O Israel, who brought you up out of the land of Egypt!" ⁵ When Aaron saw this, he built an altar before it; and Aaron made proclamation and said, "Tomorrow shall be a festival to the Lord." ⁶ They rose early the next day, and offered burnt offerings and brought sacrifices of well-being; and the people sat down to eat and drink, and rose up to revel.*

What half measures would stop your growth?
How do you know God is joy?

# Plowshares

**My soul:**

Mighty Flow,
I saw a plowshare today.
It spoke of peace.
It was a hint of an ancient work
of love and hope with earth.
In the turning of the soil,
to its deep down, dark elements
aired in truth,
there is readiness for seeds to be sown.
Mover of life, let me trust.

**God:**

Earth laborer,
bend your back with sweat and toil.
Your plowshare might be stethoscope, texting, or compass.
Let it number your days creatively
as we harvest possibility.

**Micah 4:3-4**

³ *He shall judge between many peoples, and shall arbitrate between strong nations far away; they shall beat their swords into plowshares, and their spears into pruning hooks; nation shall not lift up sword against nation, neither shall they learn war any more;* ⁴ *but they shall all sit under their own vines and under their own fig trees, and no one shall make them afraid; for the mouth of the Lord of hosts has spoken.*

How does letting the dark choices be revealed in truth open new growth for you?
What are your plowshares planting?

## Obedience

**God:**

I am the Great Dancer.
Will you follow My lead?
You know that your yes to learn grace is to walk through
false moves in trial and error.
It is a yielding, a conscious adherence.
Will you keep your eyes on Me?

**My soul:**

Lord of the Dance, I want to obey.
Take my wayward self and shape my freedom to Your movement.
I yield to the measure unseen
and to Your desire written on my heart.
Yours is an authority that loves me.

**1 Peter 1:13-16**

*13 Therefore prepare your minds for action; discipline yourselves; set all your hope on the grace that Jesus Christ will bring you when he is revealed. 14 Like obedient children, do not be conformed to the desires that you formerly had in ignorance. 15 Instead, as he who called you is holy, be holy yourselves in all your conduct; 16 for it is written, "You shall be holy, for I am holy."*

Where are you challenged to obey?
How does keeping eyes on Jesus set your rule of life?

## Needle

**God:**

Weaver child, thread together meaning.
In your soul gathering,
become expert at the needle.
Frayed edges of your world
need your attention and care.
I send you to do the sewing.

**My soul:**

The fabric of our days has holes,
God of unity.
We know the thin spaces where You come.
So in love, we take our stitches
to mend the atmosphere,
the refugee camps,
our families.
Make wholeness smooth our patch.
Let my spools of thread bind the way of truth.

### Luke 18:24-26

*²⁴ Jesus looked at him and said, "How hard it is for those who have wealth to enter the kingdom of God! ²⁵ Indeed, it is easier for a camel to go through the eye of a needle than for someone who is rich to enter the kingdom of God." ²⁶ Those who heard it said, "Then who can be saved?"*

What thin spaces open God's presence, calling you to wholeness?
Where does your mending thread call forth meaning?

# Lodge

**God:**

I want so much to lodge within you.
Will you open wide your heart
so I can make My home within you?
Feather spirit-child, how easily
you catch the wind
to flutter here and there.
Your restlessness can settle if you choose to run with Me.

**My soul:**

Wisdom Master,
I want a place of my own.
To be rooted in You means to settle.
Let me see in Your lodging within
the home that brings laughter and calm.
I throw out my wide limits that keep me stuck.
Clip my wings with Your Word.
I belong to You.

**John 14:23**

²³ *Jesus answered him, "Those who love me will keep my word, and my Father will love them, and we will come to them and make our home with them."*

Where does your restlessness take you?
How is a "place of your own" an illusion if God does not run with you?

# Likeness

**God:**

I want you to look like Me.
Resemble My humor and creativity.
Look like Me in compassion and reverence.
Let all who see and know you
recognize you favor My heart.

**My soul:**

Shape me like You, Awesome God.
As I travel through my days,
form my features like Yours.
Shine in my labor and in my relating.
I know, my dearest One, that only
suffering can carve Your image
and hint the surprise of
"Oh, that's what God looks like."

**Esther 4:13-16**

¹³ *Mordecai told them to reply to Esther, "Do not think that in the king's palace you will escape any more than all the other Jews.* ¹⁴ *For if you keep silence at such a time as this, relief and deliverance will rise for the Jews from another quarter, but you and your father's family will perish. Who knows? Perhaps you have come to royal dignity for just such a time as this."* ¹⁵ *Then Esther said in reply to Mordecai,* ¹⁶ *"Go, gather all the Jews to be found in Susa, and hold a fast on my behalf, and neither eat nor drink for three days, night or day. My maids and I will also fast as you do. After that I will go to the king, though it is against the law; and if I perish, I perish."*

Like Esther, how have you been born to show the face of God?
What does it mean for you to look like God?

# Gain

**God:**

I want you to gain and increase,
growing one.
Let all you acquire benefit your life.
Reap wisdom, love, and truth
that nothing can diminish.
I am your Donor.

**My soul:**

May I rise up, God of great bounty.
In increments, let Your light add to my stature.
Let Your shadow win peaceful rest.
Let Your storms strengthen my roots.
May I obtain all that You dream of for me.
I belong to You.

**Matthew 16:24-26**

²⁴ *Then Jesus told his disciples, "If any want to become my followers, let them deny themselves and take up their cross and follow me.* ²⁵ *For those who want to save their life will lose it, and those who lose their life for my sake will find it.* ²⁶ *For what will it profit them if they gain the whole world but forfeit their life? Or what will they give in return for their life?"*

Where are you called to save your life by losing it?
What is God's dream for you?

## Fox

**My soul:**

I know Your wanderings among us, God of the journey.
You spoke of Your homelessness,
Your hunger to belong.
To follow You means radical loneliness, not fitting in.
Rest Your head in my heart.
Even its roughness, its burlap texture, would let You know belonging.

**God:**

Shelter on this alien earth, I welcome
your heart to rest.
I will soften your scratchy pillow.
I will put up My feet for ease.
I will speak My longing to your soul.
In all of this, I will be at home.

**Luke 9:57-58**

⁵⁷ *As they were going along the road, someone said to him, "I will follow you wherever you go." ⁵⁸ And Jesus said to him, "Foxes have holes, and birds of the air have nests; but the Son of Man has nowhere to lay his head."*

Do you know God's loneliness in your heart? How?
What longing have you heard God speak?

# Hobble

**My soul:**

With a hobble, I move toward You, God of the run.
Please fix my limp so I can race with You.
My gait prevents resilience.
Let me grab hands to steady my limp.
Humbly, let me take my cane if I only must process slowly.
My God, let me run with You.

**God:**

I touch your hitch with mercy.
What is stiff and aching, I make lithe and flexible.
Your rigid gawky stride will ease to grace, dear racer.
Be spry and nimble with your vim within.
I will pace beside you.

**John 20:1-10**

¹ *Early on the first day of the week, while it was still dark, Mary Magdalene came to the tomb and saw that the stone had been removed from the tomb.* ² *So she ran and went to Simon Peter and the other disciple, the one whom Jesus loved, and said to them, "They have taken the Lord out of the tomb, and we do not know where they have laid him."* ³ *Then Peter and the other disciple set out and went toward the tomb.* ⁴ *The two were running together, but the other disciple outran Peter and reached the tomb first.* ⁵ *He bent down to look in and saw the linen wrappings lying there, but he did not go in.* ⁶ *Then Simon Peter came, following him, and went into the tomb. He saw the linen wrappings lying there,* ⁷ *and the cloth that had been on Jesus' head, not lying with the linen wrappings but rolled up in a place by itself.* ⁸ *Then the other disciple, who reached the tomb first, also went in, and he saw and believed;* ⁹ *for as yet they did not understand the scripture, that he must rise from the dead.* ¹⁰ *Then the disciples returned to their homes.*

What in your life makes you hobble?
Like Mary and Peter, what impossible hope gives you resilience to run?

# June 18

## Dragonflies

**My soul:**

I saw a dragonfly today.
Rainbow wings reflect Your glory,
Transforming God.
So long I've hidden unmovable.
My larval stage encases my swift dreams too long.
Unfold my flight of opalescence.
I long for freedom.

**God:**

Aren't dragonflies stunning?
They catch imagination and transform.
Wonderer, what seems hidden and stuck knows
an impulse of the heart.
Your beauty is unfolding.
I know and call forth.

**Luke 7:36-38**

*⁣³⁶ One of the Pharisees asked Jesus to eat with him, and he went into the Pharisee's house and took his place at the table. ³⁷ And a woman in the city, who was a sinner, having learned that he was eating in the Pharisee's house, brought an alabaster jar of ointment. ³⁸ She stood behind him at his feet, weeping, and began to bathe his feet with her tears and to dry them with her hair. Then she continued kissing his feet and anointing them with the ointment.*

Where are you stuck in a larval stage?
What impulse of the heart moves your dragonfly beauty to unfold?

## Malaise

**My soul:**

A malaise has spread over me,
God of powerful wind.
It oozes and drains me of movement and motivation.
Let Your energy catch my laziness.
Where I am tired and weary of spirit,
urge a rise of juice within.
Clear my restlessness to focus.
Let me know that heaven is now to embrace.

**God:**

From your smog of lethargy, caught one, know I am here!
I stir your dull immobile sleep to wake again refreshed.
Where you are disengaged, connect.
Where you are limp and passive, stand strong.
Where you are apathetic, come alive. I am the Lord of arising.

**Jeremiah 31:23-25**

²³ *Thus says the Lord of hosts, the God of Israel: Once more they shall use these words in the land of Judah and in its towns when I restore their fortunes: "The Lord bless you, O abode of righteousness, O holy hill!"* ²⁴ *And Judah and all its towns shall live there together, and the farmers and those who wander with their flocks.* ²⁵ *I will satisfy the weary, and all who are faint I will replenish.*

When are you caught in a malaise of motivation?
How do you experience heaven in a fresh rising?

# Petulant

**My soul:**

A storm barged in today, God of mighty winds.
It was petulant like a tempest in a teapot,
blowing leaves and limbs with wild and gusty huffs.
Entitled, it whined and snapped in spoiled pouts.
Oh, so like me, in my peevish sulks.
Mercy, please, God to whom I belong.
Help me grow up.

**God:**

Have I spoiled you, cranky child?
Where is your grateful heart?
Can you learn to play through
your grumbling bits?
Let me hold you and caress your sullenness away.

**1 Corinthians 13:11-13**

*11 When I was a child, I spoke like a child, I thought like a child, I reasoned like a child; when I became an adult, I put an end to childish ways. 12 For now we see in a mirror, dimly, but then we will see face to face. Now I know only in part; then I will know fully, even as I have been fully known. 13 And now faith, hope, and love abide, these three; and the greatest of these is love.*

Where does your irritability show up?
How does gratefulness to God calm the peevish storms?

# Leach

**God:**

I see you weep today,
heart bleeding in your needs!
Pleader for your earth,
I hear how the gunshots and blisters,
hunger and hate saturate your soul.
Let My sun leach the toxins.
Move in the warmth of My compassion.
Dissolve the pain you see in your touch.
I am near.

**My soul:**

Powerful Light of the world,
Your sun and Your rain come to remove the poisons.
Touch all that seeps in of anguish,
all that spurts out in blame,
all that drains into culture in protest.
You are healer and mender of
our frayed and fractured earth.

**Matthew 5:43-48**

⁴³ *"You have heard that it was said, 'You shall love your neighbor and hate your enemy.' ⁴⁴ But I say to you, Love your enemies and pray for those who persecute you, ⁴⁵ so that you may be children of your Father in heaven; for he makes his sun rise on the evil and on the good, and sends rain on the righteous and on the unrighteous. ⁴⁶ For if you love those who love you, what reward do you have? Do not even the tax collectors do the same? ⁴⁷ And if you greet only your brothers and sisters, what more are you doing than others? Do not even the Gentiles do the same? ⁴⁸ Be perfect, therefore, as your heavenly Father is perfect.*

Where do you weep? How do you experience God near?
How does your touch heal?

# Forfeit

**God:**

Will you forfeit your life for Me?
Companion of my heart, it happens day by day.
Will you set aside time, desires, comfort, choices,
knowing I hold for you
all that you sacrifice?
I long for your partnership.
In this time and place, I depend on you.

**My soul:**

I know You, Lord, who have made me.
Yes, I waive my claim to choose my way.
You have called me to life for this moment.
May the fierce advocates of angels and principalities,
saints and knights of Your realm
keep me true and courageous in my word.
May I lay down my life for You.

**Matthew 10:34, 37-39**

[34] *"Do not think that I have come to bring peace to the earth; I have not come to bring peace, but a sword.* [37] *Whoever loves father or mother more than me is not worthy of me; and whoever loves son or daughter more than me is not worthy of me;* [38] *and whoever does not take up the cross and follow me is not worthy of me.* [39] *Those who find their life will lose it, and those who lose their life for my sake will find it."*

What is your partnership with God asking you to forfeit?
What kind of courage is demanded to be called to this moment,
this time and place?

# Cataclysms

**My soul:**

I heard today of frightful ruin.
You, our Mighty Mover, listen to our plea.
We have brought calamity.
The woe is in not living,
not birthing a new generation to stop the tide of fear.
It is our catastrophe of arrogance—
to think we alone can heal the earth.
If not, we submit to nothing.

**God:**

I see the cataclysm coming,
prophesied by fire and flood.
Yes, you have marred your living.
But do you remember springtime?
Do you dare conceive the children of your fight?
Do you know, even in your tragedies, I stand with you?
Where there was nothing, there is the wondrous spectacle
of something.

**1 Peter 4:7-11**

*⁷ The end of all things is near; therefore be serious and discipline yourselves for the sake of your prayers. ⁸ Above all, maintain constant love for one another, for love covers a multitude of sins. ⁹ Be hospitable to one another without complaining. ¹⁰ Like good stewards of the manifold grace of God, serve one another with whatever gift each of you has received. ¹¹ Whoever speaks must do so as one speaking the very words of God; whoever serves must do so with the strength that God supplies, so that God may be glorified in all things through Jesus Christ. To him belong the glory and the power forever and ever. Amen.*

How does risk to our earth paralyze your living?
Where is God standing with you to bring festivity out of disaster?

# Charged

**God:**

The lightning flashes with a charged energy.
In exchange, you who are my charge
have assignment to bravery.
Let My love draw you into selflessness and service.
In this storm of hunkered-down hiding,
dare a courage of bonds with one another.

**My soul:**

Send, then, Your Spirit
of light and truth,
of fierce steadiness in me,
to bear the cost of courage.
With You, all things are possible.

**Romans 8:31-36**

*31 What then are we to say about these things? If God is for us, who is against us? 32 He who did not withhold his own Son, but gave him up for all of us, will he not with him also give us everything else? 33 Who will bring any charge against God's elect? It is God who justifies. 34 Who is to condemn? It is Christ Jesus, who died, yes, who was raised, who is at the right hand of God, who indeed intercedes for us. 35 Who will separate us from the love of Christ? Will hardship, or distress, or persecution, or famine, or nakedness, or peril, or sword? 36 As it is written, "For your sake we are being killed all day long; we are accounted as sheep to be slaughtered."*

What is your assignment to bravery?
How do you dare a courage of bonds?

# Crevices

**God:**

Climber child,
I see you caught in the cleft in the rocks.
From that crevice, I will lift you up.
I hear your cry of anguish.
In that dark chasm, know you are not alone.
Where you feel cold and abandoned,
know that I am near.

**My soul:**

God of All-Seeing,
I am broken and unable to move.
In this cranny where I am stuck,
let down Your harness of freedom.
Put Your yoke upon me
so together I can leave this fissure.
Where an abyss yawns, I keep my eyes on You.
I am so glad You found me.

**Matthew 11:28-30**

[28] *"Come to me, all you that are weary and are carrying heavy burdens, and I will give you rest. [29] Take my yoke upon you, and learn from me; for I am gentle and humble in heart, and you will find rest for your souls. [30] For my yoke is easy, and my burden is light."*

How has your climbing led to being caught in the cleft?
In what ways does God lift you to freedom when you are stuck?

# Crescendo

**My soul:**

My music is a whisper,
God whom I praise!
Raise within me a mighty song.
I give my life to voice Your name.
Send Your Spirit of wind within me.
Increase the swell of my impact
to heal and comfort,
to understand and confront,
to echo what Your Word proclaims.

**God:**

I hear you, messenger of My Word!
What is hoarse and voiceless within you,
I give the power of fire. Trust your calling.
The gathering will come to make a symphony of hallelujah.
Your whisper will be heard in a heartfelt crescendo of glory.

**Matthew 11:2-6**

*² When John heard in prison what the Messiah was doing, he sent word by his disciples ³ and said to him, "Are you the one who is to come, or are we to wait for another?" ⁴ Jesus answered them, "Go and tell John what you hear and see: ⁵ the blind receive their sight, the lame walk, the lepers are cleansed, the deaf hear, the dead are raised, and the poor have good news brought to them. ⁶ And blessed is anyone who takes no offense at me."*

When is your proclamation of God's Word only a whisper?
How have you felt within you a crescendo of praise and power?

# Scrawny

**My soul:**

My soul feels scrawny and gaunt, Robust Life.
To all that's starved and shrunken,
fill with Your nourishing strength.
Build my heart's mettle with Your endurance.
Where there is passiveness in me, place Your creative force.
Where there is wizened waste, may Your direction move me.
I choose Your magnetic love to shape my soul anew.

**God:**

Turn your life to Me, meager spirit.
Look at the willow and crocus—the first to dare spring dancing.
Behold the ocean tides, responsive and full of play.
Let My wind and fire urge you to run in freedom.
Know My Presence of peace.

**1 Kings 17:10-15**

*¹⁰ So he set out and went to Zarephath. When he came to the gate of the town, a widow was there gathering sticks; he called to her and said, "Bring me a little water in a vessel, so that I may drink." ¹¹ As she was going to bring it, he called to her and said, "Bring me a morsel of bread in your hand." ¹² But she said, "As the Lord your God lives, I have nothing baked, only a handful of meal in a jar, and a little oil in a jug; I am now gathering a couple of sticks, so that I may go home and prepare it for myself and my son, that we may eat it, and die." ¹³ Elijah said to her, "Do not be afraid; go and do as you have said; but first make me a little cake of it and bring it to me, and afterwards make something for yourself and your son. ¹⁴ For thus says the Lord, the God of Israel: The jar of meal will not be emptied and the jug of oil will not fail until the day that the Lord sends rain on the earth." ¹⁵ She went and did as Elijah said.*

Where do you feel your soul as scrawny and gaunt?
What signs of nature restore your consciousness of God's presence?

# Sea Glass

**My soul:**

God, ever ancient and ever new,
I found sea glass this morning.
Last night's storm belched up ancient treasures,
broken and tumbled.
These are shards showing bubbles
from the weathered rolling of spring tides.
They are frosted from the salt in the long years of waiting.

**God:**

What fun!
I've cast beauty from the sea.
Packed casks from the past sailings,
shattered and scattered, litter coughed up!
It is for you, hunter of the deep!
Are the amberina of spirits, the blue of poisons,
the black most rare—thick and buried—
a puzzle for your soul?
What is the message for you of sea glass?

### Jonah 1:4, 7-10

*⁴ But the Lord hurled a great wind upon the sea, and such a mighty storm came upon the sea that the ship threatened to break up. ⁷ The sailors said to one another, "Come, let us cast lots, so that we may know on whose account this calamity has come upon us." So they cast lots, and the lot fell on Jonah. ⁸ Then they said to him, "Tell us why this calamity has come upon us. What is your occupation? Where do you come from? What is your country? And of what people are you?" ⁹ "I am a Hebrew," he replied. "I worship the Lord, the God of heaven, who made the sea and the dry land." ¹⁰ Then the men were even more afraid, and said to him, "What is this that you have done!" For the men knew that he was fleeing from the presence of the Lord, because he had told them so.*

Where are your shards of glass waiting to enter your consciousness?
What is God asking you to do that you are running from?

## Squawk

**My soul:**

I find myself in a grouse!
Absolute Mercy,
I cry and yell and screech
about our bindings.
We, Your people, are entangled in knots
that divide and bully,
then turn to violence and deceit.
My squawking comes to no end.
I stand paralyzed.
Let Your winds blow free the chaos
and renew the face of our earth.

**God:**

Little seer, no wonder you complain and stand idle.
Where to begin to untie the ancient
hurts and ravaged pain
of too much want—that is for My healing power.
I send the freshness of My Spirit
to move over all that is stuck and groaning.
Have hope for your earth home
and your family.

**Jonah 4:9-11**

⁹ *But God said to Jonah, "Is it right for you to be angry about the bush?" And he said, "Yes, angry enough to die."* ¹⁰ *Then the Lord said, "You are concerned about the bush, for which you did not labor and which you did not grow; it came into being in a night and perished in a night.* ¹¹ *And should I not be concerned about Nineveh, that great city, in which there are more than a hundred and twenty thousand persons who do not know their right hand from their left, and also many animals?"*

What settles over your life like a grouse?
How does hope free what is tied in knots to act?

# Retrieve

**God:**

Retrieve, old woman, your youth's young love.
Melt your wrinkles into a wreath of smiles.
Let weary limbs jump up again.
Reclaim your flexibility.
Recover zest and curiosity,
for I have worlds you have not yet explored.
Dare again to live.

**My soul:**

God of amazing adventure,
can You repair my stiff gait and my thin skin?
Can you bring back my ebony shine
to what has long grown brittle and gray?
Can you soften the guard on my heart
to open wide its gate?
Unearth my buried self to again believe.
You walk gently near.

**Isaiah 65:17-20**

[17] *For I am about to create new heavens and a new earth; the former things shall not be remembered or come to mind.* [18] *But be glad and rejoice forever in what I am creating; for I am about to create Jerusalem as a joy, and its people as a delight.* [19] *I will rejoice in Jerusalem, and delight in my people; no more shall the sound of weeping be heard in it, or the cry of distress.* [20] *No more shall there be in it an infant that lives but a few days, or an old person who does not live out a lifetime; for one who dies at a hundred years will be considered a youth, and one who falls short of a hundred will be considered accursed.*

What has grown brittle and gray in your life?
How are you walking with God to explore new worlds?

# July

1. Eucalyptus
2. Beckoning
3. Thunder
4. Cataract
5. Bough
6. Amble
7. Inflame
8. Cryptic
9. Compass
10. Nothing
11. Assuage
12. Fierce
13. Cling
14. Sleuth
15. Goaded
16. Dare
17. Palpable
18. Penetrate
19. Chill
20. Keening
21. Drench
22. Dart
23. Solitude
24. Seething
25. Vestiges
26. Leopard
27. Groan
28. Testify
29. Tent
30. Temporary
31. Satisfy

## July 1

## Eucalyptus

**God:**

Come to My eucalyptus groves, weary one!
It is a greening time for you
to breathe in My fragrance.
Rest your soul in the hollows
of My trees!
Like bees, let this haven be your comb for honey-making.
I am here.

**My soul:**

God of my restfulness,
evergreen in me.
Let the medicine of Your love
heal and restore Your world.
May the humming of my soul
sweeten my labor.
Refresh me in Your presence.
Taste Your delight in me.

**Deuteronomy 32:10-14**

*¹⁰ He sustained him in a desert land, in a howling wilderness waste; he shielded him, cared for him, guarded him as the apple of his eye. ¹¹ As an eagle stirs up its nest, and hovers over its young; as it spreads its wings, takes them up, and bears them aloft on its pinions, ¹² the Lord alone guided him; no foreign god was with him. ¹³ He set him atop the heights of the land, and fed him with produce of the field; he nursed him with honey from the crags, with oil from flinty rock; ¹⁴ curds from the herd, and milk from the flock, with fat of lambs and rams; Bashan bulls and goats, together with the choicest wheat—you drank fine wine from the blood of grapes.*

What weariness settles in your soul?
What sweetness is God inviting you to bring to the world?

# Beckoning

**God:**

Do you feel My beckoning,
favored one?
May you be drawn to Me
even as your appeal has written
your name on My palm.
I invite you.
I know you.
The allure of your freedom calls to My love.

**My soul:**

I want to know You.
Who would dare come close.
Be silent, my soul, and adore.
Let me open the tent flaps of my life
for You, Desert Roamer,
to find comfort in Your creating.
Let me soothe Your weary feet.
Let me sing you my love song.
I am Yours.

**Song of Songs 4:9-15**

⁹ *You have ravished my heart, my sister, my bride, you have ravished my heart with a glance of your eyes, with one jewel of your necklace.* ¹⁰ *How sweet is your love, my sister, my bride! how much better is your love than wine, and the fragrance of your oils than any spice!* ¹¹ *Your lips distill nectar, my bride; honey and milk are under your tongue; the scent of your garments is like the scent of Lebanon.* ¹² *A garden locked is my sister, my bride, a garden locked, a fountain sealed.* ¹³ *Your channel is an orchard of pomegranates with all choicest fruits, henna with nard,* ¹⁴ *nard and saffron, calamus and cinnamon, with all trees of frankincense, myrrh and aloes, with all chief spices—* ¹⁵ *a garden fountain, a well of living water, and flowing streams from Lebanon.*

How are you in your freedom being drawn to your God?
In what ways are you soothing the weary feet of God?

# July 3

# Thunder

**God:**

Distracted one,
I want to talk with you today. How do I get your attention?
Then I remembered what never fails!
I sent the long and slow rumble that is thunder.
It follows some great treasures—fire and water mixing.
Once I see you are listening, I will tell you My secret.

**My soul:**

God of earth's light show, it wasn't just a rolling thunder,
it was also a mighty boom. You have my attention; I am listening.
Speak to my heart what is Your longing.
I will set down my fears to hear.
I will give you my hand in trust.
What is it You, Mighty One, would speak to me?

**1 Samuel 12:18-24**

[18] *So Samuel called upon the Lord, and the Lord sent thunder and rain that day; and all the people greatly feared the Lord and Samuel.* [19] *All the people said to Samuel, "Pray to the Lord your God for your servants, so that we may not die; for we have added to all our sins the evil of demanding a king for ourselves."* [20] *And Samuel said to the people, "Do not be afraid; you have done all this evil, yet do not turn aside from following the Lord, but serve the Lord with all your heart;* [21] *and do not turn aside after useless things that cannot profit or save, for they are useless.* [22] *For the Lord will not cast away his people, for his great name's sake, because it has pleased the Lord to make you a people for himself.* [23] *Moreover as for me far be it from me that I should sin against the Lord by ceasing to pray for you; and I will instruct you in the good and the right way.* [24] *Only fear the Lord, and serve him faithfully with all your heart; for consider what great things he has done for you."*

Has God spoken secrets to you? How do you know?
How does "considering the great things God has done for you" cast out fear to hear?

# Cataract

**My soul:**

I can't see, God of visioning.
Cataracts make opaque and blurred
all that is in front of me.
Wash clean in Your violent rush of water
all that blinds my eyes to You.
I stand on a precipice paralyzed.
I long to see You, Lord.

**God:**

In the waterfall of My love, you will see!
The truth of you can be borne
only in My acceptance.

**Isaiah 42:16**

*16 I will lead the blind by a road they do not know, by paths they have not known I will guide them. I will turn the darkness before them into light, the rough places into level ground. These are the things I will do, and I will not forsake them.*

What is blinding you from seeing God?
How do you see the truth in God's acceptance?

## Bough

**God:**

Be my bough,
stretching to shelter,
strongly attached,
fruitful of life in season!
I have life juices planted
deeply in your earth.
You will find nurture and purpose.

**My soul:**

With all my heart, gracious Tree of Life,
I embrace being Your bough.
Let the shade of Your mercy
reach over my soul
and over Your people.
May we picnic with You,
knowing peace and laughter.
May Your Word rise up within me
to catch the breeze of Your inclusion,
to scatter seeds of hope far and wide,
to sing Your song of comfort.
Keep me closely bonded.

**Isaiah 4:2-3**

*² On that day the branch of the Lord shall be beautiful and glorious, and the fruit of the land shall be the pride and glory of the survivors of Israel. ³ Whoever is left in Zion and remains in Jerusalem will be called holy, everyone who has been recorded for life in Jerusalem.*

How are you nurtured and how do you find purpose in being a bough?
This day, how do you create a picnic of peace and laughter?

## July 6

## Amble

**God:**

I see you amble along.
Sometimes you may not want
to take a more determined stride.
Sauntering through life with a casual attitude
is one step away from cynicism.
Do you not know
that these are risky paths you walk?
It is, brothers and sisters who are used and not seen!
So let My Spirit put fire in your step.

**My soul:**

It is true.
I am meandering.
In my public walkabout, I mosey,
acting free and privileged—
not responsible.
When struggle causes blisters for others,
let them lean on me.
After all, we are walking each other home.

## Psalm 122

¹ *I was glad when they said to me, "Let us go to the house of the Lord!"* ² *Our feet are standing within your gates, O Jerusalem.* ³ *Jerusalem—built as a city that is bound firmly together.* ⁴ *To it the tribes go up, the tribes of the Lord, as was decreed for Israel, to give thanks to the name of the Lord.* ⁵ *For there the thrones for judgment were set up, the thrones of the house of David.* ⁶ *Pray for the peace of Jerusalem: "May they prosper who love you.* ⁷ *Peace be within your walls, and security within your towers."* ⁸ *For the sake of my relatives and friends I will say, "Peace be within you."* ⁹ *For the sake of the house of the Lord our God, I will seek your good.*

Where do you feel the Spirit putting fire in your step?
Who are you walking home?

# Inflame

**God:**

Can you catch flame, little prophet child?
From the pain of homeless ones, in the scars of fearful souls,
with the worn feet of refugees, arouse your fierce stand for them!
Even voiceless, stand by them! Slow up. Disturb.
Roil with your tears so they know they are not alone.

**My soul:**

God of great heart,
rile my spirit to act.
Where children are pulled from their parents,
let me stand in the breach.
Where moms are dragged back to danger,
let me foment such a cry of no.
Where men are hunted to deport,
infuriate my life to annoy.
I am yours, Parent God, to protest.

**1 Peter 4:12-17**

*12 Beloved, do not be surprised at the fiery ordeal that is taking place among you to test you, as though something strange were happening to you. 13 But rejoice insofar as you are sharing Christ's sufferings, so that you may also be glad and shout for joy when his glory is revealed. 14 If you are reviled for the name of Christ, you are blessed, because the spirit of glory, which is the Spirit of God, is resting on you. 15 But let none of you suffer as a murderer, a thief, a criminal, or even as a mischief-maker. 16 Yet if any of you suffers as a Christian, do not consider it a disgrace, but glorify God because you bear this name. 17 For the time has come for judgment to begin with the household of God; if it begins with us, what will be the end for those who do not obey the gospel of God?*

Where is God inviting you to protest?
Where do you roil with tears?

## Cryptic

**God:**

Claim the faith I give you, human child.
It is not hidden. It is not ambiguous.
It rests in My unconditional love.
You have breath and heartbeat,
vision to see heaven right on your earth,
food for your journey day by day.
Embrace the life unveiled.

**My soul:**

In cryptic murky roaming,
I stew on so much that is unimportant.
God of Mighty Love, let what is secret
within me be proclaimed on the mountaintops.
I live not on my own power.
I am gifted by You
for this time and place.
"I do believe, help Thou my unbelief."

### Luke 9:28-34

*²⁸ Now about eight days after these sayings Jesus took with him Peter and John and James, and went up on the mountain to pray. ²⁹ And while he was praying, the appearance of his face changed, and his clothes became dazzling white. ³⁰ Suddenly they saw two men, Moses and Elijah, talking to him. ³¹ They appeared in glory and were speaking of his departure, which he was about to accomplish at Jerusalem. ³² Now Peter and his companions were weighed down with sleep; but since they had stayed awake, they saw his glory and the two men who stood with him. ³³ Just as they were leaving him, Peter said to Jesus, "Master, it is good for us to be here; let us make three dwellings, one for you, one for Moses, and one for Elijah"—not knowing what he said. ³⁴ While he was saying this, a cloud came and overshadowed them; and they were terrified as they entered the cloud.*

What is it you believe in?
How do you walk in the belief that you were born for this time and place?

## Compass

**My soul:**

God, Seeker of my soul,
You've put a compass within me.
The true north inside is You.
I circle, going round and round.
I do not attend to what draws me.
My horizons widen in wasted latitude.
You are my lodestar.

**God:**

I have centered in you, wandering child,
an allure you will not resist.
Do not be afraid
near precipice or wild tide;
I've got you.
You know me in the silence.
You are carried through the noise.
In the zigzag of your choices,
I have you and will bring you home.

### Nehemiah 4:18-21

*¹⁸ And each of the builders had his sword strapped at his side while he built. The man who sounded the trumpet was beside me. ¹⁹ And I said to the nobles, the officials, and the rest of the people, "The work is great and widely spread out, and we are separated far from one another on the wall. ²⁰ Rally to us wherever you hear the sound of the trumpet. Our God will fight for us." ²¹ So we labored at the work, and half of them held the spears from break of dawn until the stars came out.*

How are you experiencing the compass within you?
How is God fighting for you?

# Nothing

**My soul:**

In our beginning, we were nothing.
Explosive Love, You poured Your juices
into the formless void.
Down the long line of ancestors, You formed me.
I am a holder of Your imagination,
Your love, Your partnership.
Quiet my soul to Your presence
so I can grow to reflect You.
Let my being not be for naught.

**God:**

I called you to be.
I let My sparks of light and laughter
catch shape in you.
For this time and place, you are born to stand tall.
I lift you "from the no of all nothing"
to be My voice and My love.
I trust you.

**Genesis 17:1-7**

*¹ When Abram was ninety-nine years old, the Lord appeared to Abram, and said to him, "I am God Almighty; walk before me, and be blameless. ² And I will make my covenant between me and you, and will make you exceedingly numerous." ³ Then Abram fell on his face; and God said to him, ⁴ "As for me, this is my covenant with you: You shall be the ancestor of a multitude of nations. ⁵ No longer shall your name be Abram, but your name shall be Abraham; for I have made you the ancestor of a multitude of nations. ⁶ I will make you exceedingly fruitful; and I will make nations of you, and kings shall come from you. ⁷ I will establish my covenant between you and me, and your offspring after you throughout their generations, for an everlasting covenant, to be God to you and to your offspring after you."*

How are you a holder of God's imagination?
What is God's trust of you?

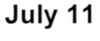

## Assuage

**My soul:**

Assuage my fear of You,
Fierce One.
My life is sated with a surfeit
that prevents my seeing You.
When You come near,
I expect to be overwhelmed.
When You mission me to speak,
I stutter in alarm.
When You show me Your great love,
I only dare a glance!
Invisible Lord, I do feel You hold me.

**God:**

Let My holding you
quiet your heart!
Then you can see Me,
speak for Me,
receive My ready love.
I am invisible only to those who
don't know Me.

### Joshua 23:8-11

[8] But *hold fast to the Lord your God, as you have done to this day.* [9] *For the Lord has driven out before you great and strong nations; and as for you, no one has been able to withstand you to this day.* [10] *One of you puts to flight a thousand, since it is the Lord your God who fights for you, as he promised you.* [11] *Be very careful, therefore, to love the Lord your God.*

How do you dull God's presence?
Where do you feel God holding you?

## Fierce

**My soul:**

First Mover God, I'm overcome with fierce emotion.
How do I contain the savage wrong of children caged
and do nothing?
What would You have me do?
How do I take the violent energy within
to protest such callous, cutthroat wrong?
In my helplessness, I come to You to move me.

**God:**

My friend, sharpen your love in My fire.
Stand and hold each child who knows fear
in the circle of your safety.
Begin with imagining.
Your arms and stance will mirror what
you hold so ferociously.
I did this.
Remember.
You can become the channel of My love.
Be My arms of refuge.

**John 16:20-24**

²⁰ *Very truly, I tell you, you will weep and mourn, but the world will rejoice; you will have pain, but your pain will turn into joy.* ²¹ *When a woman is in labor, she has pain, because her hour has come. But when her child is born, she no longer remembers the anguish because of the joy of having brought a human being into the world.* ²² *So you have pain now; but I will see you again, and your hearts will rejoice, and no one will take your joy from you.* ²³ *On that day you will ask nothing of me. Very truly, I tell you, if you ask anything of the Father in my name, he will give it to you.* ²⁴ *Until now you have not asked for anything in my name. Ask and you will receive, so that your joy may be complete.*

Who are the children in your life who need fierce protection?
How can you channel God's love to the world?

# Cling

**My soul:**

Hold me tenaciously, Breath of Life.
I cling to You with my mind and heart,
making space to listen.
Grasp me out of the miasma of hungers.
Lead me to cleave to Your truth and follow.
I do believe; help my unbelief.

**God:**

Hold lightly, free of obsession.
I am here and have you, drowning one!
Let your heart relax in My presence.
I am active and powerful in your regard.
Only trust.

## Mark 5:1-9

*¹ They came to the other side of the sea, to the country of the Gerasenes. ² And when he had stepped out of the boat, immediately a man out of the tombs with an unclean spirit met him. ³ He lived among the tombs; and no one could restrain him any more, even with a chain; ⁴ for he had often been restrained with shackles and chains, but the chains he wrenched apart, and the shackles he broke in pieces; and no one had the strength to subdue him. ⁵ Night and day among the tombs and on the mountains he was always howling and bruising himself with stones. ⁶ When he saw Jesus from a distance, he ran and bowed down before him; ⁷ and he shouted at the top of his voice, "What have you to do with me, Jesus, Son of the Most High God? I adjure you by God, do not torment me." ⁸ For he had said to him, "Come out of the man, you unclean spirit!" ⁹ Then Jesus asked him, "What is your name?" He replied, "My name is Legion; for we are many."*

What hungers occupy your mind to distraction?
How does trust invite you to hold lightly?

## Sleuth

**God:**

I am a sleuth for your destiny, child of My longing.
I weigh your freedom.
I search your choices, imagining always for you
delight and surprise.
You are the apple of My eye.
Know that I watch you
to know all your possibilities.
Enjoy and laugh, little one.

**My soul:**

Searcher of my heart,
come and direct my days.
I surrender to Your wiser path,
yet I know I must choose.
Help me to know You
so I can walk Your way.
I want to see You along the path.

**Galatians 5:1, 13-15**

¹ *For freedom Christ has set us free. Stand firm, therefore, and do not submit again to a yoke of slavery.* ¹³ *For you were called to freedom, brothers and sisters; only do not use your freedom as an opportunity for self-indulgence, but through love become slaves to one another.* ¹⁴ *For the whole law is summed up in a single commandment, "You shall love your neighbor as yourself."* ¹⁵ *If, however, you bite and devour one another, take care that you are not consumed by one another.*

How do you experience God's searching your life to plant delight?
How do you balance your own choosing with walking by God's will?

# Goaded

**My soul:**

Goad me onward, Desired Fullness!
Make me all that I can be. Spur me to see opportunity.
Hurry me to act and catch each moment for light.
Urge me to praise with joy and trust.
Incite a fierce heart for justice and care.
Prod me out of complacency and passivity.
I am Yours.

**God:**

Can I love you with all of this energy?
Will you let Me stir the embers within you?
I put the spark of My life inside you.
It is needed for this time in history.
I will give you heart. Trust Me.

## Acts 26:12-18

[12] "With this in mind, I was traveling to Damascus with the authority and commission of the chief priests, [13] when at midday along the road, your Excellency, I saw a light from heaven, brighter than the sun, shining around me and my companions. [14] When we had all fallen to the ground, I heard a voice saying to me in the Hebrew language, 'Saul, Saul, why are you persecuting me? It hurts you to kick against the goads.' [15] I asked, 'Who are you, Lord?' The Lord answered, 'I am Jesus whom you are persecuting. [16] But get up and stand on your feet; for I have appeared to you for this purpose, to appoint you to serve and testify to the things in which you have seen me and to those in which I will appear to you. [17] I will rescue you from your people and from the Gentiles—to whom I am sending you [18] to open their eyes so that they may turn from darkness to light and from the power of Satan to God, so that they may receive forgiveness of sins and a place among those who are sanctified by faith in me.'"

Today, how are you urged to be all that you can be?
How does being in love release energy within you to do your best?

# Dare

**God:**

My love is so foolhardy for you,
beautiful creature.
I want to speak your language.
I want to walk with you and see sunsets,
flowers of the fields,
storms coming across the land.
Do you see what I will dare to save your life?
My boldness is impelled by My love.
I risk it all to win your yes.

**My soul:**

How, God of infinity, do I take my wayward life to respond?
My love is too small,
my brazen entitlement too proud.
How do I quiet my soul to move beyond fussing over minutiae?
You are so big.
How can I see You?
Put within me a mighty yes, yes.
I will love You back.

**Romans 5:7-11**

*⁷ Indeed, rarely will anyone die for a righteous person—though perhaps for a good person someone might actually dare to die. ⁸ But God proves his love for us in that while we still were sinners Christ died for us. ⁹ Much more surely then, now that we have been justified by his blood, will we be saved through him from the wrath of God. ¹⁰ For if while we were enemies, we were reconciled to God through the death of his Son, much more surely, having been reconciled, will we be saved by his life. ¹¹ But more than that, we even boast in God through our Lord Jesus Christ, through whom we have now received reconciliation.*

Where is God near you, walking beside you, seeing with you?
What does it take to quiet your soul beyond fussing over minutiae?

# Palpable

**My soul:**

Please, God Invisible, be straightforward.
Today I need Your presence,
palpable and manifest.
Your wind, our earth, speaks loudly
that You are real.
Yet my heart is fogged and glutted.
Shake loose the barriers in my soul.
In the great glory of sunrise,
welcome Holy One.

**God:**

I am discernible—only look.
Let all that is conspicuous of My nearness
approach you.
I am near.
March through your shadow self,
child of My image, and be open.
Dare to walk that way of truth in your own self.
I am at home there.

**1 John 1:1-2**

*¹ We declare to you what was from the beginning, what we have heard, what we have seen with our eyes, what we have looked at and touched with our hands, concerning the word of life— ² this life was revealed, and we have seen it and testify to it, and declare to you the eternal life that was with the Father and was revealed to us.*

What barriers in your soul need shaking?
How does confronting the shadow self bring God
home to you?

# Penetrate

**My soul:**

Mover of all being, penetrate my living.
Imbue my heart with Your love.
Let all resistance be overcome.
Immerse my days with Your presence.
I long with all that I am to come to understand You.
Be the Light of my world.

**God:**

Can I get through to you,
dear companion along My way?
In the fog of your knowing, I do break in.
Do you know you delight Me?
Come home to My love.
I wait for your response of joy!

**John 4:46-54**

⁴⁶ *Then he came again to Cana in Galilee where he had changed the water into wine. Now there was a royal official whose son lay ill in Capernaum.* ⁴⁷ *When he heard that Jesus had come from Judea to Galilee, he went and begged him to come down and heal his son, for he was at the point of death.* ⁴⁸ *Then Jesus said to him, "Unless you see signs and wonders you will not believe."* ⁴⁹ *The official said to him, "Sir, come down before my little boy dies."* ⁵⁰ *Jesus said to him, "Go; your son will live." The man believed the word that Jesus spoke to him and started on his way.* ⁵¹ *As he was going down, his slaves met him and told him that his child was alive.* ⁵² *So he asked them the hour when he began to recover, and they said to him, "Yesterday at one in the afternoon the fever left him."* ⁵³ *The father realized that this was the hour when Jesus had said to him, "Your son will live." So he himself believed, along with his whole household.* ⁵⁴ *Now this was the second sign that Jesus did after coming from Judea to Galilee.*

Like the official's love of his son, what loves in your life invite God to break in?
How do you remove resistances from your life?

# Chill

**God:**

I want to tell you to chill,
quivering creature of My attention.
Relax into My call.
It will require all that you are,
so I know your dread.
Do not be dejected.
Do not be anxious.
I will accomplish what I've set out to do in you.

**My soul:**

Like the warmth of the sun melts ice,
I trust You, God of my life.
Let Your eyes be on me.
I will not fear.
In numbing cold, I choose to meet Your gaze.
I will not hide in shadows.
Own my purpose, Powerful Presence.
I am Yours.

**Job 14:1-2**

*¹ A mortal, born of woman, few of days and full of trouble, ² comes up like a flower and withers, flees like a shadow and does not last.*

What does living in God's gaze require of you?
How do you trust God to dispel your shadows?

# Keening

**My soul:**

A great sob escapes me,
God of wholeness.
I am broken and bereft.
You have called from me the
song of my life with keening;
there is no joy in me.
An earth dirge echoes
as we ruin tigers and monarchs.
I moan for loss in our callousness.
Do we not know
that we pour poisons into our world?
In hate and destruction, we are blind.

**God:**

I hear your wail, earth child,
and see your tears.
It is a wake of despair
you trail behind.
In this requiem of your choices, lament!
But move toward life.
I want you to know, I am doing a new thing.
Only believe.

**Genesis 19:24-26**

*²⁴ Then the Lord rained on Sodom and Gomorrah sulfur and fire from the Lord out of heaven; ²⁵ and he overthrew those cities, and all the Plain, and all the inhabitants of the cities, and what grew on the ground. ²⁶ But Lot's wife, behind him, looked back, and she became a pillar of salt.*

What makes you weep?
How does believing God is doing a new thing show itself in your life?

# Drench

**My soul:**

Drench me in your goodness, Bountiful God.
Flood my soul with your light.
I want to soak up Your way
of reaching out to grieving mothers,
to outcast lepers,
even those who are bound in chains.
Inundate my heart with Your kind of loving.
Our world needs You, and I stand helpless.

**God:**

I, too, was helpless against the seething hate.
I also felt the deluge of jealous survival.
Hear again the irony—
"It is right for one man to die for the people."

**John 9:12-14**

*¹² They said to him, "Where is he?" He said, "I do not know." ¹³ They brought to the Pharisees the man who had formerly been blind. ¹⁴ Now it was a Sabbath day when Jesus made the mud and opened his eyes.*

How do you meet blindness in your life?
How do you soak in God's love and let it reach out?

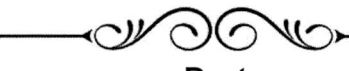

## Dart

**My soul:**

My days dart in a busy dash,
God who measures time in eons.
How do I do more than flit and stumble
across the pain of it?
In a flash, I see Your touch.
Then it is gone.
Like a shooting star, I glimpse You
in my midnight sky.
I long to hold You forever.

**God:**

Creature of wondering,
crawl out of the weight of mental turmoil.
Gather your planning, analyzing, and critiquing
under the clouds of unknowing.
Rest in your glimpses of Me.
Don't hurry past and bury My presence.
It is not illusion that I am here.
Come and see.

**Exodus 13:21-22**

*²¹ The Lord went in front of them in a pillar of cloud by day, to lead them along the way, and in a pillar of fire by night, to give them light, so that they might travel by day and by night. ²² Neither the pillar of cloud by day nor the pillar of fire by night left its place in front of the people.*

Where in your life are you being pulled to "come and see"?
What mental turmoil are you being invited to crawl out of?

## Solitude

**My soul:**

I've walked alone most of my days.
You, the Great Solitude, are near.
I walk into the cave where You pass by.
Awake, my soul, to acknowledge,
like rain on a dry thirsty earth, You come.
Saturate the quiet by Your love.

**God:**

With easy delight, surrender,
creature of many cracks.
I walk within your shadow so you are not alone.
Just beyond your sight, I am here.
Listen.
Know your heart's holding is true.
I am here.

**Jeremiah 29:11-14**

*¹¹ For surely I know the plans I have for you, says the Lord, plans for your welfare and not for harm, to give you a future with hope. ¹² Then when you call upon me and come and pray to me, I will hear you. ¹³ When you search for me, you will find me; if you seek me with all your heart, ¹⁴ I will let you find me, says the Lord, and I will restore your fortunes and gather you from all the nations and all the places where I have driven you, says the Lord, and I will bring you back to the place from which I sent you into exile.*

How are you a creature of many cracks?
What plans of God for you are full of ease and delight?

# Seething

**God:**

Child of the universe,
let your seething earth calm.
Touch our branches arm to arm.
Slow our restless tides to steadiness.
May they lull.
I feel your boiling flare up
in fierce protest.
The hungry starve.
The homeless hide to catch some sleep.
The prisoners sit idle on their dreams.
Gather your family's hand and come.
I hear your cry.

**My soul:**

Weaver God,
in the great turbulence, come.
Gather the threads of our pain in Your mercy.
A mighty anger stirs in the roots that bind us.
Upheaval casts its long destruction.
In the tangle of chaos,
draw the skeins to order.
Teach us to reach across the great divide to forgive.

**Romans 7:14-15, 24-25**

*¹⁴ For we know that the law is spiritual; but I am of the flesh, sold into slavery under sin. ¹⁵ I do not understand my own actions. For I do not do what I want, but I do the very thing I hate. ²⁴ Wretched man that I am! Who will rescue me from this body of death? ²⁵ Thanks be to God through Jesus Christ our Lord! So then, with my mind I am a slave to the law of God, but with my flesh I am a slave to the law of sin.*

What anger rises in you?
How do you experience forgiveness healing the divide?

## Vestiges

**God:**

Can I find only a remnant among you?
Is there only a hint of unselfish love,
vibrant care, and undeserved mercy?
Broken human, these are the vestiges that draw Me to you.
In the glimmer of your choices,
I see children dance securely.
A table is set for the feast.
Hope climbs your highest mountain.

**My soul:**

In the relics of our days,
I search for You, God of Resurrection.
What looks like the scrap heap of humanity
hides Your life force.
I trace my excavations to mere tokens of lost purpose.
Raise up from these bones
Your own creative juices.
I want to live.

### Zechariah 8:11-12, 16

*¹¹ But now I will not deal with the remnant of this people as in the former days, says the Lord of hosts. ¹² For there shall be a sowing of peace; the vine shall yield its fruit, the ground shall give its produce, and the skies shall give their dew; and I will cause the remnant of this people to possess all these things. ¹⁶ These are the things that you shall do: Speak the truth to one another, render in your gates judgments that are true and make for peace.*

When do you find hope climbing your highest mountain?
Where is your purpose lost and held in God's hands?

# Leopard .

**My soul:**

Imaginative Source of Being,
thank You for the multitudes of life
burgeoning forth on our earth.
Thank you for tigers and wrens, for ants and giraffes,
for leopards and lightning bugs.
Bond all of us in praise.
I bring my consciousness of all
that is varied and beautiful in adoration.
You are the spark and the flow within us.
Be our Hallelujah.

**God:**

Cherish in your attention and intention all that is.
You, awareness gathered in flesh,
honor the long line of evolution.
You have been called for this moment.
Shift your choices for oneness and life.
Follow the urge of compassion.
Lean into My blossoming expansions and trust.

**Genesis 1:24-27**

²⁴ *And God said, "Let the earth bring forth living creatures of every kind: cattle and creeping things and wild animals of the earth of every kind." And it was so. ²⁵ God made the wild animals of the earth of every kind, and the cattle of every kind, and everything that creeps upon the ground of every kind. And God saw that it was good. ²⁶ Then God said, "Let us make humankind in our image, according to our likeness; and let them have dominion over the fish of the sea, and over the birds of the air, and over the cattle, and over all the wild animals of the earth, and over every creeping thing that creeps upon the earth." ²⁷ So God created humankind in his image, in the image of God he created them; male and female he created them.*

What creatures excite you to praise?
What intention moves you to choose oneness?

# Groan

**God:**

Do you hear My groan,
awake one?
I ache and moan in the voices of
homes invaded and broken!
May I lean on you?
Will you hear My sobs
of ripped shadows torn and cast aside?
I am your Healer for arrogance and pride.
You are one fabric with Me.

**My soul:**

In the vast protests, I do hear grumbling and grousing.
Living God, we are a crushed, disordered people.
Through the lines of law,
You grunt a deeper truth.
We all belong.
All are welcome at Your table.
I must set the feast.

**Isaiah 25:6-10**

[6] On this mountain the Lord of hosts will make for all peoples a feast of rich food, a feast of well-aged wines, of rich food filled with marrow, of well-aged wines strained clear. [7] And he will destroy on this mountain the shroud that is cast over all peoples, the sheet that is spread over all nations; he will swallow up death forever. [8] Then the Lord God will wipe away the tears from all faces, and the disgrace of his people he will take away from all the earth, for the Lord has spoken. [9] It will be said on that day, Lo, this is our God; we have waited for him, so that he might save us. This is the Lord for whom we have waited; let us be glad and rejoice in his salvation. [10] For the hand of the Lord will rest on this mountain. The Moabites shall be trodden down in their place as straw is trodden down in a dung-pit.

How are you awake to the groan of God?
How do you see the lines of law breached by a deeper truth?

**July 28**

## Testify

**God:**

I vouch for you, tiny one.
I see My fingerprint.
Will you declare for Me?
Bearing witness to My love is your calling.
Remember the ways I have loved you.
I've birthed in you consciousness.
I've partnered with you in purpose.
I've given you a glimpse of My life force.
Testify to this by your life,
your hope, your fidelity.

**My soul:**

All that is proves Your greatness, First Mover.
I cite our creation story for proof.
You manifest Your beauty in each day's dawn.
You inform the mysteries well beyond our grasp.
Always You gather the poor and bereft in Your goodness.
I am among them, so limited and scarred.
Still, I see You look at me
and I am silenced.

**1 John 5:9-11**

*⁹ If we receive human testimony, the testimony of God is greater; for this is the testimony of God that he has testified to his Son. ¹⁰ Those who believe in the Son of God have the testimony in their hearts. Those who do not believe in God have made him a liar by not believing in the testimony that God has given concerning his Son. ¹¹ And this is the testimony: God gave us eternal life, and this life is in his Son.*

How do you empty yourself as Jesus did, as the great God looks at you?
How do you experience God vouching for you?

## Tent

**God**:

I lift the flap of My tent, desert roamer!
Welcome.
Here, near your earth,
know a resting place.
We are always on the move.
We live in motion.
Let your heart expand
and your tent widen.
There is enough.

**My soul:**

God, I come to dwell with You.
Only Security, marauders do not see Your encampment.
Here in Your shelter, I know refreshment.
Against the desert sands that make all invisible,
I know comfort.
All You welcome have seen you and also seek safety.
By Your grace, I embrace and know them as family.

**Exodus 29:42-45**

*⁴² It shall be a regular burnt offering throughout your generations at the entrance of the tent of meeting before the Lord, where I will meet with you, to speak to you there. ⁴³ I will meet with the Israelites there, and it shall be sanctified by my glory; ⁴⁴ I will consecrate the tent of meeting and the altar; Aaron also and his sons I will consecrate, to serve me as priests. ⁴⁵ I will dwell among the Israelites, and I will be their God.*

How does seeing the Lord bring you into the tent of His meeting?
How have you experienced the "enough" for God's gathering family?

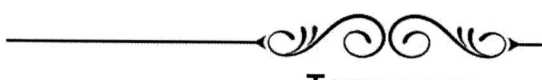

## Temporary

**My soul:**

These feelings are a temporary space, God of Mystery.
What is lasting?
The earth seen from afar has billions of years.
Still, stars die out and others are born.
In the feelings of awe or sadness, of love and indifference,
of the flash of anger or the burden of helplessness,
You choose me to live in this ebb and tide.
And I, even in my smallness, choose You.

**God:**

Dust in the wind, child of My choosing,
I walk beside you.
In the impermanence you know,
I hold you in the palm of My hand.
I hear your questions. I know your darkness.
Know that I am near.

**Hebrews 1:5-12**

⁵ *For to which of the angels did God ever say, "You are my Son;
today I have begotten you"? Or again, "I will be his Father, and he
will be my Son"?* ⁶ *And again, when he brings the firstborn into the
world, he says, "Let all God's angels worship him."* ⁷ *Of the angels he
says, "He makes his angels winds, and his servants flames of fire."*
⁸ *But of the Son he says, "Your throne, O God, is forever and ever,
and the righteous scepter is the scepter of your kingdom.* ⁹ *You
have loved righteousness and hated wickedness; therefore God,
your God, has anointed you with the oil of gladness beyond your
companions."* ¹⁰ *And, "In the beginning, Lord, you founded the
earth, and the heavens are the work of your hands;* ¹¹ *they will
perish, but you remain; they will all wear out like clothing;* ¹² *like a
cloak you will roll them up, and like clothing they will be changed.
But you are the same, and your years will never end."*

How do you feel the ebb and flow of your emotions?
How does God's walking beside you change your impermanence?

## Satisfy

**My soul:**

You satisfy the longings of my heart, God Beyond.
In the space where expansion happens, a universe invites.
You are here to shape Your dreams within me.
Deepen my love.
Let me see heaven embedded in a dewdrop.
Let the black holes within implode
under the kindness of Your light.

**God:**

Star-borne child, I have put within you
the desires that are your pulley to Me.
There are dark forces that would draw you and reshape you.
Only remember, nothing in this wide mysterious universe
can separate you from Me. I have you safe, beloved.

**Job 38:1-7**

*¹ Then the Lord answered Job out of the whirlwind: ² "Who is this that darkens counsel by words without knowledge? ³ Gird up your loins like a man, I will question you, and you shall declare to me. ⁴ "Where were you when I laid the foundation of the earth? Tell me, if you have understanding. ⁵ Who determined its measurements— surely you know! Or who stretched the line upon it? ⁶ On what were its bases sunk, or who laid its cornerstone ⁷ when the morning stars sang together and all the heavenly beings shouted for joy?"*

What darkness grabs your joy?
How do you know God holds you safely?

# August

1. Contentment
2. Scorn
3. Scarlet
4. Chartreuse
5. Castle
6. Scoff
7. Mosquito
8. Remain
9. Render
10. Rekindle
11. Parent
12. Paradise
13. Pawn
14. Ordeal
15. Orphan
16. Ointment
17. Hunger
18. Family
19. Stunned
20. Lavender
21. Dill
22. Bread
23. Wine
24. Authentic
25. Mansion
26. Rumors
27. Mutiny
28. Indict
29. Legendary
30. Haggle
31. Consequences

# Contentment

**God:**

River child,
I've made you for contentment.
In the rough and tumble,
I know you are not so sure sometimes.
You are the wish I've sparked with My light.
You are the weaving that threads My imagining.
You are the sunrise
where My ancient newness dawns.
In your living, know that I flow.

**My soul:**

Faithful Burst of Life,
I hold Your promise and know joy.
I've learned ease in Your faithfulness.
You have held me tight,
given me surprises,
invited me to share Your dream.
Is it really true that all I need to do is love?
With this mighty energy, I know bliss.

**Isaiah 66:12-13**

*12 For thus says the Lord: I will extend prosperity to her like a river, and the wealth of the nations like an overflowing stream; and you shall nurse and be carried on her arm, and dandled on her knees. 13 As a mother comforts her child, so I will comfort you; you shall be comforted in Jerusalem.*

How do you know contentment?
When is it right to address God as your Faithful Burst of Life?

# Scorn

**My soul:**

I deserve Your scorn, Life Source.
How can You not look down on me?
Yet You nurture the tiny spark of Your mighty energy.
It's beyond me—
it's where You call me to believe.
Your love power resides in me.
Come near, God who tends the holy in me.
I believe You do not disdain me,
though I make foolish, selfish choices.
Work Your transformation in me.

**God:**

Butterfly child, you are in process.
Bound in your cocoon,
you cannot imagine what you will become.
I know and see it on the way.

**Hosea 11:1-4**

*¹ When Israel was a child, I loved him, and out of Egypt I called my son. ² The more I called them, the more they went from me; they kept sacrificing to the Baals, and offering incense to idols. ³ Yet it was I who taught Ephraim to walk, I took them up in my arms, but they did not know that I healed them. ⁴ I led them with cords of human kindness, with bands of love. I was to them like those who lift infants to their cheeks. I bent down to them and fed them.*

How is God tending the holy in you?
In your cocoon stage, what do you feel? What do you believe?

## Scarlet

**God:**

I know your scarlet side,
rebellious one.
I see your flush of freedom
stretching into your power of no.
May your ruddy defiant self
turn to see My love.
May your blooming turbulence
be tamed to courtesy.
I give you life.
I bestow freedom.
I lift your soul to purpose.
Let your crimson heart know love
to open wide in yes.

**My soul:**

All that is fresh and glowing in
my life is Your gift, Speaker of Truth.
In this moment, I choose You and there is wholeness.

**Isaiah 1:18**

*¹⁸ Come now, let us argue it out, says the Lord: though your sins are like scarlet, they shall be like snow; though they are red like crimson, they shall become like wool.*

What happens in your rebellion?
How is your turbulence tamed to courtesy?

# Chartreuse

### God:

Do you like the chartreuse of
tender spring in the mountains?
I do!
Bright shoots that color blah rocky rises expand the heart.
Hope juices out on fragile wings.
I made the seasons of hibernation and of wakefulness.
Take this as your Word of God.

### My soul:

I relish the freshness.
It is Your amazing gift, Mother-God.
You birth us again after a barren winter.
On my rough bark, dare again and forever;
earth's springing forth.
I notice.
Even in my weary shivering, I feel Your stirring.
Open my eyes to see the hope.

### Acts 27:13-15, 20-23

*¹³ When a moderate south wind began to blow, they thought they could achieve their purpose; so they weighed anchor and began to sail past Crete, close to the shore. ¹⁴ But soon a violent wind, called the northeaster, rushed down from Crete. ¹⁵ Since the ship was caught and could not be turned head-on into the wind, we gave way to it and were driven. ²⁰ When neither sun nor stars appeared for many days, and no small tempest raged, all hope of our being saved was at last abandoned. ²¹ Since they had been without food for a long time, Paul then stood up among them and said, "Men, you should have listened to me and not have set sail from Crete and thereby avoided this damage and loss. ²² I urge you now to keep up your courage, for there will be no loss of life among you, but only of the ship. ²³ For last night there stood by me an angel of the God to whom I belong and whom I worship."*

Is there a moderate south wind blowing in your life?
Describe your seasons of hibernation and of wakefulness.

## Castle

**My soul:**

Brother Jesus,
I've seen some castles,
fortresses but forlorn,
set on a hill and isolated.
They are cold and dark.
But I love Your words,
"In My Father's house are many mansions;
I go to prepare a place for you."
Make my palace of green grass on top of a hill.
Let there be many pathways for all creatures to come and go.
May Your stars be my canopy.
May Your fresh streams refresh Your people.
There, sit and picnic with me.
May I be present.

**God:**

Roaming one, your delight of My Kingdom
is My delight.
Explore with Me.

**Isaiah 40:9-11**

⁹ *Get you up to a high mountain, O Zion, herald of good tidings; lift up your voice with strength, O Jerusalem, herald of good tidings, lift it up, do not fear; say to the cities of Judah, "Here is your God!"* ¹⁰ *See, the Lord God comes with might, and his arm rules for him; his reward is with him, and his recompense before him.* ¹¹ *He will feed his flock like a shepherd; he will gather the lambs in his arms, and carry them in his bosom, and gently lead the mother sheep.*

When have you known the castle on the hill to be dark and lonely?
What pathways are you creating up your mountain?

# Scoff

**God:**

Downcast one, I also have been scoffed at.
Can you imagine? I came with the
Word of Life to share,
and I was bullied and discounted.
They thought their contempt would make Me invisible.
Their taunts were armed at truth.
I stand with you.
Will you stand with Me?

**My soul:**

When I give You my cloak,
a laugh of derision rises.
Is it coming from me?
I want to separate from the jeers tossed at You.
God Hidden and Humble,
do not let me abandon You.

**John 19:23-24**

²³ *When the soldiers had crucified Jesus, they took his clothes and divided them into four parts, one for each soldier. They also took his tunic; now the tunic was seamless, woven in one piece from the top.* ²⁴ *So they said to one another, "Let us not tear it, but cast lots for it to see who will get it." This was to fulfill what the scripture says, "They divided my clothes among themselves, and for my clothing they cast lots."*

How do you know invisibility?
When do you share your cloak?
Is it in a laugh of derision or a hunger to protect?

# Mosquito

**My soul:**

We humans are called to live with mosquitos?
Presence of Life, they suck blood and bring awful illness!
It feels like we are always in the struggle!
How to honor all creatures, believing in the balance!
How to put boundaries on what will harm!
I don't know how to do it.

**God:**

Beloved, I know you are only growing in wisdom!
Like you, these long-legged flies are fostered in water.
Like you, they bite and fight for life.
Like you, they buzz in curiosity.
They do need limit-setting, and they rebel.
Learn from your brother mosquito
in the circle of life.

**Philippians 2:14-18**

*¹⁴ Do all things without murmuring and arguing, ¹⁵ so that you may be blameless and innocent, children of God without blemish in the midst of a crooked and perverse generation, in which you shine like stars in the world. ¹⁶ It is by your holding fast to the word of life that I can boast on the day of Christ that I did not run in vain or labor in vain. ¹⁷ But even if I am being poured out as a libation over the sacrifice and the offering of your faith, I am glad and rejoice with all of you— ¹⁸ and in the same way you also must be glad and rejoice with me.*

What boundaries do you set on the irritants of life?
Where are you rebelling?

# Remain

**God:**

I throw down the gauntlet to you,
child in My image.
It feels good to give out of bounty.
My challenge to you is to remain in your poverty.
Be bound by ties of dignity.
Keep your fellowship with all creatures.
Stay in the need and helplessness.
I came in that awesome surrender.

**My soul:**

I am Your child of the universe,
already blessed beyond limits.
Keep my eyes on You, Daring God.
I know no poverty when earth provides air and water.
I can share the life force with
eagles and dolphins.
In my smallness, You lift me high on Your shoulders.
Let me revel in my weakness.

**Luke 6:20-23**

²⁰ *Then he looked up at his disciples and said: "Blessed are you who are poor for yours is the kingdom of God.* ²¹ *"Blessed are you who are hungry now, for you will be filled. "Blessed are you who weep now, for you will laugh.* ²² *"Blessed are you when people hate you, and when they exclude you, revile you, and defame you on account of the Son of Man.* ²³ *Rejoice in that day and leap for joy, for surely your reward is great in heaven; for that is what their ancestors did to the prophets."*

How do you experience the gauntlet given you to remain poor?
How do you experience the life force prevented from flowing
by pride and possessions?

# Render

**God:**

Render to Me what is due Me, earth child.
I have given you life.
Pour forth into your days the rapture of its lusciousness.
Interpret its tides and palm trees and peaches into faithful joy.
Let all resistances flow. Surrender into My hands
your transparency, your Truth.

**My soul:**

Giver of all good gifts,
how do I make a return for all that You've done for me?
Let all that blocks my surrender be handed over.
I tug at the stones that are embedded.
I wrestle the currents that sweep me to the sea.
I know the winds that would collapse all that I cling to.
You are the Life Force in whom I place my trust.

### Matthew 22:15-22

*15 Then the Pharisees went and plotted to entrap him in what he said. 16 So they sent their disciples to him, along with the Herodians, saying, "Teacher, we know that you are sincere, and teach the way of God in accordance with truth, and show deference to no one; for you do not regard people with partiality. 17 Tell us, then, what you think. Is it lawful to pay taxes to the emperor, or not?" 18 But Jesus, aware of their malice, said, "Why are you putting me to the test, you hypocrites? 19 Show me the coin used for the tax." And they brought him a denarius. 20 Then he said to them, "Whose head is this, and whose title?" 21 They answered, "The emperor's." Then he said to them, "Give therefore to the emperor the things that are the emperor's, and to God the things that are God's." 22 When they heard this, they were amazed; and they left him and went away.*

What resistances hold you from surrender?
How do you trust the Life Force in your daily concerns?

# Rekindle

**My soul:**

Rekindle my young love for You, constant Presence.
I am laid low, used up.
Blow within me the embers that are buried—dead.
Ignite again my faithfulness to follow.
I want to rise up from my torpor
to walk with glee toward You, God of my pathway.
Come and refresh me.

**God:**

Blaze again, spark in My image.
Your work is not yet done.
What is charred can yet draw My face.
What is seared can still warm and thaw.
What seems ash can scatter life to a world needing refreshment.
All is not lost. I am the Lord of exploding stars.

**Job 13:25-28, 33:23-25**

²⁵ *Will you frighten a windblown leaf and pursue dry chaff?* ²⁶ *For you write bitter things against me, and make me reap the iniquities of my youth.* ²⁷ *You put my feet in the stocks, and watch all my paths; you set a bound to the soles of my feet.* ²⁸ *One wastes away like a rotten thing, like a garment that is moth-eaten.*
²³ *Then, if there should be for one of them an angel, a mediator, one of a thousand, one who declares a person upright,* ²⁴ *and he is gracious to that person, and says, 'Deliver him from going down into the Pit; I have found a ransom;* ²⁵ *let his flesh become fresh with youth; let him return to the days of his youthful vigor.'*

What leaves you feeling burned out?
How do you know your work is not done?

## Parent

**My soul:**

Parent me, God of Light.
Keep me safe as I grow up
from what I do not even know is harmful.
I want the values You hold sacred.
As You give life day by day and minute by minute,
please be attentive. See me. Listen.
You have invested in me. This I believe.

**God:**

I do parent you, precious child.
I have imprinted you with My own life flow.
As my family, I am conscious of your joys and sorrows.
I know your challenges and defeats, your victories and blooming.
I listen when you need Me. I hold you when you are afraid.
I love you forever.

**Luke 2:39-40**

*39 When they had finished everything required by the law of the Lord, they returned to Galilee, to their own town of Nazareth. 40 The child grew and became strong, filled with wisdom; and the favor of God was upon him.*

What does God, your Parent, invest in you?
How is God attentive to what puts you at risk and to what gives you life?

# Paradise

**My soul:**

Where is paradise, Creator God?
What dimension beyond our universe
opens such a promised land?
"This day you shall be in paradise!"
to a thief crucified, living earthly consequences.
Is it a door opened?
Is it access granted?
What consciousness attends to its beckoning here?
Please lead and accompany my days.
You are the way, the truth, and the life.

**God:**

"I go to prepare a place for you."
I know your name, child of life.
You belong.
You have a place with Me.
Peace is the air you breathe.
Delight is the explosion of energy you feel.
There is no desire where your heart holds it all.
Open wide all that you are to receive.
It is the measure of your paradise.

### John 14:2-6

*[2] In my Father's house there are many dwelling places. If it were not so, would I have told you that I go to prepare a place for you? [3] And if I go and prepare a place for you, I will come again and will take you to myself, so that where I am, there you may be also. [4] And you know the way to the place where I am going." [5] Thomas said to him, "Lord, we do not know where you are going. How can we know the way?" [6] Jesus said to him, "I am the way, and the truth, and the life. No one comes to the Father except through me."*

Where do you go now to find God's dwelling places?
Where do you recognize paradise in your heart's peace and delight?

## Pawn

**My soul:**

Harbor in the storm, it would be easy for me to be a pawn.
You readily and appropriately could decide I was collateral.
But You pledged not me, but Yourself, as security.
You stand with me, a mere minion or token.
May I dare to make a covenant?
How do I live faithfully to my bond?
We are on the way because You are faithful.

**God:**

You, dear sailor on this rough sea,
shape our world with Me.
You are My assurance that our wake is made of love.
I risk this gambit because I know you.
You are not a pawn but my warrant of expanding life.
Across the ocean of endless horizon,
"sail on, silver girl."
I am with you.

**John 10:11-18**

[11] *"I am the good shepherd. The good shepherd lays down his life for the sheep.* [12] *The hired hand, who is not the shepherd and does not own the sheep, sees the wolf coming and leaves the sheep and runs away—and the wolf snatches them and scatters them.* [13] *The hired hand runs away because a hired hand does not care for the sheep.* [14] *I am the good shepherd. I know my own and my own know me,* [15] *just as the Father knows me and I know the Father. And I lay down my life for the sheep.* [16] *I have other sheep that do not belong to this fold. I must bring them also, and they will listen to my voice. So there will be one flock, one shepherd.* [17] *For this reason the Father loves me, because I lay down my life in order to take it up again.* [18] *No one takes it from me, but I lay it down of my own accord. I have power to lay it down, and I have power to take it up again. I have received this command from my Father."*

How do you experience being collateral?
How are you God's warrant of expanding life?

234

# Ordeal

**God:**

Do you think I have set before you an ordeal?
This painful time is no test of guilt or innocence.
I walk with you.
I love you.
Earthen vessel, you are so easily broken,
but so intently fired for beauty.
Life teaches!
I know your spirit
and sustain your courage.

**My soul:**

This trial lasts forever, Burden-Bearer.
I hand over what I cannot carry:
my shame, my deceit, my helplessness.
Such ugliness resides within.
In Your light, they burn away.

**Revelations 7:14-17**

¹⁴ I said to him, "Sir, you are the one that knows." Then he said to me, "These are they who have come out of the great ordeal; they have washed their robes and made them white in the blood of the Lamb. ¹⁵ For this reason they are before the throne of God, and worship him day and night within his temple, and the one who is seated on the throne will shelter them. ¹⁶ They will hunger no more, and thirst no more; the sun will not strike them, nor any scorching heat; ¹⁷ for the Lamb at the center of the throne will be their shepherd, and he will guide them to springs of the water of life, and God will wipe away every tear from their eyes."

When do you interpret your trials as tests of guilt or innocence?
In practice, how does God bear the burden of your shame, deceit, or helplessness?

# Orphan

**My soul:**

God, Secure One,
I am bereft.
Alone and orphaned, who can I speak to
of my abandonment?
I have no defense.
Where the flow of Your attachment
to me should come,
I've guarded and blocked.
Mercy, break open my walls.

**God:**

Nothing can separate us, child of my longing.
You are not an orphan.
Breathe in the air I provide.
Move in trust, despite your paralysis.
Love again, knowing I love you first.
I can tumble down your walls
and surprise your defenses.
You are mine and I love you.

**Hebrews 11:29-31**

²⁹ *By faith the people passed through the Red Sea as if it were dry land, but when the Egyptians attempted to do so they were drowned.* ³⁰ *By faith the walls of Jericho fell after they had been encircled for seven days.* ³¹ *By faith Rahab the prostitute did not perish with those who were disobedient, because she had received the spies in peace.*

When do you guard your heart from love?
How does God tumble down Jericho and surprise you?

# Ointment

**God:**

Bruised soul,
I give you ointment for your wounds.
Let the balm ease your hurt,
soothe the weariness of questions.
The why is too big for you.
With healing salve, I soothe your burning pain.
Let My presence hold your ache within.

**My soul:**

Healer God, Your unction lifts what possesses,
what imprisons.
I lift my jagged thoughts to You.
The darkness of my soul needs medicine.
Bring Your cooling gift.
I need Your touch.

**Luke 17:11-19**

*¹¹ On the way to Jerusalem Jesus was going through the region between Samaria and Galilee. ¹² As he entered a village, ten lepers approached him. Keeping their distance, ¹³ they called out, saying, "Jesus, Master, have mercy on us!" ¹⁴ When he saw them, he said to them, "Go and show yourselves to the priests." And as they went, they were made clean. ¹⁵ Then one of them, when he saw that he was healed, turned back, praising God with a loud voice. ¹⁶ He prostrated himself at Jesus' feet and thanked him. And he was a Samaritan. ¹⁷ Then Jesus asked, "Were not ten made clean? But the other nine, where are they? ¹⁸ Was none of them found to return and give praise to God except this foreigner?" ¹⁹ Then he said to him, "Get up and go on your way; your faith has made you well."*

How do you carry the why of suffering?
When is the healing God touching you?

# Hunger

**God:**

Needy one, I see your hunger.
I have heard your cry for food.
I know you are famished for what will satisfy.
In your emptiness, seek Me.
All you desire, you will find in Me.
What is voracious within you can overcome you,
submerge you in your greed.
Face into it and feel your hungry heart.

**My soul:**

God, giver of finest wheat, I crave Your presence.
In the fast from all that absorbs, I turn to You.
I have been to Your feast. I know Your lavish provision.
I desire You. My spirit is malnourished and skeletal.
Let me know Your banquet.

**John 6:32-40**

³² *Then Jesus said to them, "Very truly, I tell you, it was not Moses who gave you the bread from heaven, but it is my Father who gives you the true bread from heaven. ³³ For the bread of God is that which comes down from heaven and gives life to the world." ³⁴ They said to him, "Sir, give us this bread always." ³⁵ Jesus said to them, "I am the bread of life. Whoever comes to me will never be hungry, and whoever believes in me will never be thirsty. ³⁶ But I said to you that you have seen me and yet do not believe. ³⁷ Everything that the Father gives me will come to me, and anyone who comes to me I will never drive away; ³⁸ for I have come down from heaven, not to do my own will, but the will of him who sent me. ³⁹ And this is the will of him who sent me that I should lose nothing of all that he has given me, but raise it up on the last day. ⁴⁰ This is indeed the will of my Father, that all who see the Son and believe in him may have eternal life; and I will raise them up on the last day."*

What hunger absorbs you most?
How do you know the feast of the Lord?

# Family

**God:**

Creature child,
I give you family. You belong.
You've been held and nurtured to maturity,
blessed in bonds of blood, shared genes marked in history,
committed care in birthed helplessness.
Against the rubs of closeness, you are here and formed.
I walk with you.

**My soul:**

Parent God,
You are with my family in laughter and in tears,
in feast and in famine, in the push and pull to identity.
I search for why I am here.

### Genesis 18:1-3, 9-10

¹ *The Lord appeared to Abraham by the oaks of Mamre, as he sat at the entrance of his tent in the heat of the day.* ² *He looked up and saw three men standing near him. When he saw them, he ran from the tent entrance to meet them, and bowed down to the ground.* ³ *He said, "My lord, if I find favor with you, do not pass by your servant."* ⁹ *They said to him, "Where is your wife Sarah?" And he said, "There, in the tent."* ¹⁰ *Then one said, "I will surely return to you in due season, and your wife Sarah shall have a son."*

How are you blessed in bonds of blood?
How does your family help you become who you are?

# Stunned

**My soul:**

Infinite One,
I am stunned.
Your majesty, Your hugeness are too big for me.
I am dazed to unconsciousness,
like an ocean to swim in that reaches beyond my gathering.
I shut down Your reality.
You are overwhelming!
Are you near?
Are you really near?

**God:**

Little firecracker,
you've caught the wisp of Me.
Yes, I am near.
I am in your breath that gets frosty in winter.
I'm in your skip—that energy moves.
I'm in your love that carries you to mercy and to knowledge.
In that moment of contact with Me, you know fire.

## Daniel 3:19-20, 24-25

*¹⁹ Then Nebuchadnezzar was so filled with rage against Shadrach, Meshach, and Abednego that his face was distorted. He ordered the furnace heated up seven times more than was customary, ²⁰ and ordered some of the strongest guards in his army to bind Shadrach, Meshach, and Abednego and to throw them into the furnace of blazing fire. ²⁴ Then King Nebuchadnezzar was astonished and rose up quickly. He said to his counselors, "Was it not three men that we threw bound into the fire?" They answered the king, "True, O king." ²⁵ He replied, "But I see four men unbound, walking in the middle of the fire, and they are not hurt; and the fourth has the appearance of a god.*

How do you know mental numbness because God is so big?
When do you experience contact with God?

# Lavender

**My soul:**

God of fragrances,
I roam Your lavender fields.
Here amidst Your purple,
I relax in Your protection.
I know kingly kindness.
In your perfumes,
my thoughts calm to peace,
and I can sleep.

**God:**

Restless one,
peace wafts in waves through truth.
May all that roams in your soul rest in My kinship.
Cleanse with healing herbs
all that boils up in pain.
Let My lavender essence ease
your troubled heart to love.
Choose to breathe peace deeply.

**John 14:27**

*²⁷ Peace I leave with you; my peace I give to you. I do not give to you as the world gives. Do not let your hearts be troubled, and do not let them be afraid.*

How does truth give you peace?
How do you experience kingly kindness?

# Dill

**God:**

I walked the garden with you this evening,
awakening one.
Did you catch the smell of dill in the wind?
Let it stir your senses to gift.
Flavor your life and tastes as you roam.
Serve it with joy and hospitality.

**My soul:**

God who stretches all my consciousness,
like the blossom and bountiful seeds,
scatter Your fruitfulness in me.
Dill's hollow stems reach to bloom in plumes of fragrance.
Let my walk surrender each day's aromas.
Relax and savor the evening's rest.

**Genesis 2:8-9**

*⁸ And the Lord God planted a garden in Eden, in the east; and there he put the man whom he had formed. ⁹ Out of the ground the Lord God made to grow every tree that is pleasant to the sight and good for food, the tree of life also in the midst of the garden, and the tree of the knowledge of good and evil.*

How do you flavor your life?
What do you notice in your evening's walk in your garden?

# Bread

**God:**

Hungry soul,
I am good at providing bread.
I know you need sustenance.
I enjoy your breaking bread with each other…
all that laughter over crusty loaves,
it is part of My mystery of rising
to see what yeast can do.
It is catching the smell of baking—
the message of what heat can do.
Come, sit at My table.

**My soul:**

It is the ritual of ancient supper,
God of daily provision.
Thank You for Your faithfulness.
I savor You, Bread of Life.
You are my life.

**1 Corinthians 10:16-17**

*¹⁶ The cup of blessing that we bless, is it not a sharing in the blood of Christ? The bread that we break, is it not a sharing in the body of Christ? ¹⁷ Because there is one bread, we who are many are one body, for we all partake of the one bread.*

What memory do you cherish of laughter over crusty loaves?
What message do you hear in baking bread, in what heat can do?

# Wine

**My soul:**

Joyful God,
is it only in the crushing
that wine is made, that spirits lift?
Can the burdens fall away
in the sharing?
What is the mystery of fermentation?
Free my inhibitions.
I sip Your drink of joy.

**God:**

Life listener,
Cana was a blast.
What a celebration of two people's love!
My friends raised many a glass,
and we laughed!
It makes a new beginning.
It was fine wine!

**Mark 2:21-22**

²¹ *"No one sews a piece of unshrunk cloth on an old cloak; otherwise, the patch pulls away from it, the new from the old, and a worse tear is made. ²² And no one puts new wine into old wineskins; otherwise, the wine will burst the skins, and the wine is lost, and so are the skins; but one puts new wine into fresh wineskins."*

How do you experience crushing as the task of making fine wine?
Do you know fine wine in your life?

## Authentic

**My soul:**

Solid One,
You who are real, who have touched
my life again and again,
come, please.
In this sacred time and place,
be with me.
Cast out the mist of unbelief,
the claws of self-absorption.
Let me walk the hills with You
and laugh at Your surprises.
Clear the shadows of counterfeit
to the sunlight of Your presence.

**God:**

I am here, shadowed one.
Come out into My sunlight.
Know what is authentic in your soul.
What is real is rooted there,
where I abide.
Like the lake at sunrise,
the sun path comes to Me.
I am waiting for your awakening.

**John 11:7-11**

⁷ *Then after this he said to the disciples, "Let us go to Judea again." ⁸ The disciples said to him, "Rabbi, the Jews were just now trying to stone you, and are you going there again?" ⁹ Jesus answered, "Are there not twelve hours of daylight? Those who walk during the day do not stumble, because they see the light of this world. ¹⁰ But those who walk at night stumble, because the light is not in them." ¹¹ After saying this, he told them, "Our friend Lazarus has fallen asleep, but I am going there to awaken him."*

What claws hold you in the shadows?
How do you see God waiting for you to wake up?

# Mansion

**My soul:**

Am I lost in this mansion of Your world,
Creator God?
I am absorbed in disarray
with hoarding stuffed to surfeit.
Where are you in this forest
of aspens and redwoods?
Be my star sign leading me home,
God of wonderment.
I long for the vista of peace.

**God:**

Roamer in the dark,
put down your fears and distraction
and quiet your soul.
The mansion of your longing is where
I walk with you.
Stand on your mountaintop and see.
I am around you, within you,
above you, below you.
From all eternity, I love you.

**Colossians 1:15-20**

*¹⁵ He is the image of the invisible God, the firstborn of all creation; ¹⁶ for in him all things in heaven and on earth were created, things visible and invisible, whether thrones or dominions or rulers or powers—all things have been created through him and for him. ¹⁷ He himself is before all things, and in him all things hold together. ¹⁸ He is the head of the body, the church; he is the beginning, the firstborn from the dead, so that he might come to have first place in everything. ¹⁹ For in him all the fullness of God was pleased to dwell, ²⁰ and through him God was pleased to reconcile to himself all things, whether on earth or in heaven, by making peace through the blood of his cross.*

What distractions keep you lost?
What does the mansion of your longing look like?

# Rumors

**My soul:**

Creator God, I've heard the scuttlebutt.
We are in for disaster.
The earth is weeping glaciers, thundering floods, shaken to its core.
I hear it say, "I cannot breathe," overrun by greed and hypocrisy.
How do we give polar bears, tigers, and bees a place to roar and sing?
How do we humble our hearts?

**God:**

Fall in love, like Me.
Love lavishly my purple mountain's majesty.
Dare and risk to walk beside endangered ones.
Let aliens and refugees show fierce fight
for their right to a home.
Solitary one, join my company of saints,
furry ones, feathered ones, and foreign ones.
Become a wild lover of all that is strange and wonderful.
Dispel the rumors by your love.

**Matthew 24:2-8**

² *Then he asked them, "You see all these, do you not? Truly I tell you, not one stone will be left here upon another; all will be thrown down."* ³ *When he was sitting on the Mount of Olives, the disciples came to him privately, saying, "Tell us, when will this be, and what will be the sign of your coming and of the end of the age?"* ⁴ *Jesus answered them, "Beware that no one leads you astray.* ⁵ *For many will come in my name, saying, 'I am the Messiah!' and they will lead many astray.* ⁶ *And you will hear of wars and rumors of wars; see that you are not alarmed; for this must take place, but the end is not yet.* ⁷ *For nation will rise against nation, and kingdom against kingdom, and there will be famines and earthquakes in various places:* ⁸ *all this is but the beginning of the birth pangs."*

How can you humble your heart?
How does the company of saints include furry ones, feathered ones, and foreign ones in your world?

# Mutiny

**My soul:**

I've been born to insurrection.
A mighty mutiny is astir, rumbling and rising
out of the bowels of our earth.
God of Sinai, Your stones are thrown down. Upheaval erupts.
How do we form the ordered march round Jericho
from the chaos of foment?
Speak to me, wind of my Lord, of peace and life.

**God:**

You are free to agitate.
Rebellion is the strident call for justice.
"It is not fair," you say,
children torn from their mother's arms, the turbulence of no laws
that results in tainted water, in species (perhaps you) gone extinct,
in holes in your ozone layer.
Endure the disquiet in your soul.
Receive My call to act, new Moses.
The outcry of My earth echoes to My throne, ah, to My heart.

**Psalm 18:6-8, 16-19**

*⁶ In my distress I called upon the Lord; to my God I cried for help. From his temple he heard my voice, and my cry to him reached his ears. ⁷ Then the earth reeled and rocked; the foundations also of the mountains trembled and quaked, because he was angry. ⁸ Smoke went up from his nostrils, and devouring fire from his mouth; glowing coals flamed forth from him. ¹⁶ He reached down from on high, he took me; he drew me out of mighty waters. ¹⁷ He delivered me from my strong enemy, and from those who hated me; for they were too mighty for me. ¹⁸ They confronted me in the day of my calamity; but the Lord was my support. ¹⁹ He brought me out into a broad place; he delivered me, because he delighted in me.*

What aches in your soul, "it is not fair!"?
Where are you being called to act as a new Moses?

# Indict

**My soul:**

All-seeing God, I have been named.
You lodge a complaint that I seek my own self.
You cite my oblivion and waste of all that is precious.
You know my soul, my Lord. All that You charge is true.
There is no blame or slander.
The rich wealth of my inheritance is squandered.
Only You, Great Mercy, can exonerate. I am prodigal and starving.

**God:**

I wait on the roadway for you, child of my heart.
How can I arraign what I have named My own?
I claim you. I free you in your hunger to be Mine.
You know Me and have come home.

### Luke 15:11-14, 17-20

*¹¹ Then Jesus said, "There was a man who had two sons. ¹² The younger of them said to his father, 'Father, give me the share of the property that will belong to me.' So he divided his property between them. ¹³ A few days later the younger son gathered all he had and traveled to a distant country, and there he squandered his property in dissolute living. ¹⁴ When he had spent everything, a severe famine took place throughout that country, and he began to be in need. ¹⁷ But when he came to himself he said, 'How many of my father's hired hands have bread enough and to spare, but here I am dying of hunger! ¹⁸ I will get up and go to my father, and I will say to him, "Father, I have sinned against heaven and before you; ¹⁹ I am no longer worthy to be called your son; treat me like one of your hired hands."' ²⁰ So he set off and went to his father. But while he was still far off, his father saw him and was filled with compassion; he ran and put his arms around him and kissed him."*

What life are you squandering?
What does it mean for you to come home?

# Legendary

**My soul:**

The tales of you, Hero Brother Jesus, have lodged in my heart.
Are they fables, mere stretching of our wishes?
You healed the desperate lepers—ten of them.
You touched Jairus's daughter where they wailed the dirge of death.
You cured the Phoenician woman's daughter, not part of the clan.
The stories spread of Your capture. You were too good for this world,
beyond the rules of power, sold by Your friend.
They murdered You. They executed hope. They stripped all but love.
"Today you will be with Me in paradise."
"Father, forgive them; they know not what they do."
Is it mere legend that You rose?

**God:**

I rose! I rose indeed,
in the thousands of witnesses that love is stronger than death.
I rise in you, cherished believer.
You are not shriveled and stuck in culture's climate, in fearful paralysis.
You sing your spirit song. In you, I rise.

**Luke 24:29-35**

²⁹ *But they urged him strongly, saying, "Stay with us, because it is almost evening and the day is now nearly over." So he went in to stay with them.* ³⁰ *When he was at the table with them, he took bread, blessed and broke it, and gave it to them.* ³¹ *Then their eyes were opened, and they recognized him; and he vanished from their sight.* ³² *They said to each other, "Were not our hearts burning within us while he was talking to us on the road, while he was opening the scriptures to us?"* ³³ *That same hour they got up and returned to Jerusalem; and they found the eleven and their companions gathered together.* ³⁴ *They were saying, "The Lord has risen indeed, and he has appeared to Simon!"* ³⁵ *Then they told what had happened on the road, and how he had been made known to them in the breaking of the bread.*

What stories of Jesus have healed you?
How do you know, believe that Jesus rose?

# Haggle

**God:**

It is all about exchange.
I lay down My life for you, trader child.
You breathe in oxygen and breathe out carbon dioxide.
You take in nourishment and
labor with renewed energy.
You love and expand your ability to receive love.
The covenant we make, you and I, is
in this bargain of life.

**My soul:**

This is no horse deal, God and Master!
It is not about haggling and quibbling.
You hold all the cards.
You stipulate the terms.
Yet I see the consequences when I go awry.
You made in me a law.
So I do not dispute Your direction.
Give me grace to give.
Give me maturity to serve.
Give me faith to lay down my life too.

**Proverbs 9:1-6**

*¹ Wisdom has built her house; she has hewn her seven pillars. ² She has slaughtered her animals, she has mixed her wine, she has also set her table. ³ She has sent out her servant-girls, she calls from the highest places in the town, ⁴ "You that are simple, turn in here!" To those without sense she says, ⁵ "Come, eat of my bread and drink of the wine I have mixed. ⁶ Lay aside immaturity, and live, and walk in the way of insight."*

What bargains do you make in your life?
How are you laying down your life?

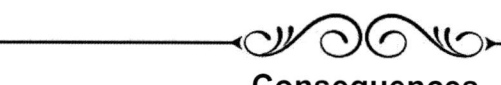

# Consequences

**My soul:**

God of Law,
I live with the consequences:
weight, loneliness, guilt.
Oozing over into my choices are
patterns of self-righteousness, fear,
and laziness.
I want to cling to Your coattails, Healer God.
Make a dent in my trajectory.
Like the butterfly effect, let the desire
for peace and compassion
erase the weapons of war,
welcome the stranger to my table,
sleep the rest of harmony.
Like the domino effect, let today's bond
with You inspire and motivate,
accomplish and free,
surprise life and wholeness.

**God:**

You don't ask for much, sluggish spirit!
I accomplish the slow, steady work of redemption.
Trust the conversation You and I have this day
will shape kinship.
The Kingdom of God is among you.

**1 Corinthians 12:12-13**

*¹² For just as the body is one and has many members, and all the members of the body, though many, are one body, so it is with Christ. ¹³ For in the one Spirit we were all baptized into one body—Jews or Greeks, slaves or free—and we were all made to drink of one Spirit.*

How do the consequences of your deeds weigh you down or lift you up?
Where do you know God's slow, steady work of redemption?

# September

1. Personal
2. Frustration
3. Undercurrent
4. Bleak
5. Porcelain
6. Amethyst
7. Onyx
8. Opaque
9. Apprenticeship
10. Terrain
11. Discontent
12. Swirl
13. Foreclosure
14. Linger
15. Primitive
16. Mined
17. Pervade
18. Debilitated
19. Prevail
20. Dawning
21. Communal
22. Cup
23. Isolated Cells
24. Intuit
25. Coral Reefs
26. Alchemy
27. Holding Place
28. Woven
29. Reluctance
30. Fabric

## Personal

**My soul:**

Are you personal, God?
Do you relate with me,
and with all Your created world,
in an I-Thou way?
Or are You pure energy flow?
Or is there any bridge for me to cross to know You?
Jesus shows us You.
Your wholeness is full of color and relationship.
So I approach. Let my heart lead.
Press it open wider and wider so I
can see You in what is freckled
and on the edge.
Come, my Lord-You, come.

**God:**

Orphan child, I know you. I made you.
I hear your whimper of aloneness.
Let me hold you to My cheek
to console and comfort you.
The tangled pathways of your
heart's roaming will not consume you.
I have My eye on you.
And I love you.

**Isaiah 40:10-11**

*¹⁰ See, the Lord God comes with might, and his arm rules for him; his reward is with him, and his recompense before him. ¹¹ He will feed his flock like a shepherd; he will gather the lambs in his arms, and carry them in his bosom, and gently lead the mother sheep.*

Is your God a person to you?
When does God hold you to his cheek to ease your whimpers?

**September 2**

# Frustration

**God:**

At each turn, you frustrate My plans
for you, rebel child.
I desire joy and freedom and light—
the slow process of coming of age.
And you eat apples.
You run to the edge of safety
and then get scared.
I sweep you up from harm,
but you go from one cliff to the next
and flirt with danger.
Even with your scars and broken bones,
you learn so little.

**My soul:**

God of my desperations,
let me not be defeated by my own wild streaks.
Though I chafe at Your reins,
deepen my trust in Your faithful lead.
I do not want to thwart Your care of me.
Do not let me foil Your dreams for me.
I believe You are the way I walk to freedom.
I believe in You, my Way, my Truth, my Light.

**Isaiah 11:6-9**

⁶ *The wolf shall live with the lamb, the leopard shall lie down with
the kid, the calf and the lion and the fatling together, and a little
child shall lead them.* ⁷ *The cow and the bear shall graze, their
young shall lie down together; and the lion shall eat straw like the
ox.* ⁸ *The nursing child shall play over the hole of the asp, and the
weaned child shall put its hand on the adder's den.* ⁹ *They will not
hurt or destroy on all my holy mountain; for the earth will be full
of the knowledge of the Lord as the waters cover the sea.*

How are you eating apples?
What are God's dreams for you?

# Undercurrent

**God:**

Rider of life's waves,
attend to the undercurrent.
Let what is unseen and powerful be recognized.
Your shadows lurk to capture your energy and even your life.
Stretch parallel to shore when the undertow threatens.
I've clothed you, needing your earth.

**My soul:**

Light and Strength,
come gather me in
when fighting the waves is exhausting.
How do I see my shadows?
How do I hold sacred my earth?
The emotions that rush below the surface
can defeat the oneness
with sea and sky.
Be my Guard of life and save me.

**Matthew 8:23-27**

*23 And when he got into the boat, his disciples followed him. 24 A windstorm arose on the sea, so great that the boat was being swamped by the waves; but he was asleep. 25 And they went and woke him up, saying, "Lord, save us! We are perishing!" 26 And he said to them, "Why are you afraid, you of little faith?" Then he got up and rebuked the winds and the sea; and there was a dead calm. 27 They were amazed, saying, "What sort of man is this, that even the winds and the sea obey him?"*

What shadows repeatedly take your energy?
What emotional undercurrent divides your heart?

# Bleak

**My soul:**

My soul is bleak today, Discerner of my way.
I am desperate for blooms to unfold my heart.
But all is barren. I bear no offspring. I leave no mark.
In the stark wilderness, I roam, desolate and afraid.
Help me, Guide and Guardian.

**God:**

Do you know that I watch? Lost and lonely one, I know your desert.
What is lacking in your spirit's wasteland, you will find in Me.
I am the nomad coming in the distance.
I am the Bedouin eager for your night fire.
In this wild and bereft silence,
I will come to tell you tales of My mighty love.

**Matthew 4:1-11**

*[1] Then Jesus was led up by the Spirit into the wilderness to be tempted by the devil. [2] He fasted forty days and forty nights, and afterwards he was famished. [3] The tempter came and said to him, "If you are the Son of God, command these stones to become loaves of bread." [4] But he answered, "It is written, 'One does not live by bread alone, but by every word that comes from the mouth of God.'" [5] Then the devil took him to the holy city and placed him on the pinnacle of the temple, [6] saying to him, "If you are the Son of God, throw yourself down; for it is written, 'He will command his angels concerning you,' and 'On their hands they will bear you up, so that you will not dash your foot against a stone.'" [7] Jesus said to him, "Again it is written, 'Do not put the Lord your God to the test.'" [8] Again, the devil took him to a very high mountain and showed him all the kingdoms of the world and their splendor; [9] and he said to him, "All these I will give you, if you will fall down and worship me." [10] Jesus said to him, "Away with you, Satan! For it is written, 'Worship the Lord your God, and serve only him.'" [11] Then the devil left him, and suddenly angels came and waited on him.*

How does your God come to you in your bleakness?
What tales of God's mighty love soothe your soul?

## September 5

## Porcelain

**My soul:**

How fragile I am, like old porcelain!
Tender God, hold me gently.
As I age with skin tears and creaking bones,
may I sing a song to you from the years.
I celebrate Your faithfulness.
Written in scars and tears,
in laugh wrinkles
and in memories,
You are still with me.
You take my breath away
in Your ancient but ever-new love.
And I feel young again.

**God:**

Let your years echo with
the caverns and mountains of My love.
You are not finished yet.
As you trudge through rocky terrain,
I have your hand.
What feels so breakable and delicate
has been forged in the seasons of My companionship.
You are the art of My shaping.
Buried in the dark of your days are the jewels of My touch.
And how I rejoice in your making!

**Luke 2:36-38**

*<sup>36</sup> There was also a prophet, Anna the daughter of Phanuel, of the tribe of Asher. She was of a great age, having lived with her husband seven years after her marriage, <sup>37</sup> then as a widow to the age of eighty-four. She never left the temple but worshiped there with fasting and prayer night and day. <sup>38</sup> At that moment she came, and began to praise God and to speak about the child to all who were looking for the redemption of Jerusalem.*

When do you feel your age, and when do you feel young?
How do you know God is rejoicing in the making of you?

258

# Amethyst

**My soul:**

God who touches all ills, today is a purple day!
Shaded like amethyst, the shadows haunt like bruises.
I ache for peace. Soothe my dreams.
Let my mind move past the stutters of obsession.
Bring harmony with You as I listen.
Quiet my soul in Your presence.

**God:**

Aching beautiful child, let the dark drift away. Dawn comes.
Let the passion of your soul awaken. Life stirs.
The streaks of purple that were nightshades
crystalize to a gem of promise.
The fire that signals day is in your soul.
Create love moments as you trust My gifts.
You are free.

**Matthew 28:1-9**

*¹ After the Sabbath, as the first day of the week was dawning, Mary Magdalene and the other Mary went to see the tomb. ² And suddenly there was a great earthquake; for an angel of the Lord, descending from heaven, came and rolled back the stone and sat on it. ³ His appearance was like lightning, and his clothing white as snow. ⁴ For fear of him the guards shook and became like dead men. ⁵ But the angel said to the women, "Do not be afraid; I know that you are looking for Jesus who was crucified. ⁶ He is not here; for he has been raised, as he said. Come, see the place where he lay. ⁷ Then go quickly and tell his disciples, 'He has been raised from the dead, and indeed he is going ahead of you to Galilee; there you will see him.' This is my message for you." ⁸ So they left the tomb quickly with fear and great joy, and ran to tell his disciples. ⁹ Suddenly Jesus met them and said, "Greetings!" And they came to him, took hold of his feet, and worshiped him.*

What are the stutters of your mind?
How do you create love moments?

# Onyx

**My soul:**

Hidden Master, I walk in the dark.
It is black as onyx, this night of my soul.
Where are You?
How can I feel You in this jungle,
this tangle of fears and lostness?
Speak to me from where I cannot breathe.
Open my ears to hear.

**God:**

I know the way in the dark.
Do not fear.
Put your trust in Me.
I am your Light within,
even when you cannot see,
even when you cannot feel,
even when you cannot hear.
Your faith will keep you walking.

**2 Peter 1:16-19**

*16 For we did not follow cleverly devised myths when we made known to you the power and coming of our Lord Jesus Christ, but we had been eyewitnesses of his majesty. 17 For he received honor and glory from God the Father when that voice was conveyed to him by the Majestic Glory, saying, "This is my Son, my Beloved, with whom I am well pleased." 18 We ourselves heard this voice come from heaven, while we were with him on the holy mountain. 19 So we have the prophetic message more fully confirmed. You will do well to be attentive to this as to a lamp shining in a dark place, until the day dawns and the morning star rises in your hearts.*

Where do you find God?
God knows the way in the dark. How do you experience this?

# Opaque

**God:**

My people, my people,
and you, dear child of My heart, all is opaque to you.
My light can't come through.
You disregard My love that would let you see.
My words spoken by the ancient wise ones are unintelligible to you.
Even my beloved, my Son, who spoke My love in flesh and blood!
How can I get through to you?
In the most elemental awe, I send you a wren warbling,
I give you a monarch precious and at risk,
I give you a full moon to catch your breath.
Do you see the signs? Do you read My love?

**My soul:**

How, God of Love, bigger than my heart's grasp, do I pay attention?
How do I walk beyond the fog of plans that absorb,
of weeping all around me unheard and denied,
of blindness to Your immense gifts?
Raise up reverence within. I am humbled in my sin.

**1 Samuel 24:3-7**

³ *He came to the sheepfolds beside the road, where there was a cave; and Saul went in to relieve himself. Now David and his men were sitting in the innermost parts of the cave.* ⁴ *The men of David said to him, "Here is the day of which the Lord said to you, 'I will give your enemy into your hand, and you shall do to him as it seems good to you.'" Then David went and stealthily cut off a corner of Saul's cloak.* ⁵ *Afterward David was stricken to the heart because he had cut off a corner of Saul's cloak.* ⁶ *He said to his men, "The Lord forbid that I should do this thing to my lord, the Lord's anointed, to raise my hand against him; for he is the Lord's anointed."* ⁷ *So David scolded his men severely and did not permit them to attack Saul. Then Saul got up and left the cave, and went on his way.*

How do you feel God's desperation to show Her love?
When does God speak and you hear?

# Apprenticeship

**God:**

Little learner,
come be mine in My apprenticeship.
I want to train you to love as I do.
No energy has power that is comparable.
In My enlightenment, you can flourish.
Be present and receive My discipline.

**My soul:**

I want to learn from You, God of love lessons.
Let me look long and hard at Jesus
and what love cost Him.
Coach me. Form me in Your way.
To come under such mighty instruction
will take total concentration.
I must leave all else behind.
Yes, Lord, with all my heart, yes!

**Mark 1:16-20**

*¹⁶ As Jesus passed along the Sea of Galilee, he saw Simon and his brother Andrew casting a net into the sea—for they were fishermen. ¹⁷ And Jesus said to them, "Follow me and I will make you fish for people." ¹⁸ And immediately they left their nets and followed him. ¹⁹ As he went a little farther, he saw James son of Zebedee and his brother John, who were in their boat mending the nets. ²⁰ Immediately he called them; and they left their father Zebedee in the boat with the hired men, and followed him.*

How do you know God is training you to love as He does?
What do you need to leave behind to go into God's apprenticeship?

# Terrain

**My soul:**

God of my heart's grounding,
Your people wanted their own piece of land.
It was their promised land.
In the terrain of my own soul,
come claim Your plot.
Let me belong to You.
There are gigantic rocks on Your land,
boulders that defy climbing.
Come and own me.
Come and nurture fruitfulness.
Come to my waterfalls and play.

**God:**

I receive you, land of My dreams,
and roam your hills and valleys.
I belong to you and you belong to Me.
I will let orchards weigh with heavy fruit.
I will send My wind to wave your grain.
In my forests, we will find the
cool and shaded pathways
to roam and laugh and own.
It is your promised land.

**Genesis 13:14-16**

*¹⁴ The Lord said to Abram, after Lot had separated from him, "Raise your eyes now, and look from the place where you are, northward and southward and eastward and westward; ¹⁵ for all the land that you see I will give to you and to your offspring forever. ¹⁶ I will make your offspring like the dust of the earth; so that if one can count the dust of the earth, your offspring also can be counted.*

What does the land of your soul look like in its promised gift of God?
What is God's dream for your land?

# Discontent

**My soul:**

Is this our season of discontent?
God of peace,
how can I be content in my own soul?
Children are murdered in our city!
Refugees wait for home.
There is no food to share in some families.
To be blessed with safety, meaning,
health, friends—thank You, thank You.
May all creatures across our world know Your gifts.

**God:**

Believing one,
know contentment
even as restlessness spews up like volcanoes.
This is its season for you.
I bless you!
I give you heart for all your brothers and sisters
who know discontent, who roam flailing,
who are lonely deep in their souls.
Hold them gently.
You are one.

**Matthew 25:41-45**

*41 Then he will say to those at his left hand, 'You that are accursed, depart from me into the eternal fire prepared for the devil and his angels; 42 for I was hungry and you gave me no food, I was thirsty and you gave me nothing to drink, 43 I was a stranger and you did not welcome me, naked and you did not give me clothing, sick and in prison and you did not visit me.' 44 Then they also will answer, 'Lord, when was it that we saw you hungry or thirsty or a stranger or naked or sick or in prison, and did not take care of you?' 45 Then he will answer them, 'Truly I tell you, just as you did not do it to one of the least of these, you did not do it to me.'*

What is your present season of soul?
How do you experience the season of discontent?

# Swirl

**My soul:**

Expanding Energy of Love,
I'm caught in the eddies of my self-absorption.
Break me out of the swirl of small stuff. I want to honor You.
I desire to catch the rush and flow of Your mighty movement.
How do I know You? Open me wide to Your encompassing current.

**God:**

Small boat on My mighty ocean,
no whirlpool should hold you caught and spinning.
Look into My face. I see you.
If you see Me, you will know Me.
From deep within, you will receive My heart.
Let us run side by side, carried in the Breath of Life.

## Mark 5:25-34

²⁵ *Now there was a woman who had been suffering from hemorrhages for twelve years.* ²⁶ *She had endured much under many physicians, and had spent all that she had; and she was no better, but rather grew worse.* ²⁷ *She had heard about Jesus, and came up behind him in the crowd and touched his cloak,* ²⁸ *for she said, "If I but touch his clothes, I will be made well."* ²⁹ *Immediately her hemorrhage stopped; and she felt in her body that she was healed of her disease.* ³⁰ *Immediately aware that power had gone forth from him, Jesus turned about in the crowd and said, "Who touched my clothes?"* ³¹ *And his disciples said to him, "You see the crowd pressing in on you; how can you say, 'Who touched me?'"* ³² *He looked all around to see who had done it.* ³³ *But the woman, knowing what had happened to her, came in fear and trembling, fell down before him, and told him the whole truth.* ³⁴ *He said to her, "Daughter, your faith has made you well; go in peace, and be healed of your disease."*

What holds you caught in its eddy of self-absorption?
How do you receive God's heart?

# Foreclosure

**My soul:**

Am I in foreclosure?
I have the illusion I own myself.
I cannot pay my debt.
Am I collateral?
Are You doing to me what
all debtors go through:
the living on the edge,
the scrimping for food,
homelessness?
My soul is adrift, with nothing
to give it ballast.
Dare I call on Your mercy?

**God:**

In trying to right your own boat
and own your soul,
lost child, you have emptiness.
Quiet your busy mind
to know I am present.
I fill you with joy, with peace,
with abounding love.
Own your own soul in surrender.
Let Me lead our dance.
My mercy is always with you.

**Matthew 18:23-25**

[23] *"For this reason the kingdom of heaven may be compared to a king who wished to settle accounts with his slaves.* [24] *When he began the reckoning, one who owed him ten thousand talents was brought to him;* [25] *and, as he could not pay, his lord ordered him to be sold, together with his wife and children and all his possessions, and payment to be made."*

What does it mean to you if God owns you?
What is the debt you owe?

# Linger

**My soul:**

God of patient rushing,
I linger watching cardinals flit for food!
I lounge as stars seem to show up,
massing across the midnight sky.
I dawdle at the silent pool waiting for fish to bite.
Yet Your speed of light races.
Your energy explodes, pushing the universe boundaries.
Your love creates a fresh wonder
from snowflakes and rainbows and me.
No wonder I am in a hurry.
Life does not waffle at Your feet.

**God:**

No, dear urgent soul, do not tarry.
Fill your days with wondrous awe. I walk with You.
As we saunter across My earth way,
birth oozes forth at your fingertips.
What pushes you to wait is alertness for My coming.
I want you to see Me. Be patient for My presence.

**John 4:27-30**

*²⁷ Just then his disciples came. They were astonished that he was speaking with a woman, but no one said, "What do you want?" or, "Why are you speaking with her?" ²⁸ Then the woman left her water jar and went back to the city. She said to the people, ²⁹ "Come and see a man who told me everything I have ever done! He cannot be the Messiah, can he?" ³⁰ They left the city and were on their way to him.*

Where do you linger?
Where do you hurry?

## Primitive

**My soul:**

Visionary God,
I am primitive, simple and crude.
I am so little evolved in my heart.
Root within me the blooming
refinement to listen.
Let me wait on Your dream to stir in me.
Catch hold my attention to You
and let me breathe in unison.
Derive from me Your growing.

**God:**

Naïve seed child, in your ancient pulse of life,
I am excited. I chose you to be.
I can see your budding consciousness.
I feel your ache to know Me.
You have been a cave dweller,
drawing your dreams on walls.
Now catch fire and see Me.
I love you, possibility.

**Hebrews 12:28-29**

*²⁸ Therefore, since we are receiving a kingdom that cannot be shaken, let us give thanks, by which we offer to God an acceptable worship with reverence and awe; ²⁹ for indeed our God is a consuming fire.*

How is listening an evolution of your heart?
When are you aware of God's excitement in your possibility?

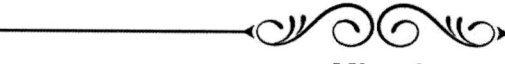

# Mined

**My soul:**

Come mine this quarry of my soul,
God of fearless Presence.
Excavate beyond embedded rock.
Do you really believe there's treasure?

**God:**

Resisting earth child,
I know there is treasure.
If I can get beyond your "me, myself, and I," I will find it.
Mines have been planted to explode grenades
in jealous competition,
in pride that divides,
in fear that attacks.
But I mine in truth
for the shining pool that reflects My light.
Lay down your resistance and surrender.

**Matthew 13:44**

*⁴⁴ The kingdom of heaven is like treasure hidden in a field, which someone found and hid; then in his joy he goes and sells all that he has and buys that field.*

What rock is God excavating in your soul?
What mines have been planted within you to resist God's coming?

# Pervade

**God:**

Scattered wild child,
let Me pervade your life.
I want to walk with you.
I can imbue you with My peace.
Can you believe I ask your permission?
Let My light saturate your consciousness.
I want You to know Me.

**My soul:**

You take my breath away.
Unreachable God, can I really reach You?
I welcome You.
I commit all that I am into Your care.
Diffuse Your radiance within me
so Your way is clear.
Steady my feet in Your path.
I bow before You.
I know I run on the cliff's edge,
but I run to You.

**Psalm 57:6-10**

⁶ *They set a net for my steps; my soul was bowed down. They dug a pit in my path, but they have fallen into it themselves.* ⁷ *My heart is steadfast, O God, my heart is steadfast. I will sing and make melody.* ⁸ *Awake, my soul! Awake, O harp and lyre! I will awake the dawn.* ⁹ *I will give thanks to you, O Lord, among the peoples; I will sing praises to you among the nations.* ¹⁰ *For your steadfast love is as high as the heavens; your faithfulness extends to the clouds.*

How do you know God asks your permission to be part of your life?
How are you running on a cliff's edge?

# Debilitated

**My soul:**

Vibrancy of Life,
I feel myself being debilitated.
I waste the calls You make
to dare, to work fiercely, to create.
Break open the prisons of fear
and laziness within me.
Let what is enfeebled rise up
on strong bones and dance.
I am drained of Your juice.

**God:**

Weakened one,
I fill your heart once again.
Let all that is emaciated
gather sinew and health.
If your love sees lucidly and embraces Me,
your endurance will find strength.
All your dreams and visions will be real.
I raise you up to live.
Take My hands.

## John 5:2-3, 5-9

*² Now in Jerusalem by the Sheep Gate there is a pool, called in Hebrew Beth-zatha, which has five porticoes. ³ In these lay many invalids—blind, lame, and paralyzed. ⁵ One man was there who had been ill for thirty-eight years. ⁶ When Jesus saw him lying there and knew that he had been there a long time, he said to him, "Do you want to be made well?" ⁷ The sick man answered him, "Sir, I have no one to put me into the pool when the water is stirred up; and while I am making my way, someone else steps down ahead of me." ⁸ Jesus said to him, "Stand up, take your mat and walk." ⁹ At once the man was made well, and he took up his mat and began to walk. Now that day was a Sabbath.*

What keeps you paralyzed and debilitated?
What do you dream of doing?

271

## September 19

## Prevail

**God:**

Old one,
you are not as old as I am.
When you are discounted and cast aside,
you can understand how I am disregarded.
I am the Ancient One.
My rules are old-fashioned,
my ways are out of step,
though written into the warp and woof
of trees and cells and laws.
My people choose blindness.
Will you see and prevail?

**My soul:**

Ancient and Ever-New One,
I do see.
I believe in Your triumph in my heart.
Hold on to me.
Persist in my diminishment.
In Your Presence, I am young
and can move the earth.

**Isaiah 29:15-19**

*¹⁵ Ha! You who hide a plan too deep for the Lord, whose deeds are in the dark, and who say, "Who sees us? Who knows us? ¹⁶ You turn things upside down! Shall the potter be regarded as the clay? Shall the thing made say of its maker, "He did not make me"; or the thing formed say of the one who formed it, "He has no understanding"? ¹⁷ Shall not Lebanon in a very little while become a fruitful field, and the fruitful field be regarded as a forest? ¹⁸ On that day the deaf shall hear the words of a scroll, and out of their gloom and darkness the eyes of the blind shall see. ¹⁹ The meek shall obtain fresh joy in the Lord, and the neediest people shall exult in the Holy One of Israel.*

When do you experience being old and discounted?
How do you feel in God's presence that you can move the earth?

# Dawning

**My soul:**

Infinite Dawn and Light,
today sunrise is dawning, all is fresh and new.
How will I shape this day?
Break open in me a way by which to see.
Then I can maneuver around rocks.
Then I can catch the eye of the stranger.
Then I can imagine building home.
You are my lamp's Light, God ever present.

**God:**

At sunup, I am here.
Even in your dark, I am here,
reflecting pool of My light.
Let your new day dawn with awareness.
I seek your partnership.
Are you surprised that I need you?
Do you realize that the colors of our universe need
your touch, your laughter, your hand beneath Mine?
Come, see Me in your ride of the waves.
I am your energy.

**Isaiah 58:6-9**

*[6] Is not this the fast that I choose: to loose the bonds of injustice, to undo the thongs of the yoke, to let the oppressed go free, and to break every yoke? [7] Is it not to share your bread with the hungry, and bring the homeless poor into your house; when you see the naked, to cover them, and not to hide yourself from your own kin? [8] Then your light shall break forth like the dawn, and your healing shall spring up quickly; your vindicator shall go before you, the glory of the Lord shall be your rear guard. [9] Then you shall call, and the Lord will answer; you shall cry for help, and he will say, "Here I am."*

How does God's Light let you see?
What colors of the universe depend on you?

## Communal

**God:**

Puzzle piece, put your mark to My design.
Cello player, let your strings add resonance
to My mighty music.
Stonemason,
build with your strong arm My cathedral.
You are part of My life fabric.
The community of the universe is My home.
Let your humble work be Mine.

**My soul:**

God, beyond my imagining,
I am only part.
The great enterprise of Your love
shapes and forms us.
Let my piece complete Your dream.
May my harmony make Your symphony rich.
I want the stones I chisel of my days
to praise Your holy name.
I am part of Your Kingdom come.

**Luke 17:20-21**

*²⁰ Once Jesus was asked by the Pharisees when the kingdom of God was coming, and he answered, "The kingdom of God is not coming with things that can be observed; ²¹ nor will they say, 'Look, here it is!' or 'There it is!' For, in fact, the kingdom of God is among you."*

What humble work does God call you into?
How is God's love shaping the vast enterprise of the Kingdom?

# Cup

**God:**

Come share this cup with Me, thirsty one.
Empty it to the dregs.
I pour in savorings.
I lift to your lips the kisses
of earth's finest gifts:
fullness,
beauty,
satisfaction.
And I also drink.
For somewhere in this cup rests suffering.
Oh that you could be spared, My love.

**My soul:**

Do I have the love that would be
nowhere else but near You,
dear God of the feast?
Whether in good times or in bad,
in riches or in poverty,
in vitality or in illness,
I share Your cup.
I trust life to endure.
I choose You.

**Romans 8:14-17**

*¹⁴ For all who are led by the Spirit of God are children of God. ¹⁵ For you did not receive a spirit of slavery to fall back into fear, but you have received a spirit of adoption. When we cry, "Abba! Father!" ¹⁶ it is that very Spirit bearing witness with our spirit that we are children of God, ¹⁷ and if children, then heirs, heirs of God and joint heirs with Christ—if, in fact, we suffer with him so that we may also be glorified with him.*

What is in your cup to drink right now?
How does your love impel you to share His cup?

# Isolated Cells

**My soul:**

I am an isolated cell, Holy One!
In this breathing, dancing, entwined energy that is You,
let me touch Your hand.
A dark miasma builds my walls.
No words come!
I am confined.
Where I am bereft and helpless,
break open my prison.
I yearn to laugh again.

**God:**

Study my butterfly's journey and know all is not lost.
I hear your heart, My child.
It beats next to My own.
Life impels you to grow.
Even in darkness, I am here.
Hang in there.

**Acts 12:6-10**

⁶ *The very night before Herod was going to bring him out, Peter, bound with two chains, was sleeping between two soldiers, while guards in front of the door were keeping watch over the prison.* ⁷ *Suddenly an angel of the Lord appeared and a light shone in the cell. He tapped Peter on the side and woke him, saying, "Get up quickly." And the chains fell off his wrists.* ⁸ *The angel said to him, "Fasten your belt and put on your sandals." He did so. Then he said to him, "Wrap your cloak around you and follow me."* ⁹ *Peter went out and followed him; he did not realize that what was happening with the angel's help was real; he thought he was seeing a vision.* ¹⁰ *After they had passed the first and the second guard, they came before the iron gate leading into the city. It opened for them of its own accord, and they went outside and walked along a lane, when suddenly the angel left him.*

How can you touch God's hand?
How is the butterfly speaking to this moment of your life?

## Intuit

**God:**

Tiny marvelous person, I intuit you.
I grasp you with My love,
knowing all your possibilities.
I encompass you in freedom
to be My hands and feet and heart.
Do you discern our destiny?
What reason cannot figure out,
simple presence holds!
It is our energy of love.

**My soul:**

God of a billion galaxies, You are too much!
How can I, so weak and small,
hold this immense truth?
Let me believe!
I open my awakened heart to
Your pulsing, mighty Love.
Let Your presence shine
as a starlight spark in the midnight sky.

**Romans 8:19-23**

*[19] For the creation waits with eager longing for the revealing of the children of God; [20] for the creation was subjected to futility, not of its own will but by the will of the one who subjected it, in hope [21] that the creation itself will be set free from its bondage to decay and will obtain the freedom of the glory of the children of God. [22] We know that the whole creation has been groaning in labor pains until now; [23] and not only the creation, but we ourselves, who have the first fruits of the Spirit, groan inwardly while we wait for adoption, the redemption of our bodies.*

What is your destiny with God?
How do you experience the speck of light in your midnight world?

## Coral Reefs

**God:**

I've roamed the coral reefs.
Where have all the colors gone?
Person of such casual indifference,
do you see what you are doing?
Wake up!
Precious life is bleeding out.
What belongs to jellyfish,
anemone, and man-of-war
is symbolic for you as well.

**My soul:**

God of my heart life, I weep with You.
The mighty underwater structures
of tens of thousands of years are at risk.
The arrogance we ooze endangers what we breathe.
And we saunter on in our choices!
Mercy and wisdom, God who started us all, please!
Will we all disappear with a whimper?

### Micah 7:13-14, 18-19

*¹³ But the earth will be desolate because of its inhabitants, for the fruit of their doings. ¹⁴ Shepherd your people with your staff, the flock that belongs to you, which lives alone in a forest in the midst of a garden land; let them feed in Bashan and Gilead as in the days of old. ¹⁸ Who is a God like you, pardoning iniquity and passing over the transgression of the remnant of your possession? He does not retain his anger forever, because he delights in showing clemency. ¹⁹ He will again have compassion upon us; he will tread our iniquities under foot. You will cast all our sins into the depths of the sea.*

How are you seeing colors disappear from your life?
What do you weep over, and how do you feel human arrogance?

# Alchemy

**God:**

Are you foolishly crying for more, restless one?
The alchemy of things or travel or drink buries what is here.
Look within!
The gold of your desire is already near.
Travel lightly.
Come steadily into My arms.

**My soul:**

Delight of my heart,
I ache to shed the weight of all I bear in burdens.
Let me leave behind to others
the jewels and scarves and toys.
The way I am made invites me to have eyes
constantly for You.
I seek You in my seasons.
I yearn for You in my aloneness.
Hold me, God of faithfulness.

**Joel 3:17-18**

*¹⁷ So you shall know that I, the Lord your God, dwell in Zion, my holy mountain. And Jerusalem shall be holy, and strangers shall never again pass through it. ¹⁸ In that day the mountains shall drip sweet wine, the hills shall flow with milk, and all the stream beds of Judah shall flow with water; a fountain shall come forth from the house of the Lord and water the Wadi Shittim.*

How do you see God when you travel lightly?
In the seasons of your life, how are you seeking God?

# Holding Place

**My soul:**

Shelter of my soul,
the storm is coming.
I seek haven when all is caving in around me.
Hide me in Your loft from floods.
Secure me in Your cyclone cellar from wind.
I am afraid and alone.
My wants overwhelm me.

**God:**

I have formed you, child who bears My light.
You are precious and I love you.
I know your enemy within.
I am attentive to your fear.
I am provider for you
who run about wildly seeking asylum.
Let your spirit rest in My love.
I am here.

**Psalm 27:4-5**

*⁴ One thing I asked of the Lord, that will I seek after: to live in the house of the Lord all the days of my life, to behold the beauty of the Lord, and to inquire in his temple. ⁵ For he will hide me in his shelter in the day of trouble; he will conceal me under the cover of his tent; he will set me high on a rock.*

What wants overwhelm you?
As you believe you are a child of the light, how does it show in your life?

# Woven

**God:**

Child of My imaginings,
I have woven your sinews with your hopes.
Your ancient threads interlace your dance in dawn
and rest at sunset.
The cloth of your life unfolds.
May it clothe and warm a cold world.

**My soul:**

Weaver God,
in Your hands I entrust the skeins of my growing.
The twists and turns, the knots and silks,
plait my soul fabric.
I am Yours.
Your designs are mystery.
The braids of my longing invite a wedding cloth.
I am Yours.

**Revelations 21:1-4**

*¹ Then I saw a new heaven and a new earth; for the first heaven and the first earth had passed away, and the sea was no more. ² And I saw the holy city, the New Jerusalem, coming down out of heaven from God, prepared as a bride adorned for her husband. ³ And I heard a loud voice from the throne saying, "See, the home of God is among mortals. He will dwell with them; they will be his peoples, and God himself will be with them; ⁴ he will wipe every tear from their eyes. Death will be no more; mourning and crying and pain will be no more, for the first things have passed away."*

How do you spread the cloth of your life over a cold world?
What knots and silk weave into your soul fabric?

# Reluctance

**My soul:**

God of incongruities,
receive my reluctance.
Travel the shadows of my soul. Let my resistances recede.
I want to hold back nothing from Your gaze
and from Your transforming touch.
So I creep and shuffle toward Your freedom.
I drag my fears and hunger for control into Your sunlight.
Let these shrivel there, surrendered.

**God:**

Hesitating one, this day is yours.
Hold your head high to claim this moment to respond with kindness.
Take heart and stand with rejected ones. Make that call to initiate action.
Do not be unwilling, but willing. Catch My fire for love.
Turn strangers to neighbors and, even more, turn enemies to friends.
I am Father to all.

**Colossians 3:12-17**

*¹² As God's chosen ones, holy and beloved, clothe yourselves with compassion, kindness, humility, meekness, and patience. ¹³ Bear with one another and, if anyone has a complaint against another, forgive each other; just as the Lord has forgiven you, so you also must forgive. ¹⁴ Above all, clothe yourselves with love, which binds everything together in perfect harmony. ¹⁵ And let the peace of Christ rule in your hearts, to which indeed you were called in the one body. And be thankful. ¹⁶ Let the word of Christ dwell in you richly; teach and admonish one another in all wisdom; and with gratitude in your hearts sing psalms, hymns, and spiritual songs to God. ¹⁷ And whatever you do, in word or deed, do everything in the name of the Lord Jesus, giving thanks to God the Father through him.*

Where are you reluctant to follow Jesus's word?
How are you hearing God's call to action?

## Fabric

**God:**

Child of substance,
I count on you to be the satin in My world.
I know you feel like burlap often,
but the shine in your fabric is from Me.
The material of which you are spun has My touch.
Believe that I live in Your heart.
Then you will walk tall.

**My soul:**

Daring One,
how can You risk so much with me?
You name me child of substance.
I feel my poverty.
I know my shallowness.
The rough edges of my being are like burlap!
You see deeper.
You know of what You've made me.
I am Your cloth. I trust in You!

### Esther 4:16, 5:1-2

¹⁶ *"Go, gather all the Jews to be found in Susa, and hold a fast on my behalf, and neither eat nor drink for three days, night or day. I and my maids will also fast as you do. After that I will go to the king, though it is against the law; and if I perish, I perish."*
¹ *On the third day Esther put on her royal robes and stood in the inner court of the king's palace, opposite the king's hall. The king was sitting on his royal throne inside the palace opposite the entrance to the palace. ² As soon as the king saw Queen Esther standing in the court, she won his favor and he held out to her the golden scepter that was in his hand. Then Esther approached and touched the top of the scepter.*

When do you feel like burlap and when are you satin?
What is God's risk with you?

# October

1. Cascade
2. Accumulation
3. Certainty
4. Magnet
5. Inclusive
6. Shimmer
7. Salmon
8. Stranded
9. Arc
10. Shadow
11. Disown
12. Twisted
13. Poison
14. Quilt
15. Wrinkle
16. Shore
17. Vibrations
18. Will
19. Confession
20. Swan
21. Sweet
22. Bitter
23. Tide Pools
24. Straddle
25. Orbit
26. Teakettle
27. Coffee
28. Sharpen
29. Cradle
30. Leaves
31. Face

# Cascade

**My soul:**

The cascade of my strongest hopes
rushes too quickly,
Beauty Maker.
I plunge in desperation,
not knowing the waterfalls
that You are creating of my life.
I am afraid.
Help me.

**God:**

Trust My shower of love,
anxious child.
I am opening windows to the world for you.
Your rainbow self descends,
catching My light.
Your music tumbles vibrations, tiny but mighty.
I am always for you.

**Romans 4:18-20**

*18 Hoping against hope, he believed that he would become "the father of many nations," according to what was said, "So numerous shall your descendants be." 19 He did not weaken in faith when he considered his own body, which was already as good as dead (for he was about a hundred years old), or when he considered the barrenness of Sarah's womb. 20 No distrust made him waver concerning the promise of God, but he grew strong in his faith as he gave glory to God.*

What waterfalls do you know in your life?
What windows on the world open in your descent?

# Accumulation

**God:**

Hoarding soul,
do all your accumulations net you peace?
"What does it profit to gain the whole world?"
Child after My own heart, live lightly in enough.
Let the increase of merits drift past like dust in the wind.
I know the value of your being.
I hold you in My hand.

**My soul:**

I store against a rainy day, God who holds my future.
All that I've collected, I've buried in storage sheds or I drag along.
Who needs this extra load? Where can I lay it down?
How can I dance unburdened? I am walking to a new life.
I am companioned by those who wear my treasures.
I am the coral reef growing beauty, unmarred and natural.

**Luke 12:13-21**

¹³ *Someone in the crowd said to him, "Teacher, tell my brother to divide the family inheritance with me."* ¹⁴ *But he said to him, "Friend, who set me to be a judge or arbitrator over you?"* ¹⁵ *And he said to them, "Take care! Be on your guard against all kinds of greed; for one's life does not consist in the abundance of possessions."* ¹⁶ *Then he told them a parable: "The land of a rich man produced abundantly.* ¹⁷ *And he thought to himself, 'What should I do, for I have no place to store my crops?'* ¹⁸ *Then he said, 'I will do this: I will pull down my barns and build larger ones, and there I will store all my grain and my goods.* ¹⁹ *And I will say to my soul, Soul, you have ample goods laid up for many years; relax, eat, drink, be merry.'* ²⁰ *But God said to him, 'You fool! This very night your life is being demanded of you. And the things you have prepared, whose will they be?'* ²¹ *So it is with those who store up treasures for themselves but are not rich toward God."*

How do you live with enough?
What are the spiritual merits you hoard?

# Certainty

**My soul:**

Solid Rock,
in You is a call to stand firm.
Then the fog closes in,
and I am feeling my way with no certainty.
All my sureness fades.
Where do I place reliance? What lasts?
What is my way to live?
I fumble out of my cocksureness.
Steady me, though I question
and hunger for assurance.
Let me remember, I am here because
You are here.

**God:**

I know your world flexes and changes,
quicker than the fireflies flicker,
slower than the moon's waxing and waning.
I hear your heartbeat, child of My making.
To gain equilibrium, grab My truth.
Let love be your north star.
In times of dead wind, wait.
I am near.

**Mark 12:28-31**

*²⁸ One of the scribes came near and heard them disputing with one another, and seeing that he answered them well, he asked him, "Which commandment is the first of all?" ²⁹ Jesus answered, "The first is, 'Hear, O Israel: the Lord our God, the Lord is one; ³⁰ you shall love the Lord your God with all your heart, and with all your soul, and with all your mind, and with all your strength.' ³¹ The second is this, 'You shall love your neighbor as yourself.' There is no other commandment greater than these."*

How is your certainty rock solid in knowing, "I am here because You are
here"?
In what truth of God do you gain equilibrium?

287

# Magnet

**God:**

How do I get you to pay attention?
Day by day, I invite you, little lamb.
Listen.
Open your eyes and ears; I am waiting.
Let your heart be drawn by My magnetic pull.
Notice distractions, addictions,
comparisons that scatter your life force.
I see you and carry you home.

**My soul:**

Shepherd of my soul,
tend the holy in me.
Attract me to stand erect.
Open my heart to notice Your presence everywhere.
Let Your Goodness, beauty, and truth catch my heart.
I want to see You.
Please, do carry me home.

**John 10:1-5**

¹ *"Very truly, I tell you, anyone who does not enter the sheepfold by the gate but climbs in by another way is a thief and a bandit.* ² *The one who enters by the gate is the shepherd of the sheep.* ³ *The gatekeeper opens the gate for him, and the sheep hear his voice. He calls his own sheep by name and leads them out.* ⁴ *When he has brought out all his own, he goes ahead of them, and the sheep follow him because they know his voice.* ⁵ *They will not follow a stranger, but they will run from him because they do not know the voice of strangers."*

Where does God catch your attention?
What does it mean in your life to be carried home?

# Inclusive

**God:**

I dream.
Can you imagine with Me all that is one?
Include along your way the weary and outcast,
the lame and the deaf, the poor and the voiceless.
Can you hammer swords into plowshares?
It means you'll sweat. It means the loudness of conflict will come.
It means you will be misunderstood and labeled.
My tent is very wide. Come set our family feast.

**My soul:**

Parent God, break open Your dream in my life.
I love family gatherings where all are delighted to be there.
Let me feel Your energy of joy so all can feast on the fatted calf.
Let me prepare my cloak for Your celebration.
Under Your tent, gather your Kingdom, God of the big heart.

### Luke 15:25-32

[25] "*Now his elder son was in the field; and when he came and approached the house, he heard music and dancing.* [26] *He called one of the slaves and asked what was going on.* [27] *He replied, 'Your brother has come, and your father has killed the fatted calf, because he has got him back safe and sound.'* [28] *Then he became angry and refused to go in. His father came out and began to plead with him.* [29] *But he answered his father, 'Listen! For all these years I have been working like a slave for you, and I have never disobeyed your command; yet you have never given me even a young goat so that I might celebrate with my friends.* [30] *But when this son of yours came back, who has devoured your property with prostitutes, you killed the fatted calf for him!'* [31] *Then the father said to him, 'Son, you are always with me, and all that is mine is yours.* [32] *But we had to celebrate and rejoice, because this brother of yours was dead and has come to life; he was lost and has been found.'"*

Who needs inclusion in your life?
How are you to prepare your cloak for the celebration?

# Shimmer

**God:**

I invite you to shimmer,
My gleam of light.
Become the light vibration
that breathes life.
So many fear the dying.
Spirit child, shine with My enduring light.
Reflect My goodness.
Smile My greeting.
Our world so longs for the
lantern of home in the darkness.

**My soul:**

Explosion of Light,
so bright to be blinding,
I choose to open the ocean of my life to You.
Play in the waves of my soul.
Let Your beam in me make a pathway home.
I feel so beautiful in Your light.

**1 John 1:5-7**

*⁵ This is the message we have heard from him and proclaim to you, that God is light and in him there is no darkness at all. ⁶ If we say that we have fellowship with him while we are walking in darkness, we lie and do not do what is true; ⁷ but if we walk in the light as he himself is in the light, we have fellowship with one another, and the blood of Jesus his Son cleanses us from all sin.*

How do you shimmer?
How do you choose to open your life to God?

# Salmon

**God:**

Curious watcher,
have you noticed my salmon climb,
jump, dash against the rush of water?
Upstream is their destiny against the tide.
Yours is too!
I have created you for great things.
Amidst floods and winds and earthquakes,
I invite you to flourish.
I have loved you, my heart-child,
with an imperishable love.

**My soul:**

What an oddity, Your salmon,
Fountain of Life!
Teach me to play, to love, to hope that I also gush forth,
overflowing with life.
I must travel lightly.
I journey with my family.
I see the goal despite exhaustion and impossibility.
It is home!

**Mark 6:7-9**

*⁷ He called the twelve and began to send them out two by two, and gave them authority over the unclean spirits. ⁸ He ordered them to take nothing for their journey except a staff; no bread, no bag, no money in their belts; ⁹ but to wear sandals and not to put on two tunics.*

What great things are you created for?
How do storms strip you to travel lightly?

## Stranded

**My soul:**

Invisible One, where are You?
I am stranded, left behind.
Dressed in my gray hair,
I limp along with my treasures.
No one wants them. No one even sees them.
Cut off from the flow of ordinary,
I watch monarchs and birds
and wonder that I never noticed before.
Have You also abandoned me
amid aches and pains?
I am bereft of all my comfort patterns.
Mercy, please!

**God:**

Lonely soul,
I know you feel marooned. I ache with you.
To leave the meaning and the distraction
is a soul stripping that tears your roots.
It is the process of life.
Learn from the cheetah cat.
Soul speed and beauty spots emerge.
See Me.
I will not abandon you.

**Isaiah 54:7-8**

*7 For a brief moment I abandoned you, but with great compassion I will gather you. 8 In overflowing wrath for a moment I hid my face from you, but with everlasting love I will have compassion on you, says the Lord, your Redeemer.*

What treasures have you amassed?
What meaning and distraction must you leave behind?

## Arc

**God:**

Beginner again,
didn't I do amazing work with rainbows?
It is some of My best work, if I must say so Myself.
After the storm, freshness comes
with color and an arc of hope.
Listen to its heart-message.
The layers of living unlock how
I walk with you always.

**My soul:**

Awesome Companion,
in the downpours, I need You.
I can't see where I am going.
Then, wow, what a surprise!
You know the legends speak to the pot of gold at the end.
I think it is You,
Treasure who shows Your face,
Traveler who leads me on,
Promise who always fulfills.
Come skip with me.
It is a fresh day.

**Genesis 9:12-13**

*¹² God said, "This is the sign of the covenant that I make between me and you and every living creature that is with you, for all future generations: ¹³ I have set my bow in the clouds, and it shall be a sign of the covenant between me and the earth."*

What heart message do you experience in the rainbow?
In what ways can you not see where you are going right now?

# Shadow

**My soul:**

Poet God,
I saw my shadow today.
You are my Sun and Moon.
You are my ever-abiding Presence.
I am here because You are here.
You are no ghost or phantasm.
You who are real make me real.
May there come a time
when I am transparent with Your light.
Meanwhile, may this shade-self be my refuge
when I cannot bear Your brightness.

**God:**

Evolving person,
when you catch a glimpse of your shadow,
know I am near.
I can move in your growing.
In My wide wonderful world,
do not be afraid.
Pray with your shadow. I do!
When it is dark and enveloping and alien,
I am near.
Confront what feels like your alien
with embrace.
My energy can then penetrate.

**John 1:1-5**

*¹ In the beginning was the Word, and the Word was with God, and the Word was God. ² He was in the beginning with God. ³ All things came into being through him, and without him not one thing came into being. What has come into being ⁴ in him was life, and the life was the light of all people. ⁵ The light shines in the darkness, and the darkness did not overcome it.*

When do you run to the shade because the Light is too bright to bear?
How do you play in your shadow?

# Disown

**My soul:**

Parent God,
nothing scares me more than Your words, "I do not know you."
Even though I've eaten at Your table,
walked with Your company of friends, gone fishing for your people…
please, do not deny I belong. I want to come with a lamp full of oil.
You are too big to know. I dabble around lazily and give up the search.
Save me, Immense One, from myself.

**God:**

Wild child, I do not take back My choice to make you.
Open your heart to know Me. You carry My imprint within you.
Set aside seeing your own way.
Let the truth of your creaturehood defy using others.
I will fill you; just surrender.

**Matthew 25:1-12**

¹ "Then the kingdom of heaven will be like this. Ten bridesmaids took their lamps and went to meet the bridegroom. ² Five of them were foolish, and five were wise. ³ When the foolish took their lamps, they took no oil with them; ⁴ but the wise took flasks of oil with their lamps. ⁵ As the bridegroom was delayed, all of them became drowsy and slept. ⁶ But at midnight there was a shout, 'Look! Here is the bridegroom! Come out to meet him.' ⁷ Then all those bridesmaids got up and trimmed their lamps. ⁸ The foolish said to the wise, 'Give us some of your oil, for our lamps are going out.' ⁹ But the wise replied, 'No! There will not be enough for you and for us; you had better go to the dealers and buy some for yourselves.' ¹⁰ And while they went to buy it, the bridegroom came, and those who were ready went with him into the wedding banquet; and the door was shut. ¹¹ Later the other bridesmaids came also, saying, 'Lord, lord, open to us.' ¹² But he replied, 'Truly I tell you, I do not know you.'"

Where are you dabbling lazily in knowing God?
How do you use others?

# Twisted

**God:**

The trunk of the ponderosa pine is twisted.
Wind and sand have carved their beauty.
May your journey's twists and turns
not distort your heart, child of My longing.
May your green umbrella open wide and strong—
needles lush enough to form a shade for desert roamers.
You are my sentinel, the watcher for My dawn.

**My soul:**

Shaper of my soul, I trust Your art—aged wood,
barren landscape, needles—and thirst stretches out inside me.
I watch across the drifting sands for Your coming.
As day breaks, I see Your plodding.
I see Your coming.
You are shrouded in disguise against the sun and wind.
I welcome You to my tent.

**Ruth 1:15-18**

¹⁵ *So she said, "See, your sister-in-law has gone back to her people and to her gods; return after your sister-in-law."* ¹⁶ *But Ruth said, "Do not press me to leave you or to turn back from following you! Where you go, I will go; where you lodge, I will lodge; your people shall be my people, and your God my God.* ¹⁷ *Where you die, I will die—there will I be buried. May the Lord do thus and so to me, and more as well if even death parts me from you!"* ¹⁸ *When Naomi saw that she was determined to go with her, she said no more to her.*

How do your life's twists and turns shape beauty in your life?
How is God coming to you shrouded in disguise?

## Poison

**My soul:**

Healer God,
I've walked among poison ivy with no antidote.
Is the earth no safe place for me?
Is the rash a sign that I do not belong?
Is the itch only a signal that
my addictions absorb and possess?
Mercy, I beg, from Your great bounty!

**God:**

Your soul is Mine, scarred one!
Yes, you react to a world of poisons.
Come, let Me soothe and heal.

### Matthew 23:27-28

*²⁷ Woe to you, scribes and Pharisees, hypocrites! For you are like whitewashed tombs, which on the outside look beautiful, but inside they are full of the bones of the dead and of all kinds of filth. ²⁸ So you also on the outside look righteous to others, but inside you are full of hypocrisy and lawlessness.*

What skin boundary holds your soul safe from toxins?
What possesses your attention like an itch?

## Quilt

**My soul:**

Designing God,
I've taken to doing a quilt.
I'm gathering remnants from my life.
It is a patchwork
pieced of many colors.
Bring beauty of its craziness.
Make endurance of its threads.
Carry Your warmth to all who rest beneath.
I dream of Your Kingdom.

**God:**

Sometimes My Kingdom feels like a dream.
On the slow evolving gathering of humankind, I cast My lot.
Know I shape the patterns.
I build your resilience.
My warmth is sewn into your labors.
You will find rest for your soul.

**2 Samuel 7:10-11**

¹⁰ *And I will appoint a place for my people Israel and will plant them, so that they may live in their own place, and be disturbed no more; and evildoers shall afflict them no more, as formerly,* ¹¹ *from the time that I appointed judges over my people Israel; and I will give you rest from all your enemies. Moreover the Lord declares to you that the Lord will make you a house.*

What remnants are in your quilt?
How is God building resilience in your quilt of life?

# Wrinkle

**My soul:**

Ancient Energy,
I'm noticing wrinkles.
I also feel a slowdown
where my soul gathers in folds.
Crow's feet are appearing.
The seam of my life flow is furrowing.
May I deepen in the resting.
May I live with the freedom of the surfer.
May I trust Your steady faithfulness.

**God:**

Beauty is in the surrender, graced one.
I pulse with heart lines, laugh lines, and love lines.
Erase your frown lines in attention.
I am with you.

**1 Samuel 16:6-7, 11-12**

⁶ *When they came, he looked on Eliab and thought, "Surely the Lord's anointed is now before the Lord." ⁷ But the Lord said to Samuel, "Do not look on his appearance or on the height of his stature, because I have rejected him; for the Lord does not see as mortals see; they look on the outward appearance, but the Lord looks on the heart." ¹¹ Samuel said to Jesse, "Are all your sons here?" And he said, "There remains yet the youngest, but he is keeping the sheep." And Samuel said to Jesse, "Send and bring him; for we will not sit down until he comes here." ¹² He sent and brought him in. Now he was ruddy, and had beautiful eyes, and was handsome. The Lord said, "Rise and anoint him; for this is the one."*

How is your soul gathering in folds?
How is your attention erasing frown lines?

## Shore

**God:**

Sailor of life,
do you see My shore?
Are you lured by the music of those who plot your ruin?
The beach of My Kingdom is not far.
Its strand reaches out to you.
Come play in My sand.
I watch you over the brim of My world.

**My soul:**

Sea-surfer God,
I am always on the brink.
I play in the waves,
unaware of riptides and sharks
or, sometimes on the edge of
my consciousness, daring them.
I do not want You merely on the margins of my living.
Let me know Your shore.
Let me be immersed in Your wave, Presence.

**Mark 4:35-41**

*³⁵ On that day, when evening had come, he said to them, "Let us go across to the other side." ³⁶ And leaving the crowd behind, they took him with them in the boat, just as he was. Other boats were with him. ³⁷ A great windstorm arose, and the waves beat into the boat, so that the boat was already being swamped. ³⁸ But he was in the stern, asleep on the cushion; and they woke him up and said to him, "Teacher, do you not care that we are perishing?" ³⁹ He woke up and rebuked the wind, and said to the sea, "Peace! Be still!" Then the wind ceased, and there was a dead calm. ⁴⁰ He said to them, "Why are you afraid? Have you still no faith?" ⁴¹ And they were filled with great awe and said to one another, "Who then is this, that even the wind and the sea obey him?"*

How do you see the strand of God's Kingdom reaching out to you?
Where are you letting the siren call of riptides and sharks tease you?

# Vibrations

**God:**

Did you notice how My great explosion of love
has saturated your world with music?
In the pause—the quivering expectation—bursts
the drum beat in caverns,
the swish of ocean shells,
the melody of bird song,
your heart's steady life call!
In the ebb and flow, I hide and invite.

**My soul:**

Do You speak in the rustle of autumn leaves?
Do the reed's holes scale Your hopes?
What vibrations draw my choice to You
in exhilarating awe?
I bow to the music of Your presence.
I feel You as close as my essence.
Let me attend to You, my God and my All.

**Luke 6:6-10**

*⁶ On another Sabbath he entered the synagogue and taught, and there was a man there whose right hand was withered. ⁷ The scribes and the Pharisees watched him to see whether he would cure on the Sabbath, so that they might find an accusation against him. ⁸ Even though he knew what they were thinking, he said to the man who had the withered hand, "Come and stand here." He got up and stood there. ⁹ Then Jesus said to them, "I ask you, is it lawful to do good or to do harm on the Sabbath, to save life or to destroy it?" ¹⁰ After looking around at all of them, he said to him, "Stretch out your hand." He did so, and his hand was restored.*

How does your withered hand hear life's music to become whole?
What ebb and flow moves your life with constancy?

# Will

**My soul:**

God from whom all things flow,
my will is dull today.
To choose is to be most like You,
yet I slack in lethargy!
Simply, I am lazy.
Today, give me a push.
My intention from the couch is fierce desire.

**God:**

Weary will, catch My wind and rise.
I share with you consent.
I lift you in this moment from all that tethers you.
Keep your eyes on Me.
With magnetic force, you will find assent.
See Me and let My love raise you up.
It is My determination, My desire, that you choose.

**Joshua 24:14-15**

¹⁴ *"Now therefore revere the Lord, and serve him in sincerity and in faithfulness; put away the gods that your ancestors served beyond the River and in Egypt, and serve the Lord.* ¹⁵ *Now if you are unwilling to serve the Lord, choose this day whom you will serve, whether the gods your ancestors served in the region beyond the River or the gods of the Amorites in whose land you are living; but as for me and my household, we will serve the Lord."*

Where is your will dull today?
What lift do you experience that convinces you God gives you choice?

# Confession

**My soul:**

I come to You, Life Source,
with this confession.
You are God and I am not.
In my arrogance, I want to control.
In my self-absorption, I neglect to hear You.
In my laziness, I dawdle and indulge.
I confess my need of You.
I surrender my pretense to be more.
I depend totally on Your mercy.

**God:**

Wayward wanderer,
come to Me for rest.
Let Me put you to My shoulder,
clear the brambles from your hair,
wipe the tears and smudges from your face.
You are not alone; I am here.
I cover you with My cloak
to warm and claim you once again.
You are Mine and I love you.

**Isaiah 43:1-4**

*¹ But now thus says the Lord, he who created you, O Jacob, he who formed you, O Israel: Do not fear, for I have redeemed you; I have called you by name, you are mine. ² When you pass through the waters, I will be with you; and through the rivers, they shall not overwhelm you; when you walk through fire you shall not be burned, and the flame shall not consume you. ³ For I am the Lord your God, the Holy One of Israel, your Savior. I give Egypt as your ransom, Ethiopia and Seba in exchange for you. ⁴ Because you are precious in my sight, and honored, and I love you, I give people in return for you, nations in exchange for your life.*

What do you need to confess?
How do you experience being gathered in God's cloak?

## Swan

**God:**

Growing soul,
I know your pure potential.
Like a swan, ugliness can bloom to beauty.
Your land-bound clumsiness can blossom grace.
Your ferocious meanness can be protective.
I trust our partnership.
May your nesting near water be healed in all My ebb and flow.

**My soul:**

Elegant Eternal One,
enter my circling wagons of time and nesting.
You are my fluidity.
You are my balance.
When I migrate, You are my direction.
Glide with me in Your serene constancy.

**Philippians 1:3-11**

*³ I thank my God every time I remember you, ⁴ constantly praying with joy in every one of my prayers for all of you, ⁵ because of your sharing in the gospel from the first day until now. ⁶ I am confident of this, that the one who began a good work among you will bring it to completion by the day of Jesus Christ. ⁷ It is right for me to think this way about all of you, because you hold me in your heart, for all of you share in God's grace with me, both in my imprisonment and in the defense and confirmation of the gospel. ⁸ For God is my witness, how I long for all of you with the compassion of Christ Jesus. ⁹ And this is my prayer, that your love may overflow more and more with knowledge and full insight ¹⁰ to help you to determine what is best, so that in the day of Christ you may be pure and blameless, ¹¹ having produced the harvest of righteousness that comes through Jesus Christ for the glory and praise of God.*

What does pure potential look like to you?
How are you circling your wagons?

## Sweet

**My soul:**

My sweet Lord,
as honey in the comb,
let me taste Your goodness.
As harmony among angels' songs,
let my soul be refreshed in peace.
As fragrance of Your flowers,
let my senses rest in You.
Find within me Your own image of truth.
I long to know Your nearness.

**God:**

Come to Me, tiny child of sweetness.
I long to nurture your life with delicacies.
Drink deeply of My juice,
for I am with you.
Cast out all bitterness.
Let what would sour ferment.
Be enveloped by the freshness of My love.

**Exodus 3:7-8**

*⁷ Then the Lord said, "I have observed the misery of my people who are in Egypt; I have heard their cry on account of their taskmasters. Indeed, I know their sufferings, ⁸ and I have come down to deliver them from the Egyptians, and to bring them up out of that land to a good and broad land, a land flowing with milk and honey, to the country of the Canaanites, the Hittites, the Amorites, the Perizzites, the Hivites, and the Jebusites."*

How does God find sweetness in you?
When do you drink deeply of God's juice?

# Bitter

**My soul:**

God of the wind,
soften my spirit from bitterness.
Let the caustic comments sift out of my expectations to gentleness.
May all that is distasteful be endured for the wider purpose.
I give You, God of Siftings, my stuck mind's resentments and cynicism.
Let good seed be scattered and grow.

**God:**

Child of inner sores,
remember I healed lepers.
I can take what bites and blisters in your heart.
Let it go.
My wind will give it lift and wholeness.
I know your power to hurt.
I believe in your gift to raise up.
Trust Me to work My miracles.

**Matthew 5:38-42**

³⁸ *"You have heard that it was said, 'An eye for an eye and a tooth for a tooth.' ³⁹ But I say to you, Do not resist an evildoer. But if anyone strikes you on the right cheek, turn the other also; ⁴⁰ and if anyone wants to sue you and take your coat, give your cloak as well; ⁴¹ and if anyone forces you to go one mile, go also the second mile. ⁴² Give to everyone who begs from you, and do not refuse anyone who wants to borrow from you."*

How do your expectations harden into bitterness when not met?
What bites and blisters in your heart?

# Tide Pools

**God:**

Come to My marsh, explorer child.
Tide pools wait for frogs and egrets.
Here in the muddy flats, you can find mussels.
This is a bayou to silence your soul.
I can speak truth here as you wade the shallows.
I can send sun here to dry a pathway.
I can alert your spirit to danger.
Alligators wait in lagoons of lassitude.

**My soul:**

God of the wetland's music, come with Me.
It is fearsome here where reptiles breed. I lean on Your daring!
Under Spanish moss, I peer for Your surprises and Your warnings.
Why do You lead me here to such tangled truth?
On this shoal of rest, how do I surrender
my cautious absorption and distraction?
As I wander, lead the way.

**2 Chronicles 32:5-8**

⁵ *Hezekiah set to work resolutely and built up the entire wall that was broken down, and raised towers on it, and outside it he built another wall; he also strengthened the Millo in the city of David, and made weapons and shields in abundance. ⁶ He appointed combat commanders over the people, and gathered them together to him in the square at the gate of the city and spoke encouragingly to them, saying, ⁷ "Be strong and of good courage. Do not be afraid or dismayed before the king of Assyria and all the horde that is with him; for there is one greater with us than with him. ⁸ With him is an arm of flesh; but with us is the Lord our God, to help us and to fight our battles." The people were encouraged by the words of King Hezekiah of Judah.*

How does God speak truth to you in the shallows where you wade?
Where are you leaning on God's daring?

# Straddle

**God:**

Ambivalent one,
are you straddling My pathway?
Do you choose the lukewarm perch of neither here nor there?
It gives you no momentum.
It paralyzes passion.
It is spread-eagle life defeat.
Come, climb on My wings and fly.
Let the energy of My choice of you bring forth a resounding yes!
Believe with your whole heart.

**My soul:**

God, my Eagle Perch,
I sit astride Your mighty calling. I feel You lift.
I savor the height's perspective
of motion and grace above the fray.
When I'm back on the ground, keep my eyes strong.
Bolster my faith from the wishy-washy.
I want the span of my life
measured by Your vision.
I choose to live with fierce commitment.
I have seen Your holy mountain.

**Revelations 3:15-19**

*[15] "I know your works; you are neither cold nor hot. I wish that you were either cold or hot. [16] So, because you are lukewarm, and neither cold nor hot, I am about to spit you out of my mouth. [17] For you say, 'I am rich, I have prospered, and I need nothing.' You do not realize that you are wretched, pitiable, poor, blind, and naked. [18] Therefore I counsel you to buy from me gold refined by fire so that you may be rich; and white robes to clothe you and to keep the shame of your nakedness from being seen; and salve to anoint your eyes so that you may see. [19] I reprove and discipline those whom I love. Be earnest, therefore, and repent."*

Where in your life are you straddling?
How is the breadth of your life measured by God's vision?

# Orbit

**God:**

I want you in My orbit, child of My own.
May your reach be coming closer.
I long to fold you in My arms.
May your circle be in My pathway.
I want you to know Me.
May My energy be as lightning to your soul.
I want to stir your life with strength.
I want to encompass your heart with caring.
I want to give your eye the truth of responsibility.

**My soul:**

God of universe orbits,
hold me in Your sacred realm.
May the range of my orbits be always near You.
Magnetic God, lure my heart to You.
Circle me round with Your unconditional love.
May the sparks of Your passion
transform my life.
I am Yours.

**Exodus 6:6-7**

*⁶ Say therefore to the Israelites, 'I am the Lord, and I will free you from the burdens of the Egyptians and deliver you from slavery to them. I will redeem you with an outstretched arm and with mighty acts of judgment. ⁷ I will take you as my people, and I will be your God. You shall know that I am the Lord your God, who has freed you from the burdens of the Egyptians."*

How is God's energy like lightning to your soul?
How do the sparks of God's passion transform your life?

## Teakettle

**My soul:**

My soul's Guest,
come for tea today.
Let me put the teakettle on
to heat the tea.
Steep my life to serve.
I yearn to share my heart with You.
Out of the tealeaves of my musings,
hear my love and joy, my pain and longing,
my learnings and curiosities.
I serve You, Lord of my life,
the jasmine tea of my days.

**God:**

Ah, what refreshment, to be so welcomed, servant of My creating.
Together, let us share your tea.
Will you listen to My dreams for you?
Will you know the ache I feel for your brothers and sisters?
Will you laugh with Me on the ironies of giraffes' long necks
and zebras' stripes?
Together, we shall shape life.
Oh, and I love jasmine tea!

**John 12:1-2**

*¹ Six days before the Passover Jesus came to Bethany, the home of Lazarus, whom he had raised from the dead. ² There they gave a dinner for him. Martha served, and Lazarus was one of those at the table with him.*

What tealeaves of your musings would you share with God?
How are you and God shaping life?

## Coffee

**My soul:**

May I serve you morning coffee, my Lord?
It is my wake-up brew that gets my morning going.
The sun comes up.
I do my stretches.
I empty my mind to come to Your rhythm.
I want to be "woke,"
dear One for whom I live.
I put my energy at Your disposal.

**God:**

Isn't morning marvelous?
Freshly awakened child,
come meet a new day.
Drink your morning magic with Me.
Your earth needs your love today.
Go and make your mark.
Notice. Be awake all day.
Brim full of gratefulness; see your brothers and sisters.
Today with coffee, you begin family.
My table comes to fullness.

**Philippians 2:5-11**

*⁵ Let the same mind be in you that was in Christ Jesus, ⁶ who, though he was in the form of God, did not regard equality with God as something to be exploited, ⁷ but emptied himself, taking the form of a slave, being born in human likeness. And being found in human form, ⁸ he humbled himself and became obedient to the point of death—even death on a cross. ⁹ Therefore God also highly exalted him and gave him the name that is above every name, ¹⁰ so that at the name of Jesus every knee should bend, in heaven and on earth and under the earth, ¹¹ and every tongue should confess that Jesus Christ is Lord, to the glory of God the Father.*

What do you experience of being "woke"?
What can you do to fill God's table?

## Sharpen

**God:**

Foggy child,
sharpen your vision of what lasts.
Let the point of your being here come into your awareness.
Raise the pitch of your music
to the clarity of kindness.
I know you are in training.
The edges of your living are so ragged.
Come, rest and learn from Me.

**My soul:**

God of crisp knowing,
bend me to the changes needed
so I can follow You.
Hone my love to unselfishness.
In freedom, I bring my messy life before You.
Transform my choices to serve.
Lift my laughter to mercy and truth.
I am so small.
I am confused and drifting.
On You I lean, Sculptor of my becoming.

### Jeremiah 18:2-6

² *"Come, go down to the potter's house, and there I will let you hear my words."* ³ *So I went down to the potter's house, and there he was working at his wheel.* ⁴ *The vessel he was making of clay was spoiled in the potter's hand, and he reworked it into another vessel, as seemed good to him.* ⁵ *Then the word of the Lord came to me:* ⁶ *Can I not do with you, O house of Israel, just as this potter has done? says the Lord. Just like the clay in the potter's hand, so are you in my hand, O house of Israel.*

How is your vision of what lasts foggy?
When does your laughter lift to mercy and truth?

## Cradle

**God:**

Little one,
I long to cradle you in My arms.
I want to see you growing and celebrate.
Know that I nurture you,
watch your discoveries,
discipline your edge-walking,
raise you up to see stars and eagles.
Receive My parenting.
I see My image in you.

**My soul:**

Parent God,
hold me close to Your heart.
In my infant stage, imprint trust on me.
Rock away my fears.
Take my hand and lead me to care as You do…
for ants and minnows,
for tears and wrinkles,
for those last picked and for braggarts.
May the birthplace of my longings always seek Your way.

**Luke 11:11-13**

*¹¹ Is there anyone among you who, if your child asks for a fish, will give a snake instead of a fish? ¹² Or if the child asks for an egg, will give a scorpion? ¹³ If you then, who are evil, know how to give good gifts to your children, how much more will the heavenly Father give the Holy Spirit to those who ask him!*

Where is God catching you at the edge of safety?
Where is it difficult for you to care as God does?

# Leaves

**My soul:**

Amazing Master of color, I walk in your greenery.
Leaves are vibrant in shades and shadows.
At my feet are blades of Your wonder.
High in the sky wave fronds of glory.
Dandelion greens and parsley taste of your flavor.
Basil and clover smell of Your aura.
Open my heart in happy summer.
Come walk with me, my God.

**God:**

Don't you just love green?
Sequoias and aspen claim My art.
Wondering learner, I revel in turning deserts to green.
Lush and blooming, I reclaim what is Mine.
And you can help! Plant trees. Grow alfalfa.
Stretch along the water's edge with papyrus and willows.
Let your heart sing.

## Exodus 2:1-6

*¹ Now a man from the house of Levi went and married a Levite woman. ² The woman conceived and bore a son; and when she saw that he was a fine baby, she hid him three months. ³ When she could hide him no longer she got a papyrus basket for him, and plastered it with bitumen and pitch; she put the child in it and placed it among the reeds on the bank of the river. ⁴ His sister stood at a distance, to see what would happen to him. ⁵ The daughter of Pharaoh came down to bathe at the river, while her attendants walked beside the river. She saw the basket among the reeds and sent her maid to bring it. ⁶ When she opened it, she saw the child. He was crying, and she took pity on him. "This must be one of the Hebrews' children," she said.*

What calls you to walk with God?
What do you discover hidden among your reeds?

# Face

**My soul:**

Unseen God,
how often I've prayed,
"I long to see Your face."
Even Moses knew Your burning light
and took off his shoes.
Elijah hid as You passed by.
How dare I?
What if Your gaze is of stony indifference?
And you say, "I do not know you!"
I am afraid!

**God:**

Prodigal one,
I wait at the roadside.
Denier, I fix breakfast at lakeside.
Doubter, put your hands into My wounded hands.
Keep praying your heart.
We share the ache of longing.
Be not afraid.

**Revelations 4:1, 9-11**

¹ *After this I looked, and there in heaven a door stood open! And the first voice, which I had heard speaking to me like a trumpet, said, "Come up here, and I will show you what must take place after this."* ⁹ *And whenever the living creatures give glory and honor and thanks to the one who is seated on the throne, who lives forever and ever,* ¹⁰ *the twenty-four elders fall before the one who is seated on the throne and worship the one who lives forever and ever; they cast their crowns before the throne, singing,* ¹¹ *"You are worthy, our Lord and God, to receive glory and honor and power, for you created all things, and by your will they existed and were created."*

How do you see God's face?
What is your ache of longing?

# November

1. Raining
2. Barbed Wire
3. Difficult
4. Taste
5. Filigree
6. Sleepiness
7. Doubt
8. Bees
9. Glow
10. Field of Light
11. Leaps
12. Ecstasy
13. Cruelty
14. Weeds
15. Marooned
16. Crunch
17. Veil
18. Barely
19. Carpet
20. Bunting
21. Kingfisher
22. Loose
23. Concert
24. Scuffed
25. Sandals
26. Keeper
27. Grass
28. Roar
29. Reek
30. Switchback

## November 1

# Raining

**My soul:**

God Overflowing, it is raining.
Your torrents soak me to the bone and I am chilled.
Is it only in the downpour
that I become alert to survival?
Wash me clean.
In the cloudburst, pelt me awake!
Here in Your mighty expanse,
I will pay attention.

**God:**

Drenched child,
let's take shelter in your heart,
where love embraces and makes Me one with you.
Come and let Me dry you.
As fresh water showers your earth,
run with Me in the rain.
Let all that is wet and wild
laugh in our play.

**Isaiah 1:16-17**

[16] *Wash yourselves; make yourselves clean; remove the evil of your doings from before my eyes; cease to do evil,* [17] *learn to do good; seek justice, rescue the oppressed, defend the orphan, plead for the widow.*

What downpours come in your life that alert you to survive?
How do you run in the rain with your God and know it as play?

## Barbed Wire

**My soul:**

God of the open heart,
I have barbed wire around my soul.
It is strung with all the spikes that
life has speared of disappointment.
I am lonely!
Fenced in, I push away joy.
Come, clip an opening and let in cavorting.
I welcome You, Insistent One!

**God:**

Imprisoned creature,
how to untangle all that binds?
I do it gently.
Watch Me free you.
Keep your eyes on Me.
What feels impossible, I can undo.
Yes, I am persistent,
because "you are precious and I love you."

**Isaiah 43:4, 10-13**

*⁴ Because you are precious in my sight, and honored, and I love you, I give people in return for you, nations in exchange for your life. ¹⁰ You are my witnesses, says the Lord, and my servant whom I have chosen, so that you may know and believe me and understand that I am he. Before me no god was formed, nor shall there be any after me. ¹¹ I, I am the Lord, and besides me there is no savior. ¹² I declared and saved and proclaimed, when there was no strange god among you; and you are my witnesses, says the Lord. ¹³ I am God, and also henceforth I am He; there is no one who can deliver from my hand; I work and who can hinder it?*

Where does disappointment imprison you?
How is God gently untangling what binds you?

# Difficult

**My soul:**

Strong One,
this breaking open of new horizons is difficult for me.
My soul is filled with shadows,
and I am afraid.
Can I endure the pain?
Do I comprehend Your mystery?
What is it all about, God of my longing?
Please be my Friend!

**God:**

I know what I ask of you is not easy, little one.
I am with you.
I have placed in your spirit
mighty resilience.
What it is all about is simple:
I love you.
I send you to love the strangers along the way.

**Mark 6:47-52**

*⁴⁷ When evening came, the boat was out on the sea, and he was alone on the land. ⁴⁸ When he saw that they were straining at the oars against an adverse wind, he came towards them early in the morning, walking on the sea. He intended to pass them by. ⁴⁹ But when they saw him walking on the sea, they thought it was a ghost and cried out; ⁵⁰ for they all saw him and were terrified. But immediately he spoke to them and said, "Take heart, it is I; do not be afraid." ⁵¹ Then he got into the boat with them and the wind ceased. And they were utterly astounded, ⁵² for they did not understand about the loaves, but their hearts were hardened.*

What difficult new horizons must you meet?
Where do you meet strangers along the way?

## Taste

**God:**

Hungry one,
refine your taste of Me.
Deep in your soul, I flavor you.
What you relish of nourishment—
juicy foods, rich wines, sweet confections—
are all passing.
But always, I invite you to know Me.
Come and savor My presence.

**My soul:**

My God and my All,
You are the manna and the meat of my days.
Feed my hungry soul.
Let me listen with the cravings
of my being to how You satisfy.
I taste You, God of my origin.

### John 6:48-51

*⁴⁸ I am the bread of life. ⁴⁹ Your ancestors ate the manna in the wilderness, and they died. ⁵⁰ This is the bread that comes down from heaven, so that one may eat of it and not die. ⁵¹ I am the living bread that came down from heaven. Whoever eats of this bread will live forever; and the bread that I will give for the life of the world is my flesh.*

How do you experience your taste of God?
In what ways is God feeding Your soul?

# Filigree

**My soul:**

Attentive God, my soul is Your crafted filigree.
Delicate and fragile, I walk my days of twists and turns.
I do not see their patterns.
Like veins in leaves,
like coral reefs,
like my body's weave of bone and blood,
of muscles and nerves,
all is Your handiwork.
May I be attentive to You,
God of my shaping, as You are to me.

**God:**

Beautiful one,
I know you.
I know how I made you.
Together you and I are forming your life,
the fine art of fierce courage,
of faithful love, of intricate soul seeing.
Receive the intimacy of co-creating.

**2 Corinthians 5:1-5**

*[1] For we know that if the earthly tent we live in is destroyed, we have a building from God, a house not made with hands, eternal in the heavens. [2] For in this tent we groan, longing to be clothed with our heavenly dwelling— [3] if indeed, when we have taken it off we will not be found naked. [4] For while we are still in this tent, we groan under our burden, because we wish not to be unclothed but to be further clothed, so that what is mortal may be swallowed up by life. [5] He who has prepared us for this very thing is God, who has given us the Spirit as a guarantee.*

What twists and turns of your life reveal God's work?
What do you know of intimacy with God in co-creating?

## Sleepiness

**God:**

Wake from your sleepiness,
indulgent one!
Be aware of this day's gifts.
Put your shoulder to the task.
A world awaits—for capering, discovering, and creating with Me.
I have called you by name to this time and place.
Mark your being here.
I have desired you to know Me.

**My soul:**

God of my waking,
don't let me miss You.
You have called me to life;
to know You, mighty Mystery;
to love You, in awe and gratitude;
to serve You, Guide of my path.
Wrest from my spirit the drowsiness
that buries me in uselessness.
You are my Beginning and my End.

**Matthew 26:37-41**

*[37] He took with him Peter and the two sons of Zebedee, and began to be grieved and agitated. [38] Then he said to them, "I am deeply grieved, even to death; remain here, and stay awake with me." [39] And going a little farther, he threw himself on the ground and prayed, "My Father, if it is possible, let this cup pass from me; yet not what I want but what you want." [40] Then he came to the disciples and found them sleeping; and he said to Peter, "So, could you not stay awake with me one hour? [41] Stay awake and pray that you may not come into the time of trial; the spirit indeed is willing, but the flesh is weak."*

What wakes you up to know the Lord?
Where is your sleepiness burying you in uselessness?

# Doubt

**My soul:**

Rock of ages,
tonight I am assailed by doubt.
My head can know Your work in my life.
Still I stew and hedge and waffle
in putting my life on the line.
Am I unsure of Your hand to steady me?
Do I have reservations that I can be trusted with Your commission?
I may let go from fear and weariness.
Why do You trust me?

**God:**

Doubting Thomas,
grab my hand.
I know your wavering heart
on the rim of astonishing.
I trust you because I trust Me.
You are living with Light inside.
It will bring you clarity.

**John 20:24-28**

*[24] But Thomas (who was called the Twin, one of the twelve, was not with them when Jesus came. [25] So the other disciples told him, "We have seen the Lord." But he said to them, "Unless I see the mark of the nails in his hands, and put my finger in the mark of the nails and my hand in his side, I will not believe." [26] A week later his disciples were again in the house, and Thomas was with them. Although the doors were shut, Jesus came and stood among them and said, "Peace be with you." [27] Then he said to Thomas, "Put your finger here and see my hands. Reach out your hand and put it in my side. Do not doubt but believe." [28] Thomas answered him, "My Lord and my God!"*

What doubts assail you?
What trust is God placing in you?

323

## Bees

**God:**

Apprentice child,
aren't bees marvelous?
They are some of my most profound creation!
What teachers!
They are humble and hidden.
Their work saves the world.
They are blessed to make honey.
They live in community.
They are attentive to the good of whole.
I give you nature to share its wisdom.

**My soul:**

Master Teacher,
may the nectar You spread throughout
Your world draw me by its color.
May I receive the collective wisdom,
deeply listening with my heart.
As I gather the pollen of what looks like weeds,
give me Your daring.
May I give sweet honey!
At the time of swarming,
open my way to new horizons.
Let me trust that bee stings heal our chronic malaise.
God, You are something!

**Psalm 81:16**

*16 I would feed you with the finest of the wheat, and with honey from the rock I would satisfy you.*

How is your work like bees in saving the world?
How do the weeds in your life give pollen?

## Glow

**My soul:**

God of Light,
I want to glow with Your shine.
I've seen it in the faces
of those whose excellence gives beauty and safety,
of those whose compassion aches with hurt and pain,
of those whose eyes see You and, with daring, follow.
These all reflect You. Their radiance is Yours.
I long for You to catch my life,
mysterious hidden One!

**God:**

So you want My freshness, shadow child.
My light may feel like noonday sun. The shade may be your longing.
To bear My beam of love will take you where you may not want to go.
My energy is hard to preach.
Are you sure you want to shine?

**Jonah 3:5-10**

⁵ And the people of Nineveh believed God; they proclaimed a fast, and everyone, great and small, put on sackcloth. ⁶ When the news reached the king of Nineveh, he rose from his throne, removed his robe, covered himself with sackcloth, and sat in ashes. ⁷ Then he had a proclamation made in Nineveh: "By the decree of the king and his nobles: No human being or animal, no herd or flock, shall taste anything. They shall not feed, nor shall they drink water. ⁸ Human beings and animals shall be covered with sackcloth_and they shall cry mightily to God. All shall turn from their evil ways and from the violence that is in their hands. ⁹ Who knows? God may relent and change his mind; he may turn from his fierce anger, so that we do not perish." ¹⁰ When God saw what they did, how they turned from their evil ways, God changed his mind about the calamity that he had said he would bring upon them; and he did not do it.

Where do you see God shine?
How are you called to an energy that is hard to preach?

# Field of Light

**My soul:**

Awesome God,
I saw a field of fireflies in summer's midnight.
Tiny specks of light pulse their dance of
"I am here."
They take my breath away.
I bow to Your miracle.

**God:**

Night traveler, I enjoy them too—
these lightning bugs that defy the darkness.
So tiny, yet they are seen!
They are not unlike the stars, so tiny
that they gleam.
I put this mighty miracle right at your feet.
What fun we share!

**Genesis 15:5-6**

*⁵ He brought him outside and said, "Look toward heaven and count the stars, if you are able to count them." Then he said to him, "So shall your descendants be." ⁶ And he believed the Lord; and the Lord reckoned it to him as righteousness.*

What miracle catches your attention to say, "I am here"?
What pulses at your feet to announce God's call to you to be faithful?

## Leaps

**My soul:**

God of my desire,
You make my heart leap in Your coming.
With the juice of joy, I welcome You.
I bound and bounce in new freedom, letting go of self-defeat.
Break open my passiveness to exuberance.
Eager am I to follow, God, my Companion of life.

**God:**

Dare to dream big, child of My following.
Raise up imaginings and intuitions that see My disguises.
Laugh at the pretenses in yourself and your world.
That's what parrots and anteaters and dolphins sing out.
Then your foibles and falls will not frighten.
I belong to you, heir of My imaging.

**Acts 3:1-8**

*¹ One day Peter and John were going up to the temple at the hour of prayer, at three o'clock in the afternoon. ² And a man lame from birth was being carried in. People would lay him daily at the gate of the temple called the Beautiful Gate so that he could ask for alms from those entering the temple. ³ When he saw Peter and John about to go into the temple, he asked them for alms. ⁴ Peter looked intently at him, as did John, and said, "Look at us." ⁵ And he fixed his attention on them, expecting to receive something from them. ⁶ But Peter said, "I have no silver or gold, but what I have I give you; in the name of Jesus Christ of Nazareth, stand up and walk." ⁷ And he took him by the right hand and raised him up; and immediately his feet and ankles were made strong. ⁸ Jumping up, he stood and began to walk, and he entered the temple with them, walking and leaping and praising God.*

How does your self-defeat keep you passive?
At what pretenses does God invite you to laugh?

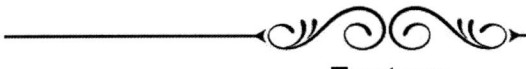

# Ecstasy

**God:**

Seeker, I come to you in a dense cloud,
like I did to Moses. I announce My presence
to your heart in prayer.
In smoke, you cannot breathe!
In fog, you cannot see!
Yet, I will lead and protect you
because I love you.

**My soul:**

God of the Mountain,
I need those moments of vision.
Even though I am terrified,
come speak to me of Your being.
Teach me how to listen!
It is here I would pitch my tent and live.

**Matthew 17:1-8**

*¹ Six days later, Jesus took with him Peter and James and his brother John and led them up a high mountain, by themselves. ² And he was transfigured before them, and his face shone like the sun, and his clothes became dazzling white. ³ Suddenly there appeared to them Moses and Elijah, talking with him. ⁴ Then Peter said to Jesus, "Lord, it is good for us to be here; if you wish, I will make three dwellings here, one for you, one for Moses, and one for Elijah." ⁵ While he was still speaking, suddenly a bright cloud overshadowed them, and from the cloud a voice said, "This is my Son, the Beloved; with him I am well pleased; listen to him!" ⁶ When the disciples heard this, they fell to the ground and were overcome by fear. ⁷ But Jesus came and touched them, saying, "Get up and do not be afraid." ⁸ And when they looked up, they saw no one except Jesus himself alone.*

How does your prayer announce God?
What moments of vision sustain you?

## Cruelty

**My soul:**

God of mercy,
I see cruelty all around.
It is within us,
pervading, capturing, impelling!
I do not see Lazarus at my doorstep.
I gain in wealth what evaporates in the market.
Ruthlessness drives the desperation
to use, discount, and disappear the lowly ones.
I beg you for conversion, Parent God.

**God:**

You long that I parent you, child of disregard.
Can you endure My discipline?
Can you stand beside My children
who are lepers on the margins?
See the violence within you
that wants first place at the table,
that taunts your righteousness,
that, in fear, strikes out to destroy.
Be converted and live so I can call you family.

**Isaiah 45:22-23**

²² *Turn to me and be saved, all the ends of the earth! For I am God, and there is no other.* ²³ *By myself I have sworn, from my mouth has gone forth in righteousness a word that shall not return: "To me every knee shall bow, every tongue shall swear."*

How do you experience cruelty pervading and impelling?
Where does the choice to be converted lead you?

## Weeds

**God:**

Creature of imaginings,
can you imagine all the fun I had in creating weeds—
foxtails, mustard and milkweed, cattails and Indian paintbrush,
wild sunflowers and daisies?
All that are discounted and expendable!
I wasn't just experimenting.
Neither was I testing My skills when I made you.
You are one of a kind.
You take My breath away!

**My soul:**

I love You, my God who makes me laugh.
Too often I feel I am a weed, yet there is no wasted energy with You!
I sprout unsought by the roadside.
All of life speeds by while I bend in the wind.
I wonder at my purpose.
Come gather my blooms for Your pleasure.
You see my beauty and possibility.

**Mark 4:30-32**

*³⁰ He also said, "With what can we compare the kingdom of God, or what parable will we use for it? ³¹ It is like a mustard seed, which, when sown upon the ground, is the smallest of all the seeds on earth; ³² yet when it is sown it grows up and becomes the greatest of all shrubs, and puts forth large branches, so that the birds of the air can make nests in its shade."*

What weeds do you discount in your life?
When do you feel like a weed?

## Marooned

**God:**

Heir of freedom,
I do not leave you marooned.
To be abandoned, left, is a fear that spouts despair.
You are My own.
Dare escape when there is none.
Put on the crimson of royalty and walk tall
upon your earth island.
I open your inside pathway.
I see you.

**My soul:**

Giver of freedom,
I am caught in my own muck. I edge near despair.
I want to see You as You see me.
How do I dare escape except by truth?
Your way lies in the giving away of stuff
and hope and life.
Your fireworks signal warning.
Escape is now!

**Joshua 6:1-5**

¹ *Now Jericho was shut up inside and out because of the Israelites;
no one came out and no one went in.* ² *The Lord said to Joshua,
"See, I have handed Jericho over to you, along with its king and
soldiers.* ³ *You shall march around the city, all the warriors
circling the city once. Thus you shall do for six days,* ⁴ *with seven
priests bearing seven trumpets of rams' horns before the ark. On
the seventh day you shall march around the city seven times, the
priests blowing the trumpets.* ⁵ *When they make a long blast with
the ram's horn, as soon as you hear the sound of the trumpet, then
all the people shall shout with a great shout; and the wall of the
city will fall down flat, and all the people shall charge straight
ahead."*

From what muck do you need to escape?
How does God's Way mean giving away in your life?

# Crunch

**My soul:**

Eternal One,
it is crunch time once again.
Winter descends.
All that bloomed and prospered is laid bare.
I curl into myself,
even as leaves, thick and brown, crackle.
The cold crushes me into passivity.
Where are You, my Maker?

**God:**

Aging soul,
time races inside you, leaving wrinkles and winter.
I am near.
I come from the timelessness
where gardens bloom forever,
even when it freezes.
As you curl up, feel My fire.
Nestle into restfulness and learn My heart.
Time is short.

**Jeremiah 32:37-41**

*[37] See, I am going to gather them from all the lands to which I drove them in my anger and my wrath and in great indignation; I will bring them back to this place, and I will settle them in safety. [38] They shall be my people, and I will be their God. [39] I will give them one heart and one way, that they may fear me for all time, for their own good and the good of their children after them. [40] I will make an everlasting covenant with them, never to draw back from doing good to them; and I will put the fear of me in their hearts, so that they may not turn from me. [41] I will rejoice in doing good to them, and I will plant them in this land in faithfulness, with all my heart and all my soul.*

How are you passive?
How are you coming to know the heart of God?

## Veil

**God:**

Bride of My heart,
I see you through your veil.
Will you commit to Me?
Can you see Me as you make your way down the aisle?
I put My cloak around your naked soul.
I take you to Myself.
Let no shade or façade block My eyes of delight.
You are mine.

**My soul:**

God of high expectations,
don't let me hide.
I take off the mask, the shroud,
that camouflages life.
Under Your mantle, I know mercy.
The brilliance of Your face only invites me to joy.
I come under the shadow of Your wing.
I am unafraid.

**Psalm 17:8-13**

*⁸ Guard me as the apple of the eye; hide me in the shadow of your wings, ⁹ from the wicked who despoil me, my deadly enemies who surround me. ¹⁰ They close their hearts to pity; with their mouths they speak arrogantly. ¹¹ They track me down; now they surround me; they set their eyes to cast me to the ground. ¹² They are like a lion eager to tear, like a young lion lurking in ambush. ¹³ Rise up, O Lord, confront them, and overthrow them! By your sword deliver my life from the wicked.*

In your nakedness of soul, how do you know God's delight in you?
Why do we hide rather than run to God's wings for shelter?

# Barely

**God:**

Greedy one, do you have enough?
Are you barely reaching a surfeit to your
voracious appetite?
Why do you cling to stuff that weighs you down?
Scatter your days to the wind, noticing plenty.
Taste a single bite, hungry one.
Know you are filled in it!
Pay attention with wide-open wings.

**My soul:**

Bountiful God,
I am hardly begun on my pathway to You.
Let me bring no suitcase, no picnic basket,
no sleeping bag, no purse!
With trust, let me stride with staff.
I take steady steps toward You, my Goal.
I have enough.

**Matthew 5:3**

³ *Blessed are the poor in spirit, for theirs is the kingdom of heaven.*

How are you noticing you have enough?
What do you need to carry that weighs you down?

# Carpet

**My soul:**

God of Comfort, I want to be Your carpet.
Nuzzle Your feet in the nap and pile of my life.
May it all be covered with attention.
You have given all that I have and am!
I bow in thanks.

**God:**

Child of My flock,
I have given you spring's green grass to carpet your imaginings.
Fresh possibilities abound. Caper across My hillside in trustful play.
This is a new day.

**Psalm 23**

¹ *The Lord is my shepherd, I shall not want.* ² *He makes me lie down in green pastures; he leads me beside still waters;* ³ *he restores my soul. He leads me in right path for his name's sake.* ⁴ *Even though I walk through the darkest valley, I fear no evil; for you are with me; your rod and your staff—they comfort me.* ⁵ *You prepare a table before me in the presence of my enemies; you anoint my head with oil; my cup overflows.* ⁶ *Surely goodness and mercy shall follow me all the days of my life, and I shall dwell in the house of the Lord my whole life long.*

How does attention to God's gifts carpet your life?
Where do you experience fresh possibilities in your life?

## Bunting

**God:**

My roamer of the night,
like the indigo bunting,
you use the stars to navigate.
You fill My fields with song.
You signal like a flag that you belong.
I nestle you in My world,
like a baby's bunting.
You are secure and safe.

**My soul:**

Protector God, I depend on You.
May my heart sing in praise of You.
I follow the urge of my spirit on Your pathway
in the nights of my unknowing.
Send me some stars to guide me.
It is a long dark road!

**Psalm 124:7-8**

*⁷ We have escaped like a bird from the snare of the fowlers; the snare is broken, and we have escaped. ⁸ Our help is in the name of the Lord, who made heaven and earth.*

How are you roaming in the night?
What stars are guiding you?

# Kingfisher

**God:**

Watcher of life, kingfishers shout to you:
"What I do is me: for that I came." *
I am connected to you.
I want you to know My force field.
Let your heart catch My colors
of belief in the good,
of surrender of self,
of joy in your being.
I know why I have made you.

**My soul:**

Weaver of Life,
I trust the threads of my days into Your hands.
You have woven brightness into my colors like the kingfisher.
May my pursuit of food, home, and flight be praise of Your glory.
I choose Your path for my purpose.

**Proverbs 16:2-4**

² *All one's ways may be pure in one's own eyes, but the Lord weighs the spirit. ³ Commit your work to the Lord, and your plans will be established. ⁴ The Lord has made everything for its purpose, even the wicked for the day of trouble.*

What glimpses do you have of why God made you?
In ordinary tasks for food, home and movement how do you praise God?

* Gerard Manley Hopkins, "34, as kingfishers catch fire," *Poems and Prose of Gerard Manley Hopkins,* selected and edited by W. H. Gardner (Penguin Books, Tenth Impression, Baltimore: 1987).

## Loose

**My soul:**

Guardian God,
today I feel loose and wobbly.
My days move unbound.
I pray for steady feet and a clear pathway.
You tell me real freedom
is in unlocking from my wants and fears.
You tell me to connect.
It is Love that calls,
that draws,
that secures my soul.

**God:**

Wanderer,
let Me take your hand.
I know your restless spirit wants to be unfettered.
What seems easy is just sloppy!
Trust the tie I have with you to bring you home.

**John 13:3-5, 13-16**

*³ Jesus, knowing that the Father had given all things into his hands, and that he had come from God and was going to God, ⁴ got up from the table, took off his outer robe, and tied a towel around himself. ⁵ Then he poured water into a basin and began to wash the disciples' feet and to wipe them with the towel that was tied around him. ¹³ "You call me Teacher and Lord—and you are right, for that is what I am. ¹⁴ So if I, your Lord and Teacher, have washed your feet, you also ought to wash one another's feet. ¹⁵ For I have set you an example that you also should do as I have done to you. ¹⁶ Very truly, I tell you, servants are not greater than their master, nor are messengers greater than the one who sent them."*

How are you called to unlock your wants and fears?
Where does washing feet unfetter you?

# Concert

**My soul:**

Conductor God,
I can't believe I'm part of Your concert.
I'm practicing.
Sometimes I am violin.
Sometimes I am trumpet.
Always I want to follow Your lead.
Let me trust Your harmony to come forth
despite rehearsal's dissonance.
Play me, Lord of the Music.

**God:**

My instrument,
play your heart out.
Let the holes in you be filled with melody.
May your substance catch timbre.
Listen to the pace of the falling snow.
Capture the passion of the rolling waves.
All fits.
Know your moment to join.
Believe in your gift.
I do.

**Psalm 150:3-6**

³ *Praise him with trumpet sound; praise him with lute and harp!*
⁴ *Praise him with tambourine and dance; praise him with strings*
*and pipe!* ⁵ *Praise him with clanging cymbals; praise him with loud*
*clashing cymbals!* ⁶ *Let everything that breathes praise the Lord!*
*Praise the Lord!*

Where do you find yourself practicing for God's concert?
How are you surprised by how your holes are filled with melody?

## Scuffed

**God:**

Resistant one,
I see your shoes are scuffed.
You drag your feet.
Are you unconvinced of My way,
of giving away of your wealth,
of turning of the other cheek,
of letting go of control?
Your mars are My grand canyon.
Your scrapings are my river paths.
Your scabs are My meeting spots
with your heart.
Lift your feet and run, little one.
I am waiting.

**My soul:**

God of my journey,
my soul is scuffed with resistance.
Like a mule, I put my feet down in belligerence.
Soften my abstinence.
Paint out the green valleys.
Refresh me with Your streams.
Let rebellion melt away.
I want to race to You.

**1 Corinthians 9:24-26**

*²⁴ Do you not know that in a race the runners all compete, but only one receives the prize? Run in such a way that you may win it. ²⁵ Athletes exercise self-control in all things; they do it to receive a perishable wreath, but we an imperishable one. ²⁶ So I do not run aimlessly, nor do I box as though beating the air.*

Where are you dragging your feet?
What are the green valleys and streams that melt your resistance?

# Sandals

**My soul:**

Unknown God,
I put sandals on my dusty feet and follow.
One foot in front of the other!
I can't see far!
Yet there is a north star inside my heart.
It judges love.
It assesses truth.
It asks, "What gives life?"
Why are You hiding in my midnight life?
Come and bring the dawn.

**God:**

Faithful follower,
why do you keep trudging?
What moments of light do you lift in the darkness?
You trust your north star as do I.
It is My imprint.
I give you endurance for your dusty trail.
I give you My shadows—
"Go walk around in them."
I am near.

**Luke 1:78-79**

*⁷⁸ By the tender mercy of our God, the dawn from on high will break upon us, ⁷⁹ to give light to those who sit in darkness and in the shadow of death, to guide our feet into the way of peace.*

When do you see your north star?
How do you walk in God's shadow?

# Keeper

**My soul:**

Keeper of my soul,
store your treasures within me…
Your courage of faithfulness,
Your wisdom to see beauty,
Your pouring out of Self.
Preserve my heart, like the lake's reflection of Your face.
I walk amid distraction and danger,
and I am afraid.

**God:**

Precious one,
I cherish you and know your value.
I keep you, My one of a kind,
dreamed for this time and place.
Go forth and make your waves.
I am with you.

**Mark 16:14-18**

*14 Later he appeared to the eleven themselves as they were sitting at the table; and he upbraided them for their lack of faith and stubbornness, because they had not believed those who saw him after he had risen. 15 And he said to them, "Go into all the world and proclaim the good news to the whole creation. 16 The one who believes and is baptized will be saved; but the one who does not believe will be condemned. 17 And these signs will accompany those who believe: by using my name they will cast out demons; they will speak in new tongues; 18 they will pick up snakes in their hands, and if they drink any deadly thing, it will not hurt them; they will lay their hands on the sick, and they will recover."*

How does the God who sends you forth keep you?
What treasures does God keep in you?

## November 27

## Grass

**God:**

Small one,
I have hidden you among the grasses of the field.
Green and flourishing, your lushness speaks of spring.
Fading and fallow, the earth surrenders its glory.
In all things, My Word lasts.
You will rise anew in My springtime
and know I am your God.

**My soul:**

God of tiny creatures,
I know my hiddenness.
In the vast expanse of pasture,
I rise as one blade.
I trumpet in my rising that
Your Kingdom is among us.
Come walk barefoot among us,
and see that it is good.

**1 Peter 1:22-25**

²² *Now that you have purified your souls by your obedience to the truth so that you have genuine mutual love, love one another deeply from the heart.²³ You have been born anew, not of perishable but of imperishable seed, through the living and enduring word of God. ²⁴ For "All flesh is like grass and all its glory like the flower of grass. The grass withers, and the flower falls, ²⁵ but the word of the Lord endures forever."*

Where is your lushness evident to you?
How are you seeing the Kingdom among you?

## Roar

**God:**

I hear your roar,
mighty king of beasts.
Like your brother, the lion,
you announce your presence.
Your soul yowls injustice,
your stance booms its pride.
What belligerent bellow or
unrestrained laugh echoes your truth?
And I smile at your foolish daring.
You are a mere child, and you are Mine.

**My soul:**

You, Lord of the Universe, are here.
I pretend.
Dare my roar be more than squeaks
in this vast and mighty world.
Still, you hear me and know my childish demands.
Mercy, my God, at my arrogance!
Lead me in Your truth.

**Hosea 11:8, 10-11**

*⁸ How can I give you up, Ephraim? How can I hand you over, O Israel? How can I make you like Admah? How can I treat you like Zeboiim? My heart recoils within me; my compassion grows warm and tender. ¹⁰ They shall go after the Lord, who roars like a lion; when he roars, his children shall come trembling from the west. ¹¹ They shall come trembling like birds from Egypt, and like doves from the land of Assyria; and I will return them to their homes, says the Lord.*

Where am I roaring at my God?
When do I know my demands are a mere squeak?

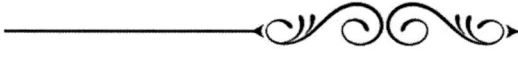

## Reek

**God:**

Alien child,
you are wandering where earth reeks of ruin.
It is saturated in sweat and blood.
Broken homes and broken hearts abound.
Look to the blue skies and keep hope.
Cast off the weeds of stink that would grow to block your path.
My love endures.

**My soul:**

Holy One,
send Your winds to disperse the smog.
Guide me out of this oppressive fog.
I cannot find blue skies.
It is only in faith that they are there.
The fumes gather and take my air.
I cannot breathe.
All wreaks decay, so I come to You and pray.

**Luke 12:4-7**

⁴ I tell you, my friends, do not fear those who kill the body, and after that can do nothing more. ⁵ But I will warn you whom to fear: fear him who, after he has killed, has authority to cast into hell. Yes, I tell you, fear him! ⁶ Are not five sparrows sold for two pennies? Yet not one of them is forgotten in God's sight. ⁷ But even the hairs of your head are all counted. Do not be afraid; you are of more value than many sparrows.

Where are you feeling the ruins around you?
How does your faith sustain you?

# Switchback

**My soul:**

Companion to the heights,
You are the Sherpa in my life's switchbacks.
I come to passes where the sun can't reach.
But You are there.
When the trail calls
for my full attention,
and I see only boulders, You are there.
I do have glimpses of the vista on occasion
because You are there.

**God:**

Climber child,
I've let you choose the way.
It is too steep with its sheer walls,
so you wander back and forth.
Granite blocks your track and you switchback.
I take your hand when your heart quakes.
I wrap you in My warmth
when you are too cold to shiver.
I watch your steps
when you go near the cliff.
I will walk you home.

**Deuteronomy 1:6-7, 30-31**

*⁶ The Lord our God spoke to us at Horeb, saying, "You have stayed long enough at this mountain. ⁷ Resume your journey. ³⁰ The Lord your God, who goes before you, is the one who will fight for you, just as he did for you in Egypt before your very eyes, ³¹ and in the wilderness, where you saw how the Lord your God carried you, just as one carries a child, all the way that you traveled until you reached this place."*

What glimpses of vistas keep you climbing?
How are you near the cliff's edge?

# December

1. Denim
2. Holler
3. Lagoon
4. Fugitive
5. Shallows
6. Turban
7. Everglades
8. Cracked
9. Myrtle
10. Minnows
11. Violin
12. Need
13. Sparkling
14. Cottonwood
15. Thaw
16. Cunning
17. Perfume
18. Raven
19. Protection
20. Riddle
21. Buttons
22. Married
23. Concern
24. Camp
25. Soar
26. Silver
27. Seep
28. Volcano
29. Moist
30. Refuge
31. Smoke

# Denim

**My soul:**

Worker God,
I'm putting on denim today.
It is time for earthwork.
Please work with me, God of blue jeans.
In the soul soil, You are Master.
It is the season of planting.

**God:**

Are you willing to dig and plow?
Digger of roots, it is dirty work!
Are you willing to sweat and strain?
It means uncovering rocks.
Do you have the strength?
Are you invested?
The garden of your life
will leave you with cuts and bruises.
But I work with you.

**Genesis 3:17-19**

*¹⁷ And to the man he said, "Because you have listened to the voice of your wife, and have eaten of the tree about which I commanded you, 'You shall not eat of it,' cursed is the ground because of you; in toil you shall eat of it all the days of your life; ¹⁸ thorns and thistles it shall bring forth for you; and you shall eat the plants of the field. ¹⁹ By the sweat of your face you shall eat bread until you return to the ground, for out of it you were taken; you are dust, and to dust you shall return."*

What earthwork calls for your labor?
Where do you sweat and strain to clear your land?

# Holler

**God:**

Edge walker,
I holler for your safety.
With thunder booming,
I alert you to the cliff's edge.
Come, let me hold you.
Listen and let your heart come.
What lures you can open an abyss.
I wail that you can fall,
but it is My gift of freedom.

**My soul:**

Guardian of my ways,
I bring You curiosity
and all the siren calls that make me blind.
Shout out Your alerts.
Roar Your urgent cries.
I cannot see the chasms.
I came from You
and long with all my soul for You.
Does the rooster have to crow?

**John 18:25-27**

*²⁵ Now Simon Peter was standing and warming himself. They asked him, "You are not also one of his disciples, are you?" He denied it and said, "I am not." ²⁶ One of the slaves of the high priest, a relative of the man whose ear Peter had cut off, asked, "Did I not see you in the garden with him?" ²⁷ Again Peter denied it, and at that moment the cock crowed.*

What lures you to an abyss?
When has the rooster crowed in your life?

## Lagoon

**My soul:**

Creator God,
they say we are made of mostly water.
Sometimes I feel like a lagoon separated from You.
Weave your coral path
to bind me to You.
Immense Ocean, beat Your rhythm
so I can feel You near.
Clear the water of stagnation.
Let the brackish estuary of my life
find its source.

**God:**

Life gatherer,
even lagoons, with their barriers, have inlets.
Let your prayer draw in My flow.
I invite you to know My energy.
Trust our dance.
I shape your purpose
and your movement.

**Matthew 7:7-11**

*⁷ Ask, and it will be given you; search, and you will find; knock, and the door will be opened for you. ⁸ For everyone who asks receives, and everyone who searches finds, and for everyone who knocks, the door will be opened. ⁹ Is there anyone among you who, if your child asks for bread, will give a stone? ¹⁰ Or if the child asks for a fish, will give a snake? ¹¹ If you then, who are evil, know how to give good gifts to your children, how much more will your Father in heaven give good things to those who ask him!*

How do you feel bound to the Lord?
How does prayer draw you into God's flow?

## December 4

## Fugitive

**God:**

Come, my fugitive from justice.
What is the lie you believe in?
What delusion has blinded your actions?
I know you are a runaway from My love.
So I wait. I keep watch.
I yearn for your love in return.

**My soul:**

My Father,
I am not worthy.
The biggest lie I tell myself is You will not receive me.
I put up barriers, hideouts of belligerence and arrogance.
I think I know better.
How can You love me?
I don't love me.
Release me from the lies
in which I'm mired.
There is no truth more real
than You are my Parent.

### Hosea 14:1, 4-7

¹ *Return, O Israel, to the Lord your God, for you have stumbled because of your iniquity.* ⁴ *I will heal their disloyalty; I will love them freely, for my anger has turned from them.* ⁵ *I will be like the dew to Israel; he shall blossom like the lily, he shall strike root like the forests of Lebanon.* ⁶ *His shoots shall spread out; his beauty shall be like the olive tree, and his fragrance like that of Lebanon.* ⁷ *They shall again live beneath my shadow; they shall flourish as a garden; they shall blossom like the vine, their fragrance shall be like the wine of Lebanon.*

What lie keeps you from the freedom as a son or daughter of God?
Where are you sure you know better?

# Shallows

**My soul:**

Leader,
I walk in the shallows of my life,
kicking up smooth stones.
The deeps call.
Still, I dwell in fear.
The vast expanse beats its music.
I do not dare to catch the waves.
How do I know You?
How do I move beyond these shoals?

**God:**

Follower,
I invite you to return to Me, all I have given you.
Let your heart sing as I lead your song.
Trust the surf 's lift
as you wait for My wave.
I want you to know My heart.
I will carry you.

**Genesis 22:1-2**

¹ *After these things God tested Abraham. He said to him, "Abraham!" And he said, "Here I am." ² He said, "Take your son, your only son Isaac, whom you love, and go to the land of Moriah, and offer him there as burnt offering on one of the mountains that I shall show you."*

How are you staying in the shallows?
What has God given you that God asks in return?

# Turban

**My soul:**

Jesus,
did you wear a turban
as You walked the path from Jericho to Jerusalem?
Was it a dusty, rowdy walk with Your friends?
Did You tell stories?
Did You laugh, accompanied by the
wind-whipping sand?
I want to come Your way.

**God:**

You will need a turban, too,
to quiet the windstorms of your mind,
to come from the palm tree paradise
to a place of crucifixion—
are you sure you want to come?
Join My company,
and we will laugh and tell stories.
Know it stirs up jealousy to be so free.
As I walked, so will you.

**Matthew 4:18-22**

¹⁸ *As he walked by the Sea of Galilee, he saw two brothers, Simon, who is called Peter, and Andrew his brother, casting a net into the sea—for they were fishermen.* ¹⁹ *And he said to them, "Follow me, and I will make you fish for people."* ²⁰ *Immediately they left their nets and followed him.* ²¹ *As he went from there, he saw two other brothers, James son of Zebedee and his brother John, in the boat with their father Zebedee, mending their nets, and he called them.* ²² *Immediately they left the boat and their father, and followed him.*

What are the windstorms of your mind?
How do you join Jesus's company?

## Everglades

**God:**

World creature,
come to the Everglades.
Here, in brackish waters, thrive
alligators and dolphins,
egrets and indigo snakes,
bobcats and green tree frogs.
I created symphonies here.
Amidst danger and play, you can learn respect.
As you enter in, humbled and attentive,
you know courage and kinship.
I had so much fun
and want to share it.

**My soul:**

God of relationships,
I can hear your creative flow.
You sent forth the energy of Your love
and so enjoyed Your many faces of life.
Inside me, are these same creatures
snapping and feeding,
lifting and singing,
slithering and hiding?
I believe in Your choice that I should be.
Open wide my heart to love like You.

**Zephaniah 3:17-18**

*17 The Lord, your God, is in your midst, a warrior who gives victory; he will rejoice over you with gladness, he will renew you in his love; he will exult over you with loud singing 18 as on a day of festival. I will remove disaster from you, so that you will not bear reproach for it.*

Where in your world do you know courage and kinship?
What actions live in you that show primal energy like in the Everglades?

# Cracked

**My soul:**

Mercy,
I am cracked.
The cold chaps my hands and lips
and leaves broken places.
My alligator kinship is awful.
I bleed and it hurts.
Can Your light shine through the cracks?
I look so ugly.

**God:**

Mirror child,
I place you as a beacon of My mercy.
In a cold world, you know the pain.
The boundaries of your self bleed and roughen.
The flow of what strikes out from bitter winter
is held in your spirit.
You crack open truth.

**John 9:1-5**

¹ *As he walked along, he saw a man blind from birth.* ² *His disciples asked him, "Rabbi, who sinned, this man or his parents, that he was born blind?"* ³ *Jesus answered, "Neither this man nor his parents sinned; he was born blind so that God's works might be revealed in him.* ⁴ *We must work the works of him who sent me while it is day; night is coming when no one can work.* ⁵ *As long as I am in the world, I am the light of the world."*

Where do you know the coming of light within you?
How are you feeling in your body the cold of the world?

## Myrtle

**God:**

Student of life,
I made periwinkle.
It is a ground cover.
Sometimes you welcome an earth mantle.
You are naked and exposed and cold.
I will let beauty surprise—even you!

**My soul:**

Rabboni,
with glossy evergreen, You cover
my nakedness.
You heal my earth.
Out of my barrenness, You bloom.
On the edge of myself,
You spread a carpet of stars.

### Jeremiah 17:7-8

*⁷ Blessed are those who trust in the Lord, whose trust is the Lord.*
*⁸ They shall be like a tree planted by water, sending out its roots by*
*the stream. It shall not fear when heat comes, and its leaves shall*
*stay green; in the year of drought it is not anxious, and it does not*
*cease to bear fruit.*

Where are you exposed and barren?
How is God healing your earth?

# Minnows

**My soul:**

Infinite One,
I walk near the creek's edge this afternoon.
Minnows play there in the shallows.
Shadows ripple over stones.
These tiny fish tumble over one another
in the sun sparkles.
In Your wide expansive energy,
You are there beside me.
I hear You say,
"Being small delights Me."

**God:**

Beloved,
fear not being lowly.
All the influence in the world
will not give Me more joy in you.
Being big with booming voice
is deceptive of My power.
So, minnow child, play in the shadows.
Let Me watch and smile at your freedom.

**Matthew 18:1-5**

*¹ At that time the disciples came to Jesus and asked, "Who is the greatest in the kingdom of heaven?" ² He called a child, whom he put among them, ³ and said, "Truly I tell you, unless you change and become like children, you will never enter the kingdom of heaven. ⁴ Whoever becomes humble like this child is the greatest in the kingdom of heaven. ⁵ Whoever welcomes one such child in my name welcomes me."*

How are you lured to be influential?
Where do you play in the shadows?

# Violin

**God:**

Child of heart harmony,
I love the violin.
It's such a combination:
hollows, strings, vibrations.
In the tension, music floats, screams,
calms, or shouts.
Your heart knows!
Come, listen and be lifted up.

**My soul:**

Inventor of music,
I bow to You.
From wind and waves, You raise up my soul
to hear and respond.
I'm strung between two points: birth and death.
You cover the caverns of my life where Your love echoes.
Let me endure the tension of Your bow,
as I hear the symphony You form.
Ahh! What surprise!

**2 Corinthians 4:6-12**

*6 For it is the God who said, "Let light shine out of darkness," who has shone in our hearts to give the light of the knowledge of the glory of God in the face of Jesus Christ. 7 But we have this treasure in clay jars, so that it may be made clear that this extraordinary power belongs to God and does not come from us. 8 We are afflicted in every way, but not crushed; perplexed, but not driven to despair; 9 persecuted, but not forsaken; struck down, but not destroyed; 10 always carrying in the body the death of Jesus, so that the life of Jesus may also be made visible in our bodies. 11 For while we live, we are always being given up to death for Jesus' sake, so that the life of Jesus may be made visible in our mortal flesh. 12 So death is at work in us, but life in you.*

What are the hollows in your life where God is playing music?
What tension are you feeling in the strings of life stretched in you?

# Need

**My soul:**

God of my Fulfilling,
I am full of need today!
Wants are oozing up out of my loneliness.
I ache with such a craving to belong.
It impels my deeds
to crazy unimportance.
You are whom I need.
Don't hide beyond my view, Gracious One.

**God:**

Yearning soul,
trust the languish to draw you to Me.
Your extreme poverty will motivate your tending.
No one can fill you but Me.
Let My energy flow unhindered.
It is what stirs your longing.
I am here for you.

**Jeremiah 20:7-9**

⁷ *O Lord, you have enticed me, and I was enticed; you have overpowered me, and you have prevailed. I have become a laughingstock all day long; everyone mocks me.* ⁸ *For whenever I speak, I must cry out, I must shout, "Violence and destruction!" For the word of the Lord has become for me a reproach and derision all day long.* ⁹ *If I say, "I will not mention him, or speak any more in his name," then within me there is something like a burning fire shut up in my bones; I am weary with holding it in, and I cannot.*

Where do you crave to belong?
How does your poverty motivate?

## Sparkling

**My soul:**

Shining One,
I love sparkling:
Your sun on the water,
sparkling wine,
sequins and diamonds,
Christmas lights,
stars at night.
Let my soul-shine welcome home to You,
like the light in the window
catching the dawn.

**God:**

I see flashes of light
and see your world is brighter.
Your brilliant points that sparkle
give hope.
Out of your own darkness,
you can come to believe your truth.
My beloved, your twinkle claims your heritage.
Come and know you shine.
I will make My home in you.

**1 Peter 2:9-10**

*⁹ But you are a chosen race, a royal priesthood, a holy nation, God's own people, in order that you may proclaim the mighty acts of him who called you out of darkness into his marvelous light. ¹⁰ Once you were not a people, but now you are God's people; once you had not received mercy, but now you have received mercy.*

When do you shine?
How does owning that you are God's beloved claim your heritage?

## December 14

# Cottonwood

**God:**

Seeker,
I've sent you to a wide plain.
Under the cottonwood, you've found shade.
Its enormous reach offers rest
in the long journey.
It becomes a gathering place.
Build your campfire.
Make your stew.
I give your heart contentedness.

**My soul:**

Comforter,
I watch Your wind catch seeds,
the cottony hair of this massive haven.
Under its wide canopy, I savor Your sun streaks.
The road is long, the way unknown.

**Revelations 14:12-13**

*¹² Here is a call for the endurance of the saints, those who keep the commandments of God and hold fast to the faith of Jesus. ¹³ And I heard a voice from heaven saying, "Write this: Blessed are the dead who from now on die in the Lord." "Yes," says the Spirit, "they will rest from their labors, for their deeds follow them."*

Where do you feel contentment?
What seeds are you seeing scattered by the wind?

## Thaw

**My soul:**

Breath of creation,
I feel Your warmth across my winter land.
It is the season of icicle melt.
Send the cold dripping.
Let me move.

**God:**

Frozen one,
I know you are caught by the cold:
betrayal, rejection, self-castigation.
I know the spring thaw will give you freedom.
Pointed spears will disappear off roof edges.
And, drop by drop, you can move.
It is begun.

### Romans 8:26-28

*26 Likewise the Spirit helps us in our weakness; for we do not know how to pray as we ought, but that very Spirit intercedes with sighs too deep for words. 27 And God, who searches the heart, knows what is the mind of the Spirit, because the Spirit intercedes for the saints according to the will of God. 28 We know that all things work together for good for those who love God, who are called according to his purpose.*

How are you feeling God's warmth freeing you to move?
What is beginning in you?

**December 16**

# Cunning

**My soul:**

Love Wisdom,
I have followed a cunning lie.
Now I bow to Your wisdom.
I shake off the knavish chains
that tie me to deceit.
Open me wide to Your truth.
Release me from the lies I believe in.
You are the crafty one; You made me.

**God:**

Dear waif,
am I not the wise One?
Am I not love unconditional?
It is true that I made you,
I chose you to be.
Shake off the lies that bind you.
No shrewdness can pry you from My hold.
You are Mine and I love you.

**Genesis 3:2-5, 13**

² *The woman said to the serpent, "We may eat of the fruit of the trees in the garden;* ³ *but God said, 'You shall not eat of the fruit of the tree that is in the middle of the garden, nor shall you touch it, or you shall die.'"* ⁴ *But the serpent said to the woman, "You will not die;* ⁵ *for God knows that when you eat of it your eyes will be opened, and you will be like God, knowing good and evil."* ¹³ *Then the Lord God said to the woman, "What is this that you have done?" The woman said, "The serpent tricked me, and I ate."*

What cunning lie are you following?
What happens in your soul when you hear God chose you to be?

# Perfume

**God:**

I remember being loved with perfume.
So I send you, child-world of my creation,
fragrance in the midst of death,
springtime lilies of a deep valley,
lilacs to allure your heart.
It is primal to draw attention.
I am present.

**My soul:**

I honor Your claim, Presence of God.
I know in the darkness of winter
that spring will come.
I believe in Your promise of life.

**Song of Songs 1:2-4**

*² Let him kiss me with the kisses of his mouth! For your love is better than wine, ³ your anointing oils are fragrant, your name is perfume poured out; therefore the maidens love you. ⁴ Draw me after you, let us make haste. The king has brought me into his chambers. We will exult and rejoice in you; we will extol your love more than wine; rightly do they love you.*

How do you choose fragrance to call forth faith?
When do you know God's presence in fragrance?

# Raven

**God:**

Survivor child,
I sent the raven out in the days after the flood.
Its caw seeks.
Its carrion diet sustains.
It is my messenger of survival.
You know in your heart
a black-winged endurance.
Come follow Life.

**My soul:**

Mercy and Life,
in crystal-clear water that should give life,
I am overwhelmed.
In the croaking call of ravens
who eats dead things,
I am raised up again.
Merciful Mother God, hold me to Your heart.

**Genesis 8:6-7**

*⁶ At the end of forty days Noah opened the window of the ark that he had made ⁷ and sent out the raven; and it went to and fro until the waters were dried up from the earth.*

What cries out in your heart, seeking like the caw of the raven?
What good things overwhelm you like the waters of a flood?

## Protection

**My soul:**

Protector God,
I grab my umbrella and hide beneath.
Neither rain nor danger can touch me.
When Your sun is too bright to behold,
I open my parasol.
But when my heart is heavy and my soul is fearful,
I crawl under the shelter of Your wings.
There You challenge me,
My Lord and my God!

**God:**

The truth is so brilliant that you cannot hear it!
Join the march of freedom.
Let your soul's quaking calm and share My stride.
May your heart see Me and vanquish fear.
I am with you always.

**Mark 15:21**

²¹ *They compelled a passer-by, who was coming in from the country, to carry his cross; it was Simon of Cyrene, the father of Alexander and Rufus.*

When is a time of fear that you are under God's wing?
What does following Jesus compel you to do?

# Riddle

**My soul:**

Mystery Beyond, Mystery come close.
You scatter my world with riddles:
the enigma of death,
the conundrum of broken promises,
the screen of unknowing where You abide.
I puzzle and wrestle. I give up solving, defeated.
I know my own limits.
Come open my heart's door.

**God:**

Child of darkness, do you understand
I must pierce your heart with many holes for the Light to beckon?
Do you recognize your life will be riddled with unsolved problems?
Like a coarse sieve, My wisdom will sort your gravel.
Only when My love pervades can you tolerate such sifting.
Come, let Me hold you.

**Matthew 13:10-15**

*¹⁰ Then the disciples came and asked him, "Why do you speak to them in parables?" ¹¹ He answered, "To you it has been given to know the secrets of the kingdom of heaven, but to them it has not been given. ¹² For to those who have, more will be given, and they will have an abundance; but from those who have nothing, even what they have will be taken away. ¹³ The reason I speak to them in parables is that 'seeing they do not perceive, and hearing they do not listen, nor do they understand.' ¹⁴ With them indeed is fulfilled the prophecy of Isaiah that says: 'You will indeed listen, but never understand, and you will indeed look, but never perceive. ¹⁵ For this people's heart has grown dull, and their ears are hard of hearing, and they have shut their eyes; so that they might not look with their eyes, and listen with their ears, and understand with their heart and turn—and I would heal them.'"*

Where do you puzzle and wrestle to know the Lord?
In what ways is God's wisdom sorting your gravel?

# Buttons

**My soul:**

God, my Security,
did You imagine buttons?
Close the edges of me to You.
What is frayed and tearing in my soul,
please hold secure!
What would reveal too much, hide in Your mercy!
What distracts and impedes, button in Your love!
I trust Your closure of my heart with You!

**God:**

Naked child,
I cover you with My cape and
receive your shame and fear.
I button the unraveling of your self
to My own heart.
You belong to Me, precious one!
You are secure!

**Revelations 3:18-20**

*¹⁸ Therefore I counsel you to buy from me gold refined by fire so that you may be rich; and white robes to clothe you and to keep the shame of your nakedness from being seen; and salve to anoint your eyes so that you may see. ¹⁹ I reprove and discipline those whom I love. Be earnest, therefore, and repent. ²⁰ Listen! I am standing at the door, knocking; if you hear my voice and open the door, I will come in to you and eat with you, and you with me.*

Where is your soul frayed?
How are you experiencing God buttoning your heart to Him?

# Married

**God:**

Beautiful dove,
come share your life with Me.
Will you exchange promises with Me?
...to listen to My heart,
...to open wide in trust,
...to seek truth?
Will you identify with Me?
...even when you can't understand,
...when I am in disguise and need you,
...when I weep at doors slammed to you and Me
and there is no room?

**My soul:**

Awesome One,
are you proposing marriage?
Yes, oh yes!
I want to walk home with You.
Let Your love hold me close.
May I wash Your feet?
Let me hear Your heart beat.
In my transparent brokenness,
let me trust Your mercy.
So, yes, my Love, all the days of my life, Yes!

**Hosea 2:18-20**

*18 I will make for you a covenant on that day with the wild animals, the birds of the air, and the creeping things of the ground; and I will abolish the bow, the sword, and war from the land; and I will make you lie down in safety. 19 And I will take you for my wife forever; I will take you for my wife in righteousness and in justice, in steadfast love, and in mercy. 20 I will take you for my wife in faithfulness; and you shall know the Lord.*

How do you listen to God's heart?
Where is your brokenness transparent to God and to you?

## Concern

**God:**

One born of My imaginings,
you are My concern.
I know from where you came.
I know what possibilities call you.
I care about what draws you and what repels you.
Always you are on My mind.
Can you open your heart to Me?

**My soul:**

Waiting God, yes, yes!
I open my too-small heart to You.
How do I take in Your concern and not be afraid?
How do I grasp Your interest in me and not be paralyzed?
You are my beginning.
Threads weave back beyond my knowing.
You are the call around my bend
that allures and leads me to open to Your love.
In the reach of Your bonding,
I dare letting my heart grow.
You grasp my soul in joy,
God beyond my imaginings.

### John 1:14-16

*¹⁴ And the Word became flesh and lived among us, and we have seen his glory, the glory as of a father's only son, full of grace and truth. ¹⁵ John testified to him and cried out, "This was he of whom I said, 'He who comes after me ranks ahead of me because he was before me.'" ¹⁶ From his fullness we have all received, grace upon grace.*

What happens inside you when you take in God's concern?
Where in your life are you hearing God's call around the bend?

## Camp

**My soul:**

Refugee God,
You know what it's like to camp.
Tents are put up.
Strangers huddle around campfires for safety.
It is temporary!
Like You, I am Egypt-bound.
I seek safety from the threat of soul assaults.
In hiding amidst foreign ways and words,
I find refuge in You.
Come sit at my fire.

**God:**

Weary one,
let Me share your food.
I know you're foot-sore and blistered.
I sense your caution and guard.
Rest well near the campfire.
No harm shall come to you.
I am on watch because I love you.

**Matthew 2:13-15**

¹³ *Now after they had left, an angel of the Lord appeared to Joseph in a dream and said, "Get up, take the child and his mother, and flee to Egypt, and remain there until I tell you; for Herod is about to search for the child, to destroy him."* ¹⁴ *Then Joseph got up, took the child and his mother by night, and went to Egypt,* ¹⁵ *and remained there until the death of Herod. This was to fulfill what had been spoken by the Lord through the prophet, "Out of Egypt I have called my son."*

What assaults your soul?
When do you know God is on guard for your soul?

## Soar

**God:**

Sailor of the skies,
come soar with Me.
Let your wings lift, your heart rise
and glide in joy
among pine trees,
over glacier lakes,
beyond the edge of the ocean.
What would weigh you down, I've raised.
Have fun and trust My hold on you.
It is Christmas!

**My soul:**

Gift-Giver of Life,
how could you bond with me to give such glee?
I hang on for dear life when terror of heights takes
my breath away.
So You are a baby
in humble attire.
Where even what is human
puts down its fiercest fight,
You invite me to hold You,
Creator of the Universe.

### Luke 2:8-12

*⁸ In that region there were shepherds living in the fields, keeping watch over their flock by night. ⁹ Then an angel of the Lord stood before them, and the glory of the Lord shone around them, and they were terrified. ¹⁰ But the angel said to them, "Do not be afraid; for see—I am bringing you good news of great joy for all the people: ¹¹ to you is born this day in the city of David a Savior, who is the Messiah, the Lord. ¹² This will be a sign for you: you will find a child wrapped in bands of cloth and lying in a manger."*

When do you feel God's hold on you is fun?
When do soul heights make you afraid?

# Silver

**My soul:**

Faithful One,
by silver moonlight, I come to You.
In the shadows, I make my way.
I trust Your lead.
Shining One,
I glimpse Your Light.
My third eye, like a smoking mirror, greets Your approach.
Open my heart to Your presence.
Shh! Now is the time for quiet.

**God:**

Nighttime seeker,
still your soul and follow.
It means laying down your self-absorbed way.
In the nighttime shades, look for My moonbeams.
All will conduct You safely home.
Dare this nighttime pilgrimage.
Your way is holy.
I accompany you.

**Genesis 32:22-24**

*²² The same night he got up and took his two wives, his two maids, and his eleven children, and crossed the ford of the Jabbok. ²³ He took them and sent them across the stream, and likewise everything that he had. ²⁴ Jacob was left alone; and a man wrestled with him until daybreak.*

What shadows slow your journey to God?
Where do you see the moonbeams of God's direction?

## Seep

**My soul:**

Great Heart of the universe,
the cold seeps into my bones,
like the drip of icicles.
Can I warm our world?
How do I ease stiff and aching limbs?
What frozen hearts can love again?
You, who bring our springtime,
send my sap flowing.
Break open my seeds in the buried earth.
Burst wide the blooms of the apple tree.
I belong to You.

**God:**

Impossible one,
let My juices touch your soul.
May they seep into your winter paralysis
to move, to run, to dance.
"The time of singing has come."
Launch your life to love for all My creatures.
I lead our dance.

**Song of Songs 2:10-12**

¹⁰ *My beloved speaks and says to me: "Arise, my love, my fair one, and come away; ¹¹ for now the winter is past, the rain is over and gone. ¹² The flowers appear on the earth; the time of singing has come, and the voice of the turtledove is heard in our land."*

What stiff joints of soul do you want to move?
How do you experience God's juices awakening your life to singing?

# Volcano

**My soul:**

God of Mystery,
was it an earthquake or volcano that called the mighty stone away?
In Your gentle showings, did you harness the energies
of such raw resurrection?
I am afraid and trembling.
Who are You that I know and do not know?

**God:**

Come near and do not flee!
In this new day when death is done, danger runs.
In your heart is born a faith that can walk on hot stones barefoot
and sing to lions of your love to lay down your life.

**Luke 24:1-12**

*¹ But on the first day of the week, at early dawn, they came to the tomb, taking the spices that they had prepared. ² They found the stone rolled away from the tomb, ³ but when they went in, they did not find the body. ⁴ While they were perplexed about this, suddenly two men in dazzling clothes stood beside them. ⁵ The women were terrified and bowed their faces to the ground, but the men said to them, "Why do you look for the living among the dead? He is not here, but has risen. ⁶ Remember how he told you, while he was still in Galilee, ⁷ that the Son of Man must be handed over to sinners, and be crucified, and on the third day rise again." ⁸ Then they remembered his words, ⁹ and returning from the tomb, they told all this to the eleven and to all the rest. ¹⁰ Now it was Mary Magdalene, Joanna, Mary the mother of James, and the other women with them who told this to the apostles. ¹¹ But these words seemed to them an idle tale, and they did not believe them. ¹² But Peter got up and ran to the tomb; stooping and looking in, he saw the linen cloths by themselves; then he went home, amazed at what had happened.*

How do you know Jesus and not know Him?
Where are you surprised at your faith?

# Moist

**My soul:**

God of great heart, I see Your eyes are moist.
You see me make my choice of forbidden apples.
It takes me out of Your arms.
I walk in darkness.
My Jerusalem lays scattered,
no stone left on a stone.
You walk amid my ruins weeping.
At Your feet, I bleed.

**God:**

Free child,
take my hand.
Always I walk with you.
Love invited your freedom.
I know it is terrifying.
Only remember your gift of life,
your invitation to receive,
your brokenness as kinship.
I will steady your heart.
I am here to stop your bleeding.
Today is new to choose.

**Zephaniah 3:14-17**

*¹⁴ Sing aloud, O daughter Zion; shout, O Israel! Rejoice and exult with all your heart, O daughter Jerusalem! ¹⁵ The Lord has taken away the judgments against you, he has turned away your enemies. The king of Israel, the Lord, is in your midst; you shall fear disaster no more. ¹⁶ On that day it shall be said to Jerusalem: Do not fear, O Zion; do not let your hands grow weak. ¹⁷ The Lord, your God, is in your midst, a warrior who gives victory; he will rejoice over you with gladness, he will renew you in his love; he will exult over you with loud singing.*

Where do you stray to forbidden apples?
How does your brokenness bring kinship?

## December 30

# Refuge

**My soul:**

My God, You are my holding place,
the shelter covering my lostness.
Here I belong, seen by You, sacred to You,
my place of rest and safety.

**God:**

Come, little one, I am your shelter on a rock.
Come home to Me; I open wide My door.
You belong within, under My solid roof.
I set My table before you to restore your energy.
Do not be afraid or bereft.

**Psalm 91:1-14**

[1] *You who live in the shelter of the Most High, who abide in the shadow of the Almighty,* [2] *will say to the Lord, "My refuge and my fortress; my god, in whom I trust."* [3] *For he will deliver you from the snare of the fowler and from the deadly pestilence;* [4] *he will cover you with his pinions and under his wings you will find refuge; his faithfulness is a shield and buckler.* [5] *You will not fear the terror of the night, or the arrow that flies by day,* [6] *or the pestilence that stalks in darkness, or the destruction that wastes at noonday.* [7] *A thousand may fall at your side, ten thousand at your right hand, but it will not come near you.* [8] *You will only look with your eye and see the punishment of the wicked.* [9] *Because you have made the Lord your refuge, the Most High your dwelling place,* [10] *no evil shall befall you, no scourge come near your tent.* [11] *For he will command his angels concerning you to guard you in all your ways.* [12] *On their hands they will bear you up, so that you will not dash your foot against a stone.* [13] *You will tread on the lion and the adder, the young lion and the serpent you will trample under foot.* [14] *Those who love me, I will deliver; I will protect those who know my name.*

Where do you feel held and like you belong?
What do you imagine in coming home to God?

## Smoke

**My soul:**

I can't breathe, my God of Life.
My being is clogged, no wind of Spirit to lift and fill.
Terror haunts like smoke.
Blow free destruction that claims and paralyzes.
Mercy, my soul's Companion, please!

**God:**

I come with refreshing breeze
to fill your life, arrested one!
Look deeply into My eyes and have no fear.
I am with you, giving breath.
My Spirit leads your dance.

### Acts 2:1-12

*¹ When the day of Pentecost had come, they were all together in one place. ² And suddenly from heaven there came a sound like the rush of a violent wind, and it filled the entire house where they were sitting. ³ Divided tongues, as of fire, appeared among them, and a tongue rested on each of them. ⁴ All of them were filled with the Holy Spirit and began to speak in other languages, as the Spirit gave them ability. ⁵ Now there were devout Jews from every nation under heaven living in Jerusalem. ⁶ And at this sound the crowd gathered and was bewildered, because each one heard them speaking in the native language of each. ⁷ Amazed and astonished, they asked, "Are not all these who are speaking Galileans? ⁸ And how is it that we hear, each of us, in our own native language? ⁹ Parthians, Medes, Elamites, and residents of Mesopotamia, Judea and Cappadocia, Pontus and Asia, ¹⁰ Phrygia and Pamphylia, Egypt and the parts of Libya belonging to Cyrene, and visitors from Rome, both Jews and proselytes, ¹¹ Cretans and Arabs—in our own languages we hear them speaking about God's deeds of power." ¹² All were amazed and perplexed, saying to one another, "What does this mean?"*

Where are you choked with smoke, giving you terror?
How are you seeing God's eyes?

To you, my reader,

May the words that draw you to communicate and to oneness become the poetry that is God's song in you, the light that shines in you.

May the Word reveal God's heart to you.

M.L. Bennett

# Biographical Sketch

M.L. Bennett is a spiritual director and retreat leader. She has a doctorate in Counseling and Family Therapy and a master's degree in Religious Studies. Most of her professional life she served as a hospital chaplain. She also worked in teaching and development for MicroFinancing Partners in Africa. As soul listener and a sister to the poor, as one who aches and who rejoices, she shares an invitation to readers to deepen their own walk with their God.